SIR CHARLES GOD DAMN

Charles G.D. Roberts, ca. 1925

SIR CHARLES GOD DAMN

The Life of Sir Charles G.D. Roberts

JOHN COLDWELL ADAMS

University of Toronto Press

Toronto Buffalo London

© University of Toronto Press 1986
Toronto Buffalo London
Printed in Canada

ISBN 0-8020-2595-1

Canadian Cataloguing in Publication Data

Adams, John Coldwell.
    Sir Charles god damn
    Includes bibliographical references and index.
    ISBN 0-8020-2595-1
    1. Roberts, Charles G. D., 1860–1943. 2. Authors,
    Canadian (English) – 20th century – Biography.*
    I. Title.
    PS8485.023Z556 1986   c818'.52   c85-090872-8
    PR9199.2R62Z52 1986

50,685

This book has been published with the help of a grant from the Canadian
Federation for the Humanities, using funds provided by the Social Sciences
and Humanities Research Council of Canada. Publication has also been
assisted by the Canada Council and Ontario Arts Council under their block
grant programs.

In memory
of my grandparents
Frank and Winnifred Coldwell

Contents

Preface

PERHAPS I SHOULD BEGIN by explaining my choice of title for this book. When Charles Roberts, as a beginning writer, decided that his middle initials would give greater distinction to his name, their 'profane' connotation may not have occurred to him. He soon discovered, however, that there was only one means by which his editors and other acquaintances could keep them straight. Thus the designation 'Charles God Damn' began as a convenient way of remembering the correct order of the letters. It would cling to him for the rest of his life. Occasionally it was used in disparagement – the Canadian modernists of the 1930s muttered it as a curse – but more often it was meant to be a jocular expression of respect. The latter usage indicates the spirit in which the title was chosen.

Although my interest in Roberts goes back to the days when I first came across his animal stories in my school readers, this book might never have been written if my wife and I had not met Elsie Pomeroy, Sir Charles' 'official' biographer, in February 1960. We saw her often during the remaining eight years of her life. As I listened to her reminiscences about Sir Charles, I was struck by all the things that she had left unsaid in the biography. That was when the idea of retelling his story originated, but it was not until much later that I began to research the subject in earnest.

I do not mean to belittle Miss Pomeroy's book. It is a valuable source of first-hand information even though she omitted anything that she considered inconsistent with the public image that Sir Charles wished to maintain. A very engaging figure emerges from its pages, one that I believe to be true to life, but not the whole truth. Until now, gossip and conjecture have supplied the details – often unfairly detrimental to Roberts – of matters upon which Miss Pomeroy remained silent. It has been my aim to present all the available facts in their proper context and let them speak for themselves.

Space does not permit me to express my gratitude to everyone who helped in the preparation of this book, but I must single out three persons: Fred Cogswell and Laurel Boone for allowing me access to their files from the Roberts Letters Project, and Betty Gerow for her assistance in checking the manuscript. I am indebted to the following members of the Roberts family for their co-operation in answering my questions: Lady Joan Roberts, Dorothy Roberts Leisner, Patricia Roberts Henderson, and Julia Roberts. Lady Roberts graciously gave me permission to use the excerpts from Roberts' letters and his poetry. I have also benefited greatly from the painstaking editorial work of Gerald Hallowell and Jean Wilson at the University of Toronto Press. Above all, I must thank my wife Mary and my daughter Cathy for their support and forbearance.

J C A
Toronto

Rev. George Goodridge Roberts and Emma Bliss Roberts, ca. 1870

From a watercolour sketch of Westcock Parsonage

Charles G.D. Roberts and May Fenety around the time of their marriage, 1880

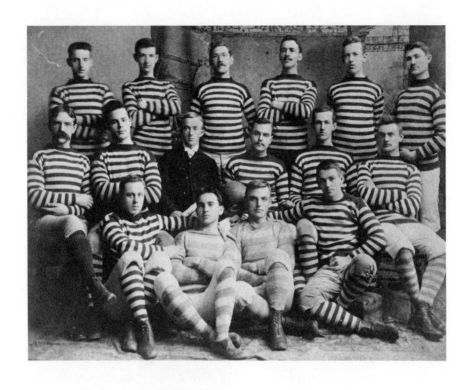

King's College football team, Windsor, NS, ca. 1891: Charles G.D. Roberts is first in second row left; Goodridge Roberts is second in third row left

George Parkin, 1876

May Roberts in Delsartre costume,
ca. 1893

The Roberts family camping near Fredericton, 18 August 1891: Charles G.D. Roberts on left; William Carman Roberts second from left; Emma Bliss Roberts fourth from left; Rev. G.G. Roberts at head of table, 'Nain' Roberts MacDonald standing bareheaded beside him

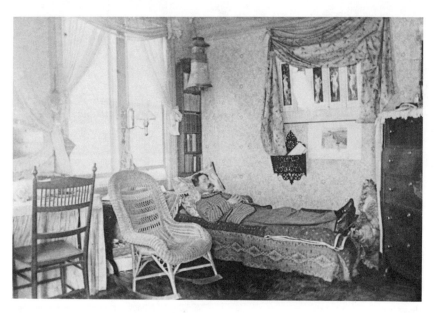

Reclining in the dressing room at 'Kingscroft,' 1893

Charles G.D. Roberts, ca. 1900

Bliss Carman, ca. 1900

Richard Hovey, ca. 1899

TOP: In camp on the Nictau, northern New Brunswick, 1905; BOTTOM: New York, ca. 1905. W.J. Keith has jokingly described Roberts as a 'dandy' in the lumber-camp and 'an elegant backwoodsman' in the drawing-room.

Major Charles G.D. Roberts during
the First World War

Roberts and his daughter Edith canoeing on the Thames, September 1921

TOP: On 27 April 1923, Roberts wrote to his son Lloyd from Brighton, England: 'A thousand thanks for the "snaps." How well and vigorous you look ... That photo of you as a wood god, climbing out of the lake on a fallen tree in the wilderness, arouses much enthusiasm over here.' BOTTOM: At Brighton, ca. 1922

With Wilson MacDonald (left) and
Bliss Carman at the Epworth Inn,
Muskoka, July 1925

With Dr Aletta Marty (centre), and
Elsie Pomeroy, beside the Marty
cottage, Muskoka, 1926

With Lloyd at 'Low Eaves,' probably 1925

Roberts at 'The Ernescliffe,' 1926

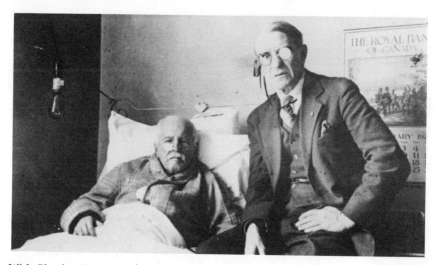

With Charles Mair in a nursing home, Victoria, British Columbia, February 1927

'Great Scribe Chief' at the Sarcee reservation near Calgary, 7 July 1928

At Hubbards Cove, Nova Scotia, August 1930

With Duncan Campbell Scott at the dedication of the Lampman memorial cairn, Morpeth, Ontario, 13 September 1930

The unveiling of the Bliss Carman memorial, Fredericton, 18 October 1930: (left to right) Lloyd Roberts, Charles G.D. Roberts, Premier J.B.M. Baxter, Sir George Foster, President C.C. Jones of UNB, Mr Justice O.S. Crockett, T.G. Roberts

Joan Montgomery (later Lady
Roberts), 1932

With Lorne Pierce, ca. 1940

On board the *Empress of Britain*, Canadian Authors' Tour of Britain, summer
1933

Roberts, E.J. Pratt, Pelham Edgar, Nathaniel Benson, ca. 1940

Roberts' eightieth birthday celebration, with Elsie Pomeroy and Nathaniel Benson

Christmas
1940

Affectionately yours
Charles G. D. Roberts

Centre Island, Toronto, summer 1940

At work, ca. 1940

With Elsie Pomeroy, Centre Island, Toronto, 1943, shortly after the publication of Miss Pomeroy's biography

Sir Charles G.D. Roberts and his bride, Joan Montgomery, 28 October 1943

SIR CHARLES GOD DAMN

CHAPTER ONE

Child of the Tantramar

1860–1873

The wide, white world is bitter still,
  (Oh, the snow lies deep in the barn-yard.)
And the dawn bites hard on the naked hill;
And the kitchen smoke from the chimney curls
Unblown, and hangs with a hue of pearls.
  (Oh, the snow lies deep in the barn-yard.)
      ('The Farmer's Winter Morning')

CHARLES G.D. ROBERTS was about forty years old
when he wrote the foregoing description of a winter dawn in rural New
Brunswick, but the day on which he was born, 10 January 1860, may have
been ushered in by just such a morning. The kitchen smoke may have
been curling from the chimney of an Anglican rectory in a country parish
about ten miles north of Fredericton. In any event, it was undoubtedly a
joyous day for the young parents: the energetic rector, who had just
turned twenty-seven on Christmas Day, and his impulsive, high-spirited
wife. Their first-born child was a healthy son, who had arrived two days
late for his mother's twenty-fourth birthday. When the time came for him
to be christened, they chose his names carefully: he was called Charles
after two uncles, George after both of his grandfathers, and Douglas after
his father's parish, the scenic countryside along the mouth of the Keswick
River.

The new father, the Reverend George Goodridge Roberts, had laboured in the parish of Douglas since his admission to the Anglican priesthood two years earlier. As a country parson he was an unqualified success, largely because 'his first object in life was to make people happier, and his second, to make them better.'[1] He was not a big man, but he was renowned for his physical strength, and he gained the respect of the local men by working as hard as any of them in the construction of the parish church. He had even built the pulpit himself, at home in his study, inadvertently mixing the shavings with the pages of his half-written sermons. Being as scholarly as he was practical, he had an excellent command of Greek, Latin, and French, and was almost as widely read in those languages as he was in his native tongue. In fact, he came from a long line of English scholars on both sides of his family. His own father had been educated at Oxford before immigrating to Fredericton, New Brunswick, where he was still serving as the headmaster of the Grammar School.

By all accounts, the rector came closer to sainthood than most other mortals, but his wife, Emma, was prone to sudden outbursts of temper. Her son Charles portrayed her in his novel *The Heart that Knows* as an 'ardent-hearted lady, always audacious'; many years later, her grandson Lloyd declared that she had 'a tongue that was sharper than thistles,' although he hastened to add that she possessed 'a heart so simple and so big that when it took you in it left nothing without to be desired.' Her father, the Honourable George Pidgeon Bliss, a former receiver-general of New Brunswick, was of United Empire Loyalist stock. His great-grandfather, the Reverend Daniel Bliss, the first pastor of Concord, Massachusetts, was also the great-grandfather of the noted American essayist and poet, Ralph Waldo Emerson. At the time of her marriage, Emma Bliss was a lively girl whose wholesome face and bright blue eyes were crowned with abundant gold-brown hair. The rector, like his counterpart in *The Heart that Knows*, was undoubtedly captivated by his wife's vibrant personality, even though he never 'got over being astonished' at her 'unexpectedness.'[2]

The district of Douglas, although sparsely populated, was geographically large, with over forty twisting miles of ill-kept roads between the places of worship. In the weeks following the birth of his son, the rector regularly left his family at home to travel through the snow to the remote areas of his parish. Sometimes the roads were impassable by sleigh, and he was forced to cover the distance on snowshoes. This difficulty would hardly have daunted a strong young man like Goodridge Roberts, but in addition to the hardships, the living was poor, and in all likelihood he was hoping for something better to come along. Early in the new year, he was offered the parishes of Westcock and Dorchester, near Sackville, down in Westmorland County where the Tantramar River empties into the Cumberland Basin at the head of the Bay of Fundy. His acceptance was probably influenced by the many acres of rich glebe land that would be available to him for raising his own produce and keeping enough livestock – cattle, sheep, pigs, and poultry – to supply the needs of his family. The cleared area comprised both upland and marsh, the latter being known to cut 100 tons of prime hay. On 4 August 1861, Goodridge arrived in Westcock to take over his new duties, supported by a grant of £200 a year from the Society for the Propagation of the Gospel in Foreign Parts. Emma and the infant Charles followed about a month later.

Technically, the old brick house into which they moved was a rectory, being the official residence of the rector of the parishes of Westcock and Dorchester. However, among the local people it was never called anything other than 'Westcock Parsonage.' Standing about half-way up a long, sloping hill, it commanded a sweeping view of the surrounding country-side. Its dormer windows on the front looked over a green terrace and orchard slopes, across upland grass and pasture lots, down to the fertile marshes of the Tantramar, and out to the bay beyond. This setting left such an imprint upon the mind of Charles G.D. Roberts that he recalled it again and again in his poetry. As Pauline Johnson stated, the Tantramar country was virtually 'undiscovered, until Roberts made the name familiar.' Through him, as his brother Theodore so gracefully phrased it, the region has 'been sung into the lyrical literature of Canada.'[3]

The tiny village of Westcock was dominated by the venerable William Botsford, a retired judge of the Supreme Court of New Brunswick, who lived in an imposing manor house on land that had been granted to his prominent Loyalist father. Although nearing ninety and almost as deaf as a post, he was still mentally alert. He took an active interest in the church and seems to have given his wholehearted support to the genial new rector. Holding a master's degree from Yale University, he was in a better position than most of the villagers to appreciate Goodridge Roberts' scholarship. His large family of ten children had been well educated, and a half dozen of his sons were occupying important positions in the province. One son, Blair, who remained in Westcock, was the high sheriff for Westmorland County.

Like most people who wrest their living from the soil and the sea, the humble folk of Westcock and Dorchester had little acquaintance with the intellectual pursuits so dear to the heart of their rector. Although he had the common touch and could mingle easily with the farmers and the seafaring men in his congregation, Goodridge Roberts was very conscious of their general indifference to academia. Furthermore, he felt that the country schoolhouse, which seemed to serve well enough for the local children, could not offer the kind of training he wanted for his own son. Consequently, Charles was not sent to school when he grew of age, but studied his lessons at home under his father's supervision. Another reason for this decision may have been a fear that constant association with children of cruder manners and speech might have an undesirable influence upon young Charles. Even though this feeling seems inconsistent with the Christian humility of the rector's character, there is a hint of this attitude of superiority in Charles' story 'The Moonlight Trails.' The central character is a boy, much like Charles, who is also the son of a rural clergyman. 'Belonging to a different class,' Charles says of him, 'he was kept from the district school and tutored at home with more or less regularity by his father.'

It seems almost certain that 'The Moonlight Trails' is largely autobiographical; as such, it provides a revealing picture of the childhood of Charles G.D. Roberts. First of all, he had little companionship of children his own age. His sister 'Nain' (christened Jane), born in 1864, and his brother Goodridge, born in 1870, were too much younger to count. Since lessons at the rectory had to be adapted to the hours when his father was home from his pastoral duties, Charles' schooling often began at a time when the village boys had been dismissed from classes. Whatever contacts he had with the latter frequently ended in fisticuffs. He had a great love for animals, and was ready to thrash any lad who dared to torture a kitten or even a snake. Fortunately, being sturdy and muscular like his father, he could command respect by sheer force, even if he did not win much popularity. 'It was a rash tyranny, and disgustingly unnatural,' in the view of the other boys, 'if they could not crush a snake's back with stones and then lay it out in the sun to die gradually, without the risk of getting a black eye and a bloodied nose for it.' Thus, Charles, 'not unnaturally, was thrust more and more into the lonely eminence of his isolation.' One of his few playmates was Alfie Barnes, from a neighbouring farm, who often went with him after supper to look for the cattle.[4] Although he sometimes played with Sheriff Botsford's younger children, catching tommy cod in season from the Botsford wharf at the mouth of the Tantramar, only a couple of the daughters were near Charles' own age. Like himself, they were being privately educated and were somewhat isolated from the rest of the village. Another occasional companion was a slightly older cousin, Courtenay Bliss, whose father was the rector at Mount Whatley, about eight miles away. Courtenay would one day marry Sheriff Botsford's daughter, Elizabeth.

Being forced upon his own resources during much of his leisure time, it was natural that Charles should turn to the surrounding forest for diversion. Just behind Westcock Parsonage 'towered groves of ancient, sombre, dark green spruce and fir, their high, serried tops populated with crows.' He was accustomed to the

> clamour of crows that fly
> In from the wide flats where the spent tides mourn
> To yon their rocking roosts   ('The Potato Harvest')

and many a time he had climbed up through dense branches in search of those treetop hideaways. 'The earliest enthusiasms which he can recollect,' he once said of himself, 'are connected with some of the furred and feathered kindred.' While still a youngster, he learned 'to follow – furtive, apprehensive, expectant, breathlessly watchful – the lure of an unknown trail.' Although he was taught how to handle a shotgun at the age of ten, shooting never really appealed to him as a sport. Like 'the boy' in another of his stories, he preferred to 'know the wild folk living, not dead.' Yet, with what he admitted was 'unabashed inconsistency,' he remained an ardent fisherman from the age of eight, when he was taken on his first fishing trip by his Uncle Ned Roberts. He could look upon the warmblooded creatures of the wild as kindred, but he found it 'hard to feel comradely towards a fish.'[5]

Charles' fascination with the outdoors was stimulated by his father, who taught him his first lessons in natural science, including the fact that 'all the snakes of the neighbourhood, without exception, were as harmless as ladybugs.' They also had many other interests in common, such as their love of reading; Charles' enthusiasm for the classics eventually rivalled that of the rector. Altogether, the Reverend Goodridge Roberts was more than a father and a teacher to his son. When Charles was twenty, an age when father-son relationships are often strained, he dedicated his first volume of poems to his father, calling him his 'dearest friend.' His father's influence remained with him all his life; and long after Goodridge Roberts was dead, important decisions were often made by pondering the question: What would Father say? In later years, he frequently dreamed about his father, and 'he rarely seemed able to dismiss them as *just dreams.*'

It was not unusual for him to remark: 'I dreamed about Father last night. It made me feel lonely all day.'[6]

His mother's influence appears to have been minor. In *The Heart that Knows*, his semi-factual novel in which he paints a dutifully affectionate portrait of her, the picture that emerges is one of a basically good-hearted woman with an unpredictable temper. In one revealing scene, she is shown arguing vehemently and irrationally with her husband even when she knows that he is in the right. Then she storms to her room in tears which eventually dry upon the satisfying reflection that she has probably made the poor man feel inexplicably in the wrong. An hour later, she steals downstairs 'in her crocheted blue bedroom slippers to mix a creamy egg-nog'[7] for the long-suffering rector. This fundamental kindness, mixed with perverseness and inconsistency, characterizes many of the females in Roberts' fiction. The model for them seems to have been his chief legacy from his mother.

While Charles was still a small lad, Mrs Roberts took a thirteen-year-old girl, named Annie Powers, into her household as a helper. Before long, the newcomer had so endeared herself to both her mistress and the rector that they decided to keep her in the parsonage to be reared and educated. Affectionately known as 'Nan,' she grew into such a willing and efficient worker that she came to be looked upon 'as a family institution – something necessary to its welfare.' It was difficult not to impose upon her, and undoubtedly everyone took her devotion for granted, but 'Nan's happiness seemed to subsist on helping others, not on being helped.' Without being formally adopted, she became in effect Charles' elder sister with 'a finger in the domestic pie,' just like any other member of the family.[8]

The farm was run with the help of a succession of hired men. Although none of them attained the family status of Annie Powers, Charles depended upon 'each in turn for some teaching that seemed more practical and timely than equations or the conjugation of *nolo, nolle, nolui*.' By the time he was twelve, he had become so mature that he could take his place beside the hired man and work for wages. His interest in farming at that time led him to write three articles that were published by *The Colonial Farmer* in Fredericton. The editor, who had assumed that the pieces came from the rector, was considerably disgruntled when he learned different-ly. Years later, Sir Gilbert Parker commented to Charles that this early achievement was 'proof that your genius was not acquired but was born with you.'[9]

The Westcock years saw young Charles' tentative explorations in the arts generally. At the age of nine, he began his first experiments in verse, but none of the results had the distinction of appearing in print, not even in *The Colonial Farmer*. At about the same time, he was taken to nearby Sackville several afternoons a week for painting lessons at the Mount Allison Ladies' College. He soon lost interest in the undertaking, however, and never again felt impelled to take up his paints and brushes. Yet, even this brief exposure may have helped develop the sure eye for colour and detail that he evinced later as a writer. He was taught the rudiments of the organ and the piano by his father, but it was obvious from the start that his musical aptitude was somewhat limited.

At an early age, Charles showed promise of becoming as athletic as his father, who could outperform 'any other man in a parish of strong and athletic men.'[10] Developing an interest in gymnastics, he practised regularly on homemade equipment that had been inspired by the pages of *The Boys' Own Annual*. He was big for his age, and at first it seemed that he might grow as tall as the six-footers in his mother's family. However, he had the rector's physical build. Later, when he was fully grown, he was a mere five foot eight, exactly the same height as his father.

The childhood of Charles G.D. Roberts coincided with the birth of the Canadian nation. He was too young to follow the arguments of the Confederationists and the anti-Confederationists prior to 1867, but the issue was so hotly debated that something of its importance must have been impressed upon his mind. In the New Brunswick election of 1865, his own county of Westmorland, ignited by the oratory of Albert J. Smith of Dorchester, was one of the hotbeds of opposition to any future union with Canada. During the campaign, voters were urged to reject union candidates on the grounds that Confederation would impose a tax on everything they owned, right down to every chicken in the barnyard. The levy of eighty cents for each resident, which had been proposed to raise money for administering the services still left to the province, came under special attack. The anti-Confederationists insisted that New Brunswickers were being asked to sell themselves to Canada like sheep for eighty cents a head. So effective were these scare tactics that in the entire province only six supporters of Confederation were elected to the forty-one-member Legislative Assembly. Mr Smith, hailed as the 'Lion of Westmorland,' became the head of the new government.

The Confederation controversy did not die out with the results of the election, however. In just over a year, the issue was taken again to the voters of New Brunswick. By that time, many people were better informed about the question of taxation and no longer looked upon it as a bogeyman. Instead, they were so thoroughly frightened by the recent prospect of Fenian invasions from the United States that they were ready to seek safety in union. Consequently, the election results in 1866 were almost an exact reversal of those in 1865. One of the few remaining holdouts was Westmorland County, retained by Mr Smith with the aid of the Acadian population, who feared the Protestant influence of Canada West. The Reverend Goodridge Roberts was never among Mr Smith's supporters. As for young Charles, his father's convictions alone were enough to engender his faith in Confederation.

In late November 1873, after thirteen years in his Westmorland parish, Goodridge Roberts moved his family to Fredericton, where he became the rector of Saint Ann's Church. The new appointment, which his grandson Lloyd has described whimsically as an advance 'from a country platter to a city plate,'[11] saw the elder Roberts settled into a position that he was to occupy until his death, thirty-two years later. The move from Westcock also marked the beginning of a new phase in the life of his son Charles: the child of the Tantramar had grown into adolescence.

CHAPTER TWO

Approaching Manhood

1873–1880

NESTLED IN A BEND of the Saint John River, Fredericton in 1873 was an undersized city of about 6,000 people. Less than ninety years earlier, it had been laid out for the occupancy of the United Empire Loyalists, whose descendants, from children to great-grandchildren, still accounted for most of the leading families. The predominant traits of their Loyalist forefathers still characterized the later generations: a strong allegiance to the British flag, a deep respect for learning, and a preoccupation with the aristocratic traditions of good breeding and gentlemanly conduct. Charles G.D. Roberts fitted naturally into that milieu, for his roots were in Fredericton, and the main branches of his family were still there. Just across the street from the rectory lived his grandmother and grandfather Roberts, the latter having only just recently retired after thirty-four years as the headmaster of the Collegiate School. Not far away lived his widowed maternal grandmother, the matriarch of the multitudinous Bliss clan. Several of her eleven children had married and remained in Fredericton, so that Charles had numerous cousins living there, including two particular favourites who were near his own age: Andy Straton and Bliss Carman.

The circumstances that led to the appointment of Charles' father as the Rector of Fredericton were far from happy. Early in July, his predecessor, Dr Charles Lee, had drowned while bathing in the Saint John River. The unfortunate man had suffered a nervous breakdown following the death of his ten-year-old son in February, and he had only recently been persuaded to take a leave of absence to regain his health. Those tragic events alone cast a cloud over the arrival of the new incumbent, but he also came with the handicap of having been a compromise candidate. There were two strong factions in the church, each with its own choice for a successor to Dr Lee, but neither group could muster the two-thirds vote required to elect its man. The stalemate continued for several weeks until the opposing sides were persuaded (probably through the intervention of John Medley, Lord Bishop of Fredericton) to invite Goodridge Roberts to fill the vacancy. He was the right man to quash the dissension and restore harmony.

The substantial old rectory on George Street was destined to be home for two generations of Roberts children. Within a year of the family's arrival from Westcock, Charles' second brother, Will (William Carman Roberts), was born in that house; and his youngest brother, Thede (George Edward Theodore Goodridge Roberts), was born there in 1877. Before either of those brothers had left the family hearth, Charles' own children were living there intermittently. Lloyd Roberts declared that he could write of the rectory as intimately as Hawthorne had done of the House of Seven Gables:

I could describe the big, bare brickiness of its exterior, the incredible thickness of its walls and partitions, its broad, open fireplace to every room, its spiral attic stairs and its windowless attic closets running the length of its eaves (the fascination of those closets!) and, with most satisfaction of all, its old-fashioned, elm-encroaching garden whence a fair share of both its physical and aesthetic substance was derived.[1]

The kitchen was in the low-beamed basement. Nan, an unparalleled cook, was ruling over that region as soon as she moved in, just as the rector ruled over the main floor, and his wife over the second storey and the attic.

Any difficulties that the family may have experienced in adjusting to their new surroundings must have been offset by the advantages that the move had brought them. Fredericton might be a small, unprogressive city from a commercial point of view, but it was unquestionably the political, educational, judicial, and ecclesiastical centre of the province. It could boast of the Parliament Buildings, Government House, the University of New Brunswick, the Normal School, and Christ Church Cathedral. Those august institutions, embodying and perpetuating the aspirations of their Loyalist founders, gave the city a social and cultural distinction out of all proportion to its size. Although Charles never outgrew the childhood influences of his beloved Tantramar country, Fredericton was probably the only location in the province that had so much to offer a receptive and impressionable teenager.

Goodridge Roberts could, at last, turn his eldest son's education over to capable hands. Charles was enrolled at once in the Collegiate School, where he was found to be adequately prepared to handle the expected grade level, although he had some catching up to do in Greek. The school was indisputably the most prestigious in the province, attracting the best teachers and grooming the greatest number of students for university. It was housed in a plain but fairly new building that stood on Brunswick Street, opposite the lower end of the cathedral property. Those grounds, leading down to the broad bank of the river, became in effect an extension of the schoolyard, where the students 'were encouraged in all kinds of sports and athletics, cricket and football in season, skating and snowshoeing in winter; swimming, canoeing and boating in summer.' Charles soon adapted to the new formality of his school life, excelling both in his studies and in athletics. For the first time he was able to participate in team sports and test his strength against boys his own age.

His particular friends from school were Jim Simons, Walter Leonard, Douglas Hazen, Andy Straton, and Bliss Carman. That most of those lads were to distinguish themselves in later life is not entirely surprising since the Collegiate boys, on the whole, were an elite group. But even among a select company, young Roberts and his friends were somewhat exceptional. Their future achievements would include two knighthoods as well as prominent careers in politics, the judiciary, the clergy, and the arts. Those destinies were still far off, however, as the six friends met in the Straton yard to practise gymnastics, or went camping up the river, and generally indulged in youthful skylarking.

Of that small band, none seemed more assured of success than Andy Straton. His mother, Sarah, the eldest daughter of Charles Roberts' grandfather, George Pidgeon Bliss, had married Francis Straton, a young barrister who later became clerk of the Executive Council. Straton and his wife lived at first with her mother in the Bliss family home where their sons, Barry, Frank, Murray, and Andrew, were born. In 1863 when Straton moved his family into a house of his own, he took his mother-in-law with him. After his wife's death the following year, he remarried and lived with his second family in a newly built upper storey which had a separate entrance. Sarah's sons lived in the original portion of the house with Grandmother Bliss. Barry, the eldest, went off to the Riel Rebellion in 1870 when he was only sixteen and did not return to Fredericton until seven years later. Andy, an acknowledged leader among his peers, was to die while still a young man, without fulfilling his early promise.

Bliss Carman's mother, Sophie, was another daughter of George Pidgeon Bliss. She had married a widower named William Carman, a barrister and a clerk of the Supreme Court, and had borne him a son and a daughter. They lived in a comfortable house on Shore Street with a side view of the river. It was there that Charles had visited once as a small boy when the Roberts family had come up briefly from Westcock. During that first acquaintance, Charles, who was a year older than Bliss, had established a seniority that had nothing to do with age, but which was to last until his cousin's death at sixty-eight. Bliss was passive by nature, and even in their boyish play looked to Charles to take the initiative. Of the group of six, he was by far the quietest, being more inclined to daydreaming than he was to boisterousness.

At Charles' prompting, Andy, Bliss, and several other boys joined together to form the T.O.Σ. (Tau Omicron Sigma) Club, a name whose significance they were sworn never to divulge. They engaged in several undertakings, including an unsuccessful attempt to publish a regular paper, but mostly they organized camping trips. Once each summer, for three years, they went off on a lengthy expedition, but for the rest of the time they ventured no farther than six miles up the river to Savage Island. This was a large, uninhabited island whose lush central meadow was surrounded by a thick growth of trees and a sandy beach. Near the upper end of it stood a deserted stone house that was rapidly falling into decay. The builder, an Englishman, had chosen a location that was too close to the river, not realizing that the spring floods would lash against his walls and batter his windows with debris. When he discovered his error, he abandoned the place forever, unwittingly providing a shelter for the T.O.Σ. campers. Nor were the boys the only ones to occupy the house. Sometimes the entire Roberts family either camped there or pitched their tents on the meadow.

The beginning of Charles Roberts' second year at the Collegiate School was marked by the return of the headmaster, George R. Parkin, who had been on a year's leave of absence at Oxford. In that dynamic teacher, his senior by only fourteen years, he was to find a friend whose influence was next to that of his father. Those two counsellors of his youth were much alike in many respects. Both men were scholarly, idealistic, and dedicated. Parkin also shared the rector's love of athletics, and had a particular fondness for snowshoeing and paddling. Whenever he joined the boys for football, as he frequently did, he enlivened the game with his characteristic energy and zest. But as much as he earned the admiration of his students on the playing field, it was in the classroom (where he taught English and the classics) that he commanded the greatest respect. Bliss Carman wrote of him:

He was a fascinating teacher, this intense and magnetic personality. There was never a dull moment in his classroom or in his society. ... In the classics, which were his chief subjects, his great appreciation of poetry and letters gave unusual scope to the day's work. The amount of Greek and Latin we read before going to college was not so great – two or three books of Virgil, a book or two of Homer, and a book of Horace, in addition to the usual Caesar and Xenophon – but much of it had to be learned by heart, and all of it minutely mastered, with a thorough knowledge of grammar and construction, and an understanding of all the poetic and mythological references. With him as an instructor, it was impossible not to feel the beauty of Virgil's lovely passages and the greatness of Homer as he read them.

Parkin would often interrupt the lesson to show how a modern writer had handled the same themes that concerned the ancients. A boy would be sent to the headmaster's rooms to bring back a book by someone such as Tennyson, or Browning, Arnold, or Rossetti, and the class would listen to another treatment of the subject. Carman declared: 'I can hear now that ringing voice in many lines of English poetry, as he read them to us, feeling all their glorious beauty.'[2]

Parkin's friendship with Carman and Roberts went beyond the normal relationship between teacher and students. Outside school hours, this tall, spare headmaster with the swinging step was often accompanied by his two favourite pupils. Those occasions were fondly remembered by Roberts:

Filling our pockets with apples (he was addicted to apples, as Adam was, but more judiciously!) he would take us favoured two for long hikes over the wooded hills behind Fredericton. He would take us as comrades, not as pupils; and his talk would weave magic for us till the austere fir-clad slopes would transform themselves before us into the soft green Cumnor Hills, and the roofs and spires of Fredericton, far below, embowered in her rich elms, would seem to us the ivied towers of Oxford. England just then was thrilling to the new music, the new colour, the new raptures of Swinburne and Rossetti; Parkin was steeped in them; and in his rich voice he would recite to us ecstatically, over and over till we too were intoxicated with them, the great choruses from 'Atlanta in Calydon,' passages from 'The Triumph of Time,' and 'Rocco,' – but above all, 'The Blessed Damozel,' which he loved so passionately that Bliss suspected him of sometimes saying it instead of his prayers.[3]

After fifteen years at the Collegiate School, Parkin went on to distinguish himself as the organizing representative of the Rhodes Scholarship Trust, the author of several books of history and biography, and a respected champion of Imperial federation. His services to the British Empire were rewarded with a knighthood, but, in the view of some observers, 'it is doubtful if he did anything more permanently valuable than stimulate the youthful imagination of Roberts and Carman.' 'Small wonder,' said Carman of Parkin's influence, 'if some of us became infected with the rhythm of the Muses...' Under the spell of Parkin's enthusiasm for Oxford, Roberts graduated as a gold medallist from the Collegiate in 1876 anticipating the day when he, too, might study at Oxford, where his paternal grandfather and great-grandfather had been educated.[4]

There was never any suggestion that Roberts would go to Oxford right away. His father could afford only to send him to the University of New Brunswick in Fredericton, but the dream remained that he would someday follow in the footsteps of his beloved Parkin. In the meantime, he was fortunate that the little university within reach was staffed with five competent men, several of whom were exceptionally able. The president, William Brydone-Jack, who taught mathematics, natural philosophy, and astronomy, had graduated from St Andrews, Scotland's oldest university, with such a brilliant record that he was invited to succeed the famous Dr John Dalton as professor of physics at New College, Manchester. For some reason, Brydone-Jack chose instead to go to the tiny provincial university in Fredericton, where he was to teach for forty-five years, serving from 1861 to 1885 as president. Loring Woart Bailey, professor of chemistry and natural science, was a graduate of Harvard, where he had studied under such renowned men as Louis Agassiz and Longfellow. Bailey remained at Fredericton for fifty years despite the attempts of Bowdin, Colby, Vassar, and McGill to lure him away. The professor of classical literature and history was George Eulas Foster, a graduate of the University of New Brunswick who had done post-graduate work at Edinburgh (where he had won a much-coveted prize in English literature) and had also studied at Heidelberg. After teaching for a few years at his alma mater, Foster embarked upon such an outstanding career in Canadian politics that he was awarded a knighthood. Too little is known about Francis Philibert Rivet, professor of French language and literature, to judge how much his instruction enabled Roberts to become a notable translator of French-Canadian literature. Roberts' favourite professor was Thomas Harrison, who taught English language and literature as well as mental and moral philosophy. A native of New Brunswick, Harrison had won high academic honours at Trinity College, Dublin, before becoming a colleague of Brydone-Jack, whom he eventually succeeded as president. Roberts obviously had the privilege of studying under some scholars of real distinction. 'They served a provincial university,' Desmond Pacey has said of them, 'but they were far from being provincial mediocrities themselves.'[5]

In 1942, looking back across the years, Roberts acknowledged that it had been 'a great piece of good fortune' to have been educated at the University of New Brunswick in the late 1870s:

My own personal debt to this small college that was then is incalculable. It confirmed and increased that love for Greek and Latin literature which had been first inspired by my father in private lessons and later nourished by Dr Bridges and Dr Parkin at the Collegiate School of Fredericton. Greek, Latin and English Literature (but Homer and Milton especially) were the formative influences to which I have chiefly owed whatever there may be of excellence, if any, in my own literary output. In the intimate teaching of this small college stress was laid upon the beauty and the wisdom of these literatures rather than upon the dry bones of grammar and rhetoric which, of necessity, underlay them. In other words, the teaching I received was inspirational before it was mechanical.[6]

Roberts' earliest extant poems, a sonnet, 'Spring,' and a lyric, 'The Dying Year,' were written when he was only fifteen, and were published three years later in *The Illustrated Canadian News*. During his first fall semester at the university, he wrote an ode 'To Winter' and a lyric, 'The Maple,' the latter soon to become a favourite of anthologists. In spite of its early popularity, 'The Maple' is not a very good poem, and although its shortcomings are not surprising in the efforts of an adolescent poet, it demonstrates a difficulty with rhyme and rhythm that frequently reappeared in his later work. It would be unfair to say that he always had a tin ear, but rhyme was often too obtrusive in his poetry and it sometimes forced his thoughts into imprecise wording.

Some of his undergraduate experiments with various verse forms echo the swift, lilting music that Parkin had chanted from Swinburne. At other times, notably in 'Ode to Drowsihood,' written when he was seventeen, the lines are suggestive of Keats: 'Breather of honeyed breath upon my face! /

Teller of balmy tales! Weaver of dreams!' The most ambitious poems of his university years were dramatic episodes from classical mythology, reworked in the manner of Shelley.

'Orion,' which is 460 lines in length, was completed while Roberts was still eighteen. It is by far the longest of the many poems he wrote throughout his career. It exceeds its closest rival, 'Ave,' written for the Shelley centenary (1892), by 150 lines. The poem begins with the return of the mighty hunter, Orion, to the court of King Oenopion of Chios after fulfilling the latter's request to rid his island kingdom of wild beasts. Oenopion, who had deemed the task to be impossible, intoxicates Orion and puts out his eyes to avoid rewarding him with his daughter's hand in marriage. Blind, Orion finds his way to a vantage point to face the rising sun, and has his sight restored by Helios, the sun god. Falling in love with Helios' sister, Eos, goddess of the dawn, Orion departs happily with her for Delos. Thus, by foreshortening and simplifying the original myth, Roberts gave it a traditional story form with a conventional happy ending. Not only did he prove adept in reshaping his material, but (given his indebtedness to his predecessors) he developed a fairly creditable blank verse style.

Although 'Orion' deals with 'alien matters in distant regions,' the youthful poet unconsciously transposed something of his Maritime background upon it. His description of an island seacoast on the Aegean (which he had never seen) is appropriate in many of its details to the coastline of his native New Brunswick. He might refer perfunctorily to the Greek vineyards, the groves of olives, and the mountain peaks of 'endless snow,' but the vivid picture of the 'writhed extremities' of the rocky formations, and such photographic images as the red sands scattered with 'stunted tufts / Of yellow beach grass,' come from the shores of the Bay of Fundy.

One noteworthy passage in 'Orion' depicts the sacrificial offering of a beast:

>   – a tawny wolf,
> Blood-stained, fast bound in pliant withes, fed fat
> On many a bleating spoil of careless folds,
> His red tongue lolling from his fangéd jaws,
> His eyes, inflamed, shrinking with terror and hate,
> His writhen sinews strained convulsively.

As the knife slit his throat, the ill-fated creature 'glared still hate upon his murderers / And died uncraven.' This episode foreshadows in several respects the animal stories Roberts wrote many years later. The description is unflinchingly graphic, and the reader's sympathy is directed towards the animal victim instead of his human 'murderers.' Here again we see the influence of Roberts' background, for his boyhood experience in the New Brunswick woods had taught him to regard the creatures of the wild with a feeling of kinship.

Roberts' cousin, Barry Straton, who returned to Fredericton from Winnipeg in 1877, was another prolific poet, although his achievement seldom rose above mediocrity. A moody fellow, Barry sometimes remained aloof even from his own family, preferring the solitude of canoeing and camping by himself on the Saint John River. Roberts claimed that his cousin's 'likes and dislikes were violent but evanescent,' but Barry's antipathy towards his stepmother was so lasting that he never spoke to her although he lived for years in another part of the same house. His interest in writing brought him close to Roberts, however, and in 1878 they collected their poems together in a single manuscript which they bundled off to a New York publisher. It was promptly rejected, and the disappointed poets dissolved their partnership.[7]

Despite the time that Roberts devoted to his poetry, he maintained a high standing in his studies. Being a natural athlete, he also excelled in all the college sports. He took as much pride in winning the running broad jump or the pole vaulting competition as he did in the honours and medals he took in philosophy, political economy, Greek, and Latin. When he was seventeen, he joined the local militia, where he eventually qualified as a captain. Nor, with all his other activities, were the expeditions of the T.O.Σ. Club entirely forgotten. The group's most memorable trip took place in the summer of 1877, after Roberts had finished his first year at the university. Joined by Bliss Carman, Andy Straton, and three other boys, Roberts journeyed by rail to Edmundston in the northern part of the province, where the party set off in three canoes up the Madawaska River into Quebec, across a chain of lakes and rivers, and back again to Edmundston for a round trip of about 140 miles. Their adventures were later recorded in a couple of articles by Roberts that appeared in *Forest and Stream* (1882) and were expanded upon in his volume of stories *Around the Campfire* (1896). In the 'campfire' stories, Roberts is referred to as the 'Old Man,' or 'O.M.' for short. The designation was a tribute that the others paid to his leadership, and had nothing to do with his actual age. 'C.G.D.R. was always known in our gang as "the Old Man",' Bliss Carman once acknowledged to Lorne Pierce. 'A familiar term of affection which fitted him exactly. Always something paternal in his strong, courageous soul ...'[8]

Fredericton, with its surrounding rivers and streams, was an ideal location for a passionate fisherman like Roberts. He found a fishing companion as ardent as himself in Will Fenety, a son of the Queen's Printer for New Brunswick. Will, who was the same age as Roberts, came from a family of eleven children that included an attractive younger sister called Mary, or May as she was known at home. Always susceptible to a pretty face, Roberts shortly became enamoured of the lovely May. At about the same time, Will was smitten by the charms of May's closest friend, Louise Black, Roberts' second cousin. Fishing was then all but forgotten as this quartet, outside of college hours, became practically inseparable.

Roberts became a regular visitor at the Fenety home, Linden Hall, 'a big yellow-gray brick house set well back from the street and much bedecked with paint and flowers.' Its furnishings were far grander than those of the rectory, for it contained 'gilded ornaments, soft carpets, heavy furniture, stained glass windows on the stairs, and even a bathroom.' It was a household ruled over with Victorian strictness by the father, George E. Fenety, a self-made man in his mid-sixties. Rising from 'selling papers to making them,' and founding the first penny newspaper in Canada, Fenety had gone on 'from printer's devil to Queen's printer.'[9] Not easy to please, he took a liking to May's young swain, and enjoyed arguing with 'Charlie' on philosophical questions, much to the astonishment of his own children, who were expected to be seen but not heard.

Neither Will nor May Fenety shared their father's intellectual pursuits. The latter, in fact, was a shy, often petulant girl, whose profoundest thought was about the decoration on her hat, or some other matter of similar consequence. There were ominous signs that she and Charles were not compatible. Once, for her birthday, he had a copy of Shelley's poems specially bound in white leather with her name imprinted on the front cover in gold letters. It cost more than he could well afford, but, as her poet-lover, he wanted to present her with a gift that was both appropriate and worthy. When she opened it, she burst into tears and threw it to the floor. She had been expecting some jewellery, she cried, and he had given her 'a horrid book.'[10] Unfortunately, incidents such as that were not enough to cure the young suitor's infatuation. Before Roberts graduated from the university, he and May Fenety were engaged to be married.

With graduation in June came another triumph to crown his work of the last three years. His poem 'Memnon' (126 lines in all) appeared in *The Century*, one of the foremost North American monthlies of the day. It seemed like a good omen for what he hoped would be a successful career as a poet. But poetry alone could not finance his dream of going to Oxford. With study abroad as his goal, he accepted the principalship of the Chatham High School and Grammar School in the hope that he could soon save enough money to travel. He assumed his duties on 10 November 1879, having grown a beard in the meantime to give himself more of an air of authority.

The town of Chatham, New Brunswick, is situated on the south shore of the Miramichi about a dozen or so miles from the point where the river empties into the Gulf of St Lawrence. Where it flows past the town, the Miramichi is nearly a mile wide and more like an arm of the sea. In Roberts' day, it was a forest of masts, with ships from all lands being twelve deep at some of the wharves, and still more ships being anchored in the channel. Behind the lumber piles on the bank, a town of close to 5,000 people extended for more than a mile. Comparing it to Fredericton, Roberts found its streets 'narrow and ill-cared for and the houses, not as a rule, in any way attractive.'[11] The High School and Grammar School, of which he was the youngest headmaster in its history, occupied five rooms in the Highland Society building.

There was great excitement among the senior students over Roberts' appointment. The report that he had been published in a leading American magazine was, in their eyes, the equivalent of having a world-wide reputation. They were prepared to give him the veneration that the world accorded to a Tennyson or a Browning. Tom Marquis, who was fifteen years old when he first saw Roberts, has recorded the students' reaction:

When the poet arrived we were amazed to find that he was little more than a boy; and had it not been for the venerable aspect given his countenance by a beard and eye-glasses, I am much afraid we would have doubted the reports, and looked upon him as being like unto ourselves. His influence soon began to be felt. He was a man who could not fail to reach the young heart, joining in our games with all the vigour of his athletic nature, and giving us his personal help in our studies with his keen young intellect. His influence over the minds of the elder pupils was very great, and the hour of his arrival gave some of us our bent.[12]

Marquis, whom Roberts regarded as one of his most promising students, was being prepared for the entrance examinations at Queen's University.

In later life, he became a prominent journalist and the author of several books on Canadian history. In retrospect, he attributed his choice of a literary career to the early influence of Charles G.D. Roberts.

In Chatham, Roberts found a former acquaintance in the person of Joseph Edmund Collins, the chubby, twenty-four-year-old editor of the town's weekly paper. Known to his friends as Edmund, Collins was a Newfoundlander who had studied law briefly in Fredericton before becoming a newspaperman. A close friendship developed between the two young men, and they spent many hours on the Miramichi in Roberts' Malicite canoe. The relationship continued even after Collins accepted a position with the Toronto *Globe* a couple of years later. By then, Collins had come within his friend's family circle, having married Roberts' second cousin, Gertrude Murphy of Fredericton.

Roberts' teaching duties left little time or energy for writing. After the great outpouring of poetry of the past three years, he grew alarmed when the flow began to dwindle as he became bogged down by the relentless pressures of marking papers and lesson preparation. With the premature despair of youth, he dramatized his plight in 'Iterumne?,' one of the few poems he composed at Chatham. Either the Muse had deserted him, he feared, or he had grown deaf and blind to her manifestations.

His main literary project during his first year at Chatham was the preparation of his modest sheaf of poems for publication. J.B. Lippincott & Co. of Philadelphia were interested in the venture, but the poet was expected to assume some of the cost. George E. Fenety, his future father-in-law, rallied to his financial assistance (as he would be obliged to do many times again) and the little volume *Orion and Other Poems* came off the press in the autumn of 1880. In Fredericton, Roberts' friend, Will Fenety, by then a partner of McMurray and Fenety, booksellers, proudly displayed the book in his shop, where it sold for one dollar. The brash young poet sent copies to Tennyson, Swinburne, and Arnold in England; and to Longfellow, Whitman, and Oliver Wendell Holmes in the United States. Neither Tennyson nor Swinburne deigned to reply, but he received acknowledgments from all the others. Arnold sent a three-page letter of encouragement, while Holmes wrote a lengthy reply with a gracious invitation for Roberts to visit him in Boston.

Several American periodicals took notice of *Orion* with surprisingly favourable reviews. The New York *Independent*, for example, overlooked the obvious signs of immaturity and called it 'a little book of choice things, with the indifferent things well weeded out.' In Canada, it was generally hailed as a new hallmark in the country's literature. A writer in the

Montreal *Gazette* predicted that Roberts was a poet who would 'confer merited fame on himself and lasting honour on his country.' Several years later, Roberts learned of the impact his book had made upon fellow poet Archibald Lampman, who was an undergraduate at Toronto's Trinity College when it appeared. In Lampman's words:

One May evening somebody lent me 'Orion and Other Poems' then recently published. Like most of the young fellows about me, I had been under the depressing conviction that we were situated hopelessly on the outskirts of civilization, where no art and no literature could be, and that it was useless to expect anything great could be done by any of our companions, still more useless to expect that we could do it ourselves. I sat up most of the night reading and re-reading 'Orion' in a state of the wildest excitement and when I went to bed I could not sleep. It seemed to me a wonderful thing that such work could be done by a Canadian, by a young man, one of ourselves. It was like a voice from some new paradise of art, calling us to be up and doing. A little after sunrise I got up and went out into the college grounds. The air, I remember, was full of the odour and cool sunshine of the spring morning. The dew was thick upon the grass, all the birds of our Maytime seemed to be singing in the oaks, and there were even a few adder's tongues and trilliums still blooming on the slope of the little ravine. But everything was transfigured for me beyond description, bathed in an old world radiance of beauty; the magic of the lines was sounding in my ears, those divine verses, as they seemed to me, with their Tennyson-like richness and strange earth-loving Greekish flavour. I have never forgotten that morning, and its influence has always remained with me.[13]

At the end of his first year at Chatham, Roberts decided that the time had nearly come for his long-awaited session at Oxford. As soon as May learned that his plans were being finalized, she accused him of reneging on his promise to marry her. In the stormy scene that followed, she would not be calmed until he had assured her that they would be married during the Christmas holidays. The dream of Oxford was abandoned forever. When his father asked if he felt that he was doing the right thing, Roberts replied, 'On most counts, no. But the engagement has been announced – I can't back out now.' His father remonstrated further that May was not very companionable, either intellectually or socially, but Roberts asserted with unwarranted confidence that he could teach her. Even Mrs Fenety cautioned him: 'You'll find May hard to live with. We do.'[14]

Upon his return to Chatham in the autumn of 1880, he rented a small cottage which his mother helped him furnish in readiness for his bride.

The wedding took place in Fredericton on 29 December, and two days later the newlyweds were ensconced in the cosy cottage. It was a far cry from Linden Hall, however, and the immature young wife was overwhelmingly homesick. Perhaps she was seized by a sudden foreboding that her life henceforth would always be lacking in worldly goods. Her tears turned to rage as her bewildered bridegroom tried in vain to reason with her. Little did he realize how sadly prophetic of their married life this inauspicious beginning would be.

CHAPTER THREE

Choosing Careers

1881–1885

AT THE AGE OF TWENTY-ONE, Charles G.D. Roberts had already been acclaimed as a young poet of great promise. In his own country, where his precocious *Orion* continued to win admiration and respect, he was being hailed as the leader of a new era in Canadian letters. It was a formidable role to thrust upon a youthful writer at the beginning of his career. Roberts was anxious to fulfil the high expectations he had raised, but he fretted that his creative efforts were being constantly hampered by his daily routine. Many years later, he told an interviewer that he 'did not enjoy'[1] teaching at Chatham, but undoubtedly his dissatisfaction arose not so much from the work itself as from the demands it made upon his time. In addition to his teaching load, he qualified for his master of arts degree at the spring convocation of the University of New Brunswick in 1881. By Christmas, he had accumulated a total of nine new poems, which he published privately in a chap-book (called *Later Poems*) for distribution to his friends.

Although he assayed the role of the poet, there was nothing of the languishing and otherworldly stereotype in either his manner or his appearance. Nor was he the dark and brooding Byronic bard. With his lithe but muscular build, he bore a greater resemblance to a fledgling prize fighter. He had inherited his physique from his father, but his face was distinguished by the characteristically rugged features of the Bliss family. Being full of lively curiosity, he turned a keen eye upon everything that came within his sphere; if the subject were feminine and pretty, the eye was inclined to linger longer than necessary in open appreciation. He soon gained a reputation as a 'ladies' man,' but men and women alike found him to be charming company, always courteous, always in blithe spirits. Whatever his personal problems might be, he invariably presented a cheerful countenance to the world.

In January 1882, Roberts was a successful applicant for the principalship of the York Street School in Fredericton, his new duties to begin on 1 February. The young couple left their tiny cottage in Chatham, with its mixed memories of their first year together, to live with the Roberts family back in their home town. Those domestic arrangements mark the first of several occasions when they sought the never-failing shelter of the old rectory during the course of their ill-starred marriage. With the birth of their son Athelstan on 10 May, a third generation was added to the family circle.

Undoubtedly, Charles and May Roberts were both happy to be back with their families and friends. Life at the rectory appears to have been remarkably harmonious, without any significant clashes between May and Emma Roberts. Perhaps May, being an indecisive person, was willing to accept the dominance of her strong-willed mother-in-law. It was good to be living near the Fenetys, but May's visits to Linden Hall were often marred by the shrewish remarks of Georgenia, her younger sister. Georgenia, who was destined to remain single, never missed an opportunity to comment disapprovingly upon the circumstances of May's married life.

For many reasons, Fredericton was more congenial to Roberts than Chatham, but his situation had greatly changed from his carefree days as a student. Now he was tied down by family responsibilities and the necessity of earning his livelihood. Both Andy Straton and Bliss Carman were still residing in the city, but, unlike their married cousin, they were unattached and had more free time at their disposal. The chances are that Roberts was not able to join them in their activities as often as he had done in the past. Nevertheless, he was in their company enough to miss them greatly when they left Fredericton later in the year.

Carman sailed from Rimouski in mid-September, bound for Oxford. However, when he arrived within sight of the hoary colleges, he was so homesick that he decided the next day to join his former classmate, Herbert Pickard, at the University of Edinburgh. Roberts, whose dream of Oxford had been denied, wrote chidingly to Carman for not sticking it out until his depression had worn off. 'Oxford would have paid you in gold,' he maintained, 'for all the copper that Edinburgh will or can give you...'[2] In the same letter he lamented Andy Straton's decision to sign on with a surveying crew in the backwoods of Maine: 'That a man of his brains should live by his muscles!'

In October 1882, young Oscar Wilde included Fredericton in his North American lecture tour. For several months, his progress had been closely followed by the press with frequent references to his wit and arrogance. When he visited 'the honeymoon capital of the world,' for example, he reportedly observed that 'Niagara Falls must be the second major disappointment of American married life.' All of those spicy tidbits gave an added fillip to his growing notoriety as an aesthete. Consequently, a large audience turned out to hear him at Fredericton's city hall. Roberts called on him at the Queen's Hotel prior to the lecture and was cordially invited to join him later in the evening. 'Could you bring along a couple of girls?' Wilde wanted to know. 'Sorry, Old Man,' Roberts replied, 'but things like that just can't be done in a small town, especially when one is the schoolmaster and one's *pater* is the rector.' He neglected to add that he had a wife at home to consider. However, they got together afterwards without the girls; and Wilde, still resplendent in ruffled shirt and velvet knee breeches, poured copious libations of gin as they took turns reading their poems to each other. When they parted in the early morning hours, Wilde expressed only one regret: 'Too bad the girls couldn't have been here!' Roberts often mused over that remark after Wilde was convicted on charges of homosexuality thirteen years later.[3]

In acknowledgment of the convivial evening they had spent listening to each other's poetry, Wilde sent Roberts a congratulatory letter on the beginning he had made and predicted that no 'height in song' would be beyond his reach. This extravagant praise greatly strengthened Roberts' self-confidence at a time when he was already excited about the part that his generation would soon be called upon to play in Canada's future. He was pinning his faith on 'the near approaching awakening of Canada in politics, art, song, intellectual effort generally.' The time was almost ripe for asserting Canadian independence, he wrote to Carman, 'and the very best of us young men will be wanted to do it.' He had the same message for Archibald Lampman, with whom he had struck up a correspondence (probably through their mutual friend, Edmund Collins, recently appointed city editor of the Toronto *Globe*): 'We want to get together literary and independent young Canada, and spread our doctrine with untiring hands.'[4]

His chap-book of new poems (again called *Later Poems*), which he printed for Christmas gifts in 1882, contained only six pieces. He had also written a couple of sketches for *Forest and Stream*, and was working on a novelette ('The Rawdon's Luck') and an article for *Picturesque Canada*. Mostly, however, he was gathering his forces in readiness 'to scribble and proselytize' in aid of Canadian independence, as he explained to Carman:

I am also studying, every spare moment, at the political questions of the day, particularly in the matter of Independence, to which I am devoted heart and soul; and to which a large party of the best and the most energetic men in Canada are rapidly gathering themselves. ... The only man I have to argue with is Parkin whom you know to be an enthusiastic Imperialist! But he stands alone now in that. His Party is dead. ... A national feeling is awakening quietly but surely. I think the change will come in a very good time, for you and me.[5]

In the spring of 1883, Edmund Collins published his *Life and Times of the Right Honourable Sir John A. Macdonald*. One of its twenty-four chapters was entitled 'Thought and Literature of Canada.' Of the chapter's sixty-three pages, seventeen were devoted to Roberts, who was called 'our greatest Canadian poet.' Moreover, Collins claimed, 'he is one of the most accomplished of our native scholars, and the master of a marrowy delightful prose that is not surpassed by that of any other Canadian writer.' As if he had not already overpaid the dues of friendship, Collins concluded his litany of superlatives by exclaiming:

How Mr Roberts would adorn one of our university chairs of English literature! Surely, if his services are available, Trinity, which has awakened from her sleep and feels a new life and impulse in her veins, and decided to endow a literature chair, might seek his services. He would, in such a place, draw all the aspiring and better ones among our young men around him; or might not our more comprehensive institution, University College, add to its excellent faculty this adorning star of native talent, this example of Canadian possibility?[6]

Collins was not the first to broach the subject of an academic appointment for Roberts in Toronto. In a two-page review of *Orion* in *Rouge et Noir*, Trinity's student publication, an anonymous writer had lamented: 'The pity is that we have not Roberts up here ... and set apart to him a chair in English literature in our College.'[7] There is no record that Roberts actively sought any such position at that time, although, had it been offered to him, in all likelihood it would have been accepted. The fact that Collins tried so hard to promote his chances suggests that his aspirations were well known among his friends. However, it is almost a certainty that the authorities at Trinity and University College never gave him a serious thought. Because they were still trying to prove that their universities were something more than academic backwaters, it is unlikely that they would have been interested in a young graduate from a tiny provincial institution in New Brunswick, regardless of his literary promise.

There was no room for him on the staff of the University of New Brunswick, but his alma mater paid tribute to his growing importance in the world of letters by inviting him to deliver the alumni oration at the convocation exercises on 28 June 1883. His subject was 'The Beginnings of a Canadian Literature,' but he also examined the role of a university in the life of a nation. 'We have,' he observed, 'what are too much universities in Canada rather than Canadian universities.' What was needed in our universities, he declared, was 'a more vivid realization of the fact that we have a country, and are making a nation; that we have a history, and are making a literature; that we have a heroic past, and are making ready for a future that shall not be inglorious.' He had, of course, put his finger on the fundamental shortcoming of all the universities in Canada at that time. When he made that assessment, he was only twenty-three years of age. Regrettably, almost his whole lifetime would pass before the universities would become significantly responsive to the Canadian milieu. As late as 1937, the University of Toronto refused a doctoral thesis on the poetry of Sir Charles G.D. Roberts, reportedly on the grounds that as a literary figure Roberts lacked sufficient world stature.

The main body of Roberts' oration examined the work of both French-Canadian and English-Canadian writers. He expressed the unorthodox view that the literature of French Canada should be 'a matter of greater interest and pride' to the rest of the country. 'It were well,' he told his thoroughly English audience, 'if we could concern ourselves more warmly with the achievements of this brother people, strive to lessen our ignorance of their doings and their characteristics, and in all ways render more apparent the ties of a national brotherhood and fellowcitizenship which binds them to us.' While his comments upon individual writers, both French-Canadian and English-Canadian, were predominantly favourable, his critical judgments were not unduly influenced by his desire to promote a national literature. He made it perfectly clear that he considered the present achievements merely as the 'beginnings' upon which to build 'large hopes.'

He concluded his oration by deploring 'that perpetual injunction to our verse writers to choose Canadian themes only.' As he saw it, English literature could not be confined by any 'boundaries of Canadian Dominion, of American Commonwealth, nor yet of British Empire.' At the same time, however, he acknowledged the importance of a distinctively Canadian flavour:

Of course the tone of a work, the quality of the handling, must be influenced by the surroundings and the local sympathies of the workman, in so far as he is a truly original and creative workman and not a mere copyist. To the assimilativeness and flexibility of genius it is as impossible that its works should lack the special flavour of race and clime, as that honey from Himettus should fail to smell of the thymy slopes. By all means let our singers preserve to the sweetness which they gather a fragrance distinctive of its origin.[8]

Early in May, Roberts had been granted a leave of absence from his duties as principal of the York Street School. He had been selected by Goldwin Smith of Toronto to edit a new paper called *The Week*, scheduled to begin publication later in the year. During the winter, he had been writing for Smith's *Bystander*, originally a monthly on public affairs, but rejuvenated as a quarterly in January after a publishing lapse of over a year. It was generally believed that Smith himself wrote all the pieces in his periodical, but in a confidential letter to Carman, Roberts claimed to have contributed 'a lot of stuff' to it. Just how he had come to Smith's attention is not known. It may have been through Edmund Collins, who had permission to dedicate his Macdonald biography to Smith. Presumably, Smith had seen a copy of the manuscript with its enthusiastic commendation of Roberts. Consequently, even though the first articles that Roberts submitted may have been unsolicited, the writer's name was not unknown to the publisher. Obviously, Roberts' work met with approval, and when Smith decided 'that the reception given to the *Bystander* seemed to warrant a larger experiment in independent journalism,' the young New Brunswicker was his choice for editor after Collins had turned down the offer because of a previous commitment.[9]

It may not have been entirely a coincidence that Roberts' request for a leave of absence came shortly after a parent named Hayes had challenged him in the Police Magistrate's Court for disciplining a pupil from a subordinate teacher's class. The Board of Education supported Roberts by amending its regulations to make it clear that the principal's authority would be upheld in such circumstances.[10] However, the incident may have been the last straw needed to convince him that the time had come to escape from the grind and harassment of teaching in a public school. The fact that he did not resign outright indicates that he was prepared to fall back upon teaching again if his other options failed.

Apparently, Goldwin Smith hired his youthful editor sight unseen, for there is no record of Roberts having had an interview with him beforehand. Following his release from the school, Roberts worked for his father-in-law, the Queen's Printer, to become familiar with all the technical aspects of publishing. In August he spent some time in Toronto, and it was probably not until then that he came face to face with Smith. Undoubtedly he was entertained at the Grange, the spacious mansion where Smith received most of the celebrated visitors who came to Toronto. It may not have been a completely satisfying meeting for Roberts, who probably found Smith a little too cold and austere in spite of his unfailing courtesy. Smith, an expatriate Englishman of sixty, had been a history professor at Oxford and was personally acquainted with many prominent Englishmen of the day, including Gladstone and the Prince of Wales. As a student he had excelled in Greek and Latin, and as an adult he had developed a talent for journalism, which owed much of its clarity and precision to his training in the classics. In his retirement in Canada, he had indeed become a bystander (as he styled himself), observing the affairs of the country, and offering his advice and criticism from the sidelines. A man of his background and interest might have seemed a natural successor to Roberts' father and Parkin as a mentor, but it was not to be.

After Roberts' return to Fredericton, he had barely a month before it was time to take up his new duties. During those last weeks he again had the company of Bliss Carman, who had recently arrived home to stay, without much to show for his year in Edinburgh. Unfortunately, there is no definite record of Carman's reactions to the handful of new poems, including 'Westmorland Revisited' (later renamed 'Tantramar Revisited'), that his cousin presented for his approval. However, the following lines, which Carman wrote shortly afterwards upon the flyleaf of one of Roberts' books, may be taken as evidence of an expanding admiration: 'My glad Greek boy in love with life, / Wake the old hollows with your song!'

On 21 September, Roberts left for Toronto, accompanied by May and sixteen-month-old Athelstan. For a few weeks, the trio boarded in the city before locating a suitable house at 471 Ontario Street at the corner of St James Avenue. It was about two miles to the office of *The Week* at 3 Jordan Street, but, weather permitting, Roberts usually walked the distance, partly for the exercise and partly to save money. Another economy measure was taken when Edmund Collins and his wife moved in with the Roberts ménage to share the rent.

In all likelihood, Roberts did not fully realize beforehand the tremendous amount of work involved in putting out a weekly magazine of about sixteen pages. Although Goldwin Smith was, as he himself expressed it, 'part proprietor and chief officer,' his only editorial contribution was to be a regular article called 'Current Events and Opinions.' To Roberts fell the task of seeking out contributors, reading through manuscripts, and writing seven or eight pages of special features such as 'Topics of the Week' and 'Book Notices.' On 3 December, he dashed off a note to Carman from the office:

I write this in a momentary lull, – am just getting first issue made up for the Press, and expect to be toiling here till midnight. We go to press tomorrow morning. ... I work from 10 to 12 hours a day, desperately, – yet am well and cheerful. I enjoy it.

On New Year's Eve, he again wrote hurriedly, enclosing a payment for Carman's 'Ma Belle Canadienne,' which had appeared in *The Week* on 27 December:

You will not wonder at the lack of time when you look at the amount of each issue of 'The Week' that comes from my devoted pen. I work almost day and night, I worked in the office on Xmas day, and entre nous I write steadily all day Sundays. I enclose the vast sum of $2.00 for the poem. But I hope to succeed soon in raising the rates a little.

By 11 January 1884, he confessed to Carman that he was wearing himself out: 'My head is in a continual whirl and I am getting to be a miserable dog from overwork.'[11]

To add to his pressures, he found himself increasingly in conflict with the views of Goldwin Smith on the matter of Canadian independence. Had Roberts been a little older and wiser when he took the job, perhaps he would have foreseen that a clash was likely to occur. Smith had been prophesying for several years that economic forces would inevitably draw Canada and the United States together. In the pages of the *Bystander*, he had enumerated the benefits that Canadians could expect from such a natural union. The price of nationhood, he argued reasonably, was a lower standard of living. He believed that as soon as Canadians realized the inescapable economic facts they would choose prosperity over patriotism and be willing to be assimilated by the United States. Naturally, he wished to promote those views in *The Week*, but Roberts steadfastly refused to print them. Smith, being a man of intellect rather than emotion, greatly underestimated the popular appeal of nationalism. To the majority of Canadians, including his young editor, an independent country was far more desirable than material advantages. At the end of February, Roberts resigned from *The Week*, exhausted from overwork, and fed up with Smith's attempted editorial interference. 'I could have got on comfortably here by being a stalking horse for G.S.,' he told Carman, 'but not otherwise.'[12]

Brief though his editorship had been, a matter of only twelve issues, Roberts had got the magazine off to a good start. He made literary history by publishing the first poem by Bliss Carman and the second poem by Archibald Lampman ever to appear outside a college journal. His own poetic masterpiece, 'Westmorland Revisited,' had graced the pages of the third issue. His aim was to publish as much Canadian poetry as possible, although he fretted over the paltry remuneration that was allowed. For beginning poets such as Carman and Lampman, the mere act of publication was a significant reward in itself; but Isabella Valancy Crawford, who inquired about The Week's rates, was one who could not afford to sacrifice her work for the pitiful sum she was offered. Under Roberts, the magazine was a judicious blend of public affairs and literature, but the result may not have been altogether satisfactory to Goldwin Smith, who was generally indifferent to contemporary litera-ture. His attitude may account for the worried tone of Roberts' query to Carman after the sixth issue: 'Does it strike you that there is any too much of a literary character about the paper?'[3] Matthew Arnold, who stayed with Goldwin Smith at the Grange during a lecture engagement in Toronto in mid-February, was sufficiently impressed with The Week to make inquiries about obtaining a subscription.

Having been granted the rest of a year's salary as severance pay, Roberts remained in Toronto throughout the spring and summer, busy with his pen, and hoping for suitable employment. His parting with Smith had not been bitter, and several of his articles appeared in The Week after his departure as editor. One of those pieces was based on his trip to New York City to explore the market possibilities there. He met many of the New York literati, and made several valuable contacts, including the acquaintance of Richard Watson Gilder, editor of The Century. The prospects in the American metropolis were tempting, and in a playful vein he wrote 'The Poet Is Bidden to Manhattan Island,' which concluded:

> You've piped at home, where none could pay,
>   Till now, I trust, your wits are riper.
> Make no delay, but come this way,
>   And pipe for them that pay the piper!

The poem was an amusing piece of light verse, but the poet's mood was serious. It was necessary, he realized, to recognize 'the side on which your bread is buttered.' Ardent nationalist though he was, if his survival as a writer stood a better chance in the United States, he was prepared to move. The best solution would be an editorial post that would allow him to become a part of the New York literary scene and keep him close to the best markets for his creative work. Over the next few months, while he was waiting for something to turn up, he implied to Carman on several occasions that he would accept a position in Canada only 'if New York fails.' At no point, apparently, did he ever seriously consider resuming his career as a school teacher. Carman, who had taught at the Collegiate under Parkin following his return from Scotland, had also abandoned the profession; unlike Roberts, his resignation in May 1884 resulted not from a conflict with his literary ambitions but from his general unsuitability for teaching.[14]

At the end of the summer, Roberts moved his family back to the rectory in Fredericton. Leaving May, who was expecting another child late in October, he set off again in search of employment. This time his hopes were centred upon Ottawa. On the way, he visited Quebec and Montreal, exploring the former in the company of three women for whose autograph albums he composed a triolet, enjoining them not to forget the day when he had guided them around the romantic old city.

'I have had a good trip, so far,' he wrote to Carman from Ottawa on 25 October, 'though laborious under the stress of divided longings.' He was referring to his infatuation with Marguerita, a young woman from Owen Sound whom he had met while he was working in Toronto. Very little is known about the circumstances of the affair, but in the autumn of 1884 Marguerita commanded such a share of his affections that, as he confessed to Carman, he travelled with 'part of me in Owen Sound, and part of me in the little Elm City.'

Socially, his visit to Ottawa was a great success. Among those who welcomed him to the capital were Archibald Lampman and Duncan Campbell Scott. He was given 'two small parties, drives, symposiums, etc.,' and wherever he recited his poetry he could count upon 'devout applause' and 'a number of fair damsels bowing down.' It was so stimulating to have all those people making a lion of him that he laughingly predicted: 'I expect the roar of the beast will soon resound throughout the nation.'

A meeting with fellow New Brunswicker, Sir Leonard Tilley, the Minister of Finance in Macdonald's cabinet, let Roberts to think about a civil service post. He had missed the 12 October deadline for applications to write the examinations, but with Tilley's intercession he was permitted to apply late. There was talk of establishing a Government Printing Bureau in the near future, and Tilley questioned him closely as to his qualifications for some sort of position within it. The more Roberts thought about it, the more attractive it seemed: 'Short hours, easy work, lots of time left for creation.' He expressed his interest in this prospect to Carman and urged the latter, who was working in a Fredericton law office, to consider a move to Ottawa:

If New York fails me, then Ottawa will stand solidly to my back. Tilley has made me the best of promises for after the Session, and has exerted himself more than once already on my behalf. I cannot help thinking, Bliss, that Fredericton will not hold you very long. You must put your whole heart into it to be a successful lawyer. ... I still fancy that we will eventually work the Ottawa Fakement, it would be a grand little city to work in, inferior only to our own dear City of Elms and Peace. It is quaint and sober, save during the Session. It has both rugged and lovely surroundings. It is characteristic and peculiar, and the air is sympathetic towards literature. A Government office gives you light work from ten to four and that's the end of it. Besides, even during hours there is abundance of time during the slack Session, for outside private work. And there are chances for all sorts of extras for a writer during Session...

After returning to Fredericton in time for the birth of his son Lloyd on 31 October, Roberts was back in Toronto in November, trying unsuccessfully to earn his living by his pen. The situation became so desperate that he was forced to write to his father-in-law for money to pay his board bill, and a $15 loan from Bliss Carman went long unpaid. It was a time of deep despair, but he had not given up the hope of finding something in New York. He resolved that he would go there again to look around just as soon as his finances permitted.

Seeking every possible advantage in the race for fame, he even considered shortening his name to plain 'Charles Roberts' in the hope that it would be more easily remembered. 'The initials are always getting mixed up,' he told Carman, 'and are useless anyway.' However, he was dissuaded from the change by his father, who convinced him that it was only his middle initials that made his name distinctive and memorable. Those 'profane' letters soon gave rise to the cognomen 'Charles God Damn.' Mostly, it was used by his friends as a term of endearment, a humorous way of expressing their affection. It clung to him for the remainder of his life. Editors found it a convenient way of remembering the order of the letters, and for a few of his detractors it was a source of malicious amusement.

To add to his depression of the moment, he could not even afford to visit Marguerita. Owen Sound was only a few hours away, but it might as well have been as distant as the moon. For the time being, he had to be satisfied with letters and the exchange of photographs. He sent her copies of his own poems and some by Carman, and she responded by exclaiming that they were both poets of the 'divine breed.' Her enthusiasm was in marked contrast to May's indifference to any poetry, including that of her husband. Marguerita's warm appreciation does not excuse Roberts' dalliance, but it does in some measure explain it. No wonder he yearned for the day when his financial circumstances would allow him 'to spend three or four dollars to satisfy my heart's desire.' However, the meeting probably never took place, for he had barely enough money to buy his ticket home for Christmas.[15]

He remained in Fredericton throughout the winter months, earning a pittance from freelancing, and recovering from a bout with typhoid fever. Accepting the advice of his father that the civil service would have a stultifying effect upon his creativity, he did not bother to take the examinations. He was now committed to a literary career; if he could not support his family by his pen alone, he would wait a little longer for something more compatible with his plans for writing.

At the 1885 spring convocation of King's College, Windsor, Nova Scotia, it was announced that Charles G.D. Roberts had been appointed Professor of English, economics, and French, his duties to commence in the fall term. Before signing his contract, he stipulated that all his classes must be held in the afternoons in order to leave his mornings free for writing. If the appointment was not as prestigious as the ones that had eluded him at Trinity College and University College in Toronto, at least it was not likely to be as demanding as an editorial post. And if he was not exactly in the groves of academe, it might be said that he was peering through the branches.

To brush up on his French, he returned to Quebec City for a few weeks during the summer. His visit coincided with that of Joaquin Miller, the middle-aged American poet who had impressed readers on both sides of the Atlantic by the vigour of his poetry about life on the frontier. Hardly any of his work has stood the test of time, but in his own day his colourful personality tended to divert attention from the inadequacies of his poetic talents. Dressing like a frontiersman, and inventing tall tales about his exploits, he hoodwinked many of his unsuspecting contemporaries. Roberts was no exception, and he praised Miller for writing 'such poems as our dilettante-ridden society is in need of.'[16]

May and the two small boys did not accompany Roberts during his first year at Windsor. Boarding in town and having the freedom of a bachelor gave him the welcome opportunity to mingle with the townspeople, but his discreet involvements with a series of charming women in the area appear to have begun at a later date. That he spent most of his time in academic pursuits is evident from a letter he wrote to Bliss Carman: 'Though happy in congenial work, I have no time or energy left me for creation.' During the first hectic year, most of the free mornings were spent, not upon his literary projects as he had planned, but upon preparation of his lectures. When he accepted a commission to write the literary chapter for *The Dominion Annual Register*, he confided to Carman: 'I am kept so confoundedly busy that every now and then I find myself compelled to go to College with lectures only half prepared.'[17]

Ten of the most significant years of Roberts' adult life were spent at Windsor, Nova Scotia. Much of his best poetry was written there, and during that period he firmly established his reputation as Canada's leading man of letters. For a whole decade, there was a stability to his domestic affairs such as he never enjoyed again. Although in time he began to chafe at the strictures of his environment, he loved Windsor and the adjacent 'Land of Evangeline' with a fervour that matched his feelings for Westcock and Fredericton.

It was not surprising that Roberts felt at home in Windsor. Although only half the size of Fredericton in population, it had much in common with his ancestral city, being steeped in the traditions of Toryism and the Anglican Church. The original French settlers had been replaced by New England Planters in 1760 and 1761, and the town later became a refuge for uppercrust United Empire Loyalists, who brought with them a devotion to their British heritage and a deep sense of their superiority in culture and breeding. It was their proud boast that they formed the most aristocratic British society outside of Britain itself. Like Fredericton, the town lay in the sweep of a river, backed by gentle hills; but Windsor's muddy Avon, with its extremes of high and low tides, emptied almost immediately into the sea, and the town had long been the home of wealthy shipowners whose enterprises were carried on in many distant ports.

Epitomizing the Loyalist traditions and attitudes of Windsor was King's College, founded in 1789, the oldest colonial university in the British Empire. Sheltered among the elm trees on a southern slope behind the town, it was comprised of a wooden building, containing students' rooms and classrooms, and a nearby Convocation Hall built of stone. At a short distance down the slope stood another stone building which housed the King's College Academy. Through the grounds of the college, a labyrinth of thick groves and tiny glens known as 'College Woods,' the road to the town wound past the gate-house of 'Clifton,' the former estate of Thomas Chandler Haliburton. As the author of the renowned 'Sam Slick' series, Haliburton was one of the college's most famous graduates. His memory still inspired the King's literary society, the Haliburton Club, of which Roberts was chairman for the entire ten years of his professorship. In the fall of 1885, King's had twenty-seven students in attendance, eleven of whom were divinity students. The newly elected president and professor of divinity was the Reverend Isaac Brock (a distant relative of the hero of Queenston Heights). In addition to Roberts, Brock was assisted by G.T. Kennedy (chemistry, geology, and mining), W.R. Butler (mathematics, natural philosophy, and engineering), and W.A. Hammond (classics).

Hammond, who had had a brilliant career as a student at Harvard (BA) and at Princeton (MA), appears to have been the most congenial of Roberts' colleagues. The two men were close in age, and, in addition to their academic interest, they shared a love of sports and outdoor life. They became two of the most valuable players on the football team and joined in frequent hiking expeditions on week-ends. Once, in a single day, they walked the width of the province, from Windsor on the Minas Basin to Chester on the Atlantic Ocean, a distance of forty miles.

Throughout Roberts' tenure at King's, there were several staff changes, including the installation of a new president, but the faculty remained small, overworked, and underpaid. Those years have sometimes been described as the halcyon period of Roberts' career; but, in fact, almost from the start, he was hoping for something more important and more lucrative to come his way. Because his beginning salary of $1,000 a year was never increased significantly, he had great difficulty in meeting the needs of his growing family. Unlike his bachelor friend Hammond, who left at the end of two years to study at Heidelberg, he was not free to further his education at some prestigious European university whose very name would be likely to impress the governors of a better-paying North American institution. His pen seemed his only hope for the time being, and he wielded it diligently, with one eye on the best markets and the other on the establishment of his reputation.

While his dissatisfaction over the modest rewards at King's in terms of professional advancement and monetary gain may have lessened his initial enthusiasm for the college, he never lost his spontaneity as a teacher. Grateful tributes received in later years from former students are ample proof of his dedication in the classroom. Hiram Alfred Cody, who entered King's in 1893 and later wrote over a score of vigorous novels in addition to fulfilling his duties as a clergyman, dedicated a poem, 'Our

Captain,' to Roberts in 1925 as a 'humble and grateful tribute' to the influence of his former professor. Another student, Robert Norwood, who later became a minor poet and a leading preacher in North America, declared at a reunion of King's College graduates in 1930: 'My success in life is due to Charles Roberts.'[18]

The Kingscroft Years

1886–1895

I N JANUARY 1886, when Roberts returned from Fredericton to Windsor after the Christmas holiday, his wife was pregnant with their third child. Daughter Edith was born in September, and shortly thereafter the family were reunited in 'Kingscroft,' a newly completed house on the edge of College Woods. Their new home was one of four modest dwellings that the college governors had decided to build for the married professors after the large faculty residence had been destroyed by fire. Because it was situated on the edge of the woods, Roberts coveted it from the beginning; and, in order to obtain it, had resorted to the subterfuge of convincing the other professors that it had the least desirable location. It was a narrow, three-storey structure of yellow clapboard, utterly unpretentious, with 'the Arts' being 'represented only by a two-column porch over the front door' and 'the Sciences' being 'concentrated in a cold-water tap over the kitchen sink and a three-compartment outhouse, air cooled both winter and summer.'[1] But they sometimes had the luxury of a maid, and there was ample room for a book-lined study and a nursery, as well as accommodation for a steady stream of relatives and other visitors.

Roberts' brother Goodridge (known in the family as 'Gool'), who entered King's in 1886 to prepare for the ministry, was a part of the Kingscroft household from the beginning. There were periodic visits from his father and mother, and from his brothers Will and Thede. His sister Nain, of whom May was particularly fond, often stayed for extended periods of time. In many ways, however, the most stimulating visits were those of his cousin Bliss Carman, with whom he could engage in mutually profitable literary debate and criticism.

In the fall of 1886, Carman had enrolled as a graduate student at Harvard. Both of his aged parents had recently died, and he had abandoned his law career with the vague idea of qualifying himself for a university post. But he applied himself half-heartedly to his studies at Harvard, and only completed one of the five courses for which he had registered. During the summer holiday he arrived in Windsor, uncertain of his future, but full of the aspirations of the would-be poet. It was his first visit to Kingscroft, although an earlier holiday in Nova Scotia had been the inspiration for his now-famous poem 'Low Tide on Grand Pré.'

For the remainder of Roberts' tenure in Windsor, Carman arrived every year for a lengthy visit, usually in the summer. He was also a frequent guest at Acadia Villa in Wolfville, the home of the Prat family, whose daughter Minnie became engaged to Goodridge Roberts. Carman struck up a close friendship with Minnie's sister, Nan, but Roberts sensed that he wished to avoid a romantic attachment. The invitation to Kingscroft for the summer of 1892 contained a cousinly caution:

Of the Villa thou would have to be a trifle sparing, on Nan's account! I fear she hankereth, so to speak, for exclusive possession! But she is not dangerous, being a sound and sensible little girl, and better pleased with half a loaf than no bread![2]

In contrast to Roberts, who was immured in Windsor, tied down by routine and responsibility, Carman was often at loose ends, free to indulge himself in reading and writing. After putting in a second year at Harvard without even registering for any courses, he spent the winter of 1888-9 rusticating at the family home in Fredericton. It was not until February 1890, when he was appointed literary editor of *The Independent* in New York City, that he settled down to regular work. His stint there, which lasted until the summer of 1892, was the longest period of steady employment in his entire lifetime. He left it to go to *Current Literature*, where he remained less than two months. During the next three years, he flitted briefly to *Cosmopolitan*, *The Chapbook*, and *The Atlantic Monthly*, never remaining in any of those editorial posts longer than a few months. His most important achievement during that period was the publication of his first book of poetry, *Low Tide on Grand Pré* (1893).

Whenever Carman was on the staff of a magazine, Canadian writers could count upon his sympathetic consideration of their submissions. In particular, he promoted the work of his cousin, the 'Old Man' – partly because Roberts thrust so much of it upon him, partly because he knew that Roberts was always in desperate financial straits, but mostly because he truly admired nearly everything that Roberts wrote. Roberts' letters to

Carman are full of gratitude for the compliments and the cash. After *The Independent* had been especially prompt in publishing his sonnet 'The Night Sky,' his acknowledgment bore this significant addendum: 'Cheque came along this morning – $7.00...' When Carman expressed pleasure with an essay on literature and politics, Roberts replied: 'Have half a dozen other screeds in view to do for you as soon as I can.' Carman was even receptive to manuscripts that Roberts had failed to place elsewhere. Two of the latter's rejects, 'The Raid from Beauséjour' and 'The Secret of the Ballot Box,' were considered by Carman to be unsuitable for *The Independent*: the first because it was primarily an adventure story for boys, and the second because its main focus was a Canadian election. However, he published 'The Star of the Marsh' (which had been returned by *Century*, *Harper's*, *Atlantic*, and *Scribner's*) apparently agreeing with Roberts' self-assessment that it was the 'best prose' he had done thus far. Yet, in spite of Carman's nepotism Roberts sometimes dispatched urgent entreaties: 'Do hurry up with those poems, and stories and articles, old man, for the cash faileth horribly.' On another occasion he pleaded: 'Publish some of my verse that I may not forget I am a poet!'[3]

His letters to Carman are the best source of information about Roberts' various affairs of the heart. Over the years he had kept in touch with Marguerita in Owen Sound, and as late as 6 February 1895, he told Carman that she had correctly identified all but one of the latter's songs in the recent *Vagabondia* volume that Carman and Richard Hovey had published jointly.[4] In the meantime, however, there were many diversions closer to home. Evidently Carman never expressed any disapproval or censure, for Roberts confessed his philanderings with the frankness of one who is sure of a sympathetic ear.

It is not known to what extent Roberts' romantic entanglements were public knowledge, but Windsor was too small a town to hold large secrets. On one occasion, he was stopped on the way to class by a student who greeted him with the shattering announcement: 'Mrs Louise Wilde, the musician, has died.' The lad made no allusion to his professor's infatuation with the lady except for the cryptic remark: 'I thought you should be told when you were alone, sir.'[5] It was to Louise Wilde that Roberts had written 'A Serenade,' which her husband had set to music. After her death he expressed his grief in several poems, including the elegy 'Grey Rocks and Greyer Sea.'

As Roberts indicated in a letter to Carman on 23 March 1890, Windsor had no scarcity of young women who were attractive enough to turn the head of a susceptible professor:

Would thou wert here for a little Friday evening Lenten club which we have had running all Lent. It containeth a dozen of us giddy young folk, – the choicest! The prettiest of the little dames! We read Shakespeare (unexpurgated) for two hours and then dance for two hours. The two fair Lawsons and their mother, Nora Harsley, Miss Dimock, Miss Locke constitute the female element, with May of course. We have a high old time, – and, with Les Belle Lawsons make grand progress! Ah!

The exclamatory sentences were his customary method of indicating his appreciation of the opposite sex. Elsewhere in the same letter he wrote: 'A word in thine ear! The little girl from Wallace is coming to Windsor to live!' Three weeks later he informed Carman: '*Jean* is here!!!'

The 'little girl' in question was Jean Carré, a young artist of considerable promise, whose family had immigrated to Nova Scotia from the island of Guernsey. A few years later, she designed the covers for several of Roberts' books. On the title-page of a friend's copy of *Barbara Ladd*, Roberts wrote: 'The cover of this novel was designed by the lady from whom I drew the heroine of the story.' Therefore, we may deduce something of the personality of Jean Carré by studying his portrait of Barbara Ladd. Although he obviously admires the strong-willed Barbara, he stresses 'her careless candour, her thoughtless self-absorption, her scorn of all opinions that differed from her own, her caprices, her passionate enthusiasms, her fierce intolerance of criticism or control.' Furthermore, he tells us that 'Barbara was one of those who colour the moods of others by their own, and are therefore apt to be at fault in their interpretation of another's motives.'[6]

Jean Carré soon began appearing in the Carman correspondence under the cumbersome pseudonym of 'she whose name is writ in music,' and although Roberts reported a few months later that she was his 'main solace in these weary days,' he was forced to acknowledge before the year was out that she was 'impatient with affairs as they are.' Just after Christmas 1891, he wrote to Carman in exasperation:

I fear that she whose name is writ in music shall henceforth have it writ in mud! She faileth me profoundly. Never before have I experienced so complete a disillusionment. I have demanded back, and taken my ring ... and have given her till the 10th of January as probation. If she comes rightly into line by then, I turn my face again to her, for I grieve to confess to thee, old man, I yet love her passing well. Verily it were better, however, were my brains in my heels. I don't see at all why I am such an ass as to remain in love with her. I must set my affections on things above!!! I will resolve firmly not to love again!!!! Like George II 'J'aurai des maîtresses,' and then, alack, first thing I know I will fall in love again, and again go on the same old sweet, ridiculous, delicious, bitter round. Ah well, all this makes philosophers of us. There is much consolation in that.

In the new year, he admitted that she still managed to keep him so miserable that his stomach felt 'like a boiled pudding.' However, by the middle of March he was able to announce: 'She is now clothed in her right mind, – which is an altogether delightful one, and a great comfort is she.' A month later, he was still exulting that 'after a long spell of unmanage-ableness she is now all music and exceeding dear.'[7]

During 1892, his infatuation with Jean Carré reached such a pitch that he finally agreed 'to chuck everything'[8] and run off with her. New Year's Eve found him outlining his resolutions in a letter to Carman:

We are working into shape a very beautiful, prudent, and feasible scheme for Italy & such like, which I verily believe will carry, & into which *thou* wouldst fit most suavely & economically & with no loss or hindrance to thy freedom. *She* plans to be daily at work at one of the art schools in one of the big Italian cities – say Pisa, Florence, Naples, Venice, Parma or Palermo. We could live cheaply & deliciously in the suburbs, & work, loaf, invite our souls, vagabondize, to our souls' content. Wilt thou not be in it, heart o' me?

With characteristic waywardness, Jean was anxious to take the plunge at once, but Roberts hesitated. He was not really ready to make the break with his family; and, since she would be satisfied with nothing less, the romance foundered. She eventually went to New York City, where she studied art at the Metropolitan League and supported herself with secretarial work. It is intriguing to note that while the affair was at its height, Roberts was contemplating a verse drama based upon the story of Lilith, but the mythological temptress, like the real one, was ultimately abandoned.

Another pseudonym appeared in the Carman correspondence for the first time on 19 December 1891, when Roberts wrote: 'Methinks the Queen of Bohemia will be a governess at Kingscroft this winter.'[9] Obviously, the identity of the woman was no mystery to Carman. Indeed, he knew her as Miss Maude Clarke, an intimate of the Roberts family circle. It was May Roberts who actually pressured that Maude be hired as governess. The request was reasonable enough since there were now four small children to look after, the youngest, Douglas (or 'Duddy'), having been born in 1888. Money was almost too scarce for such a luxury, but Roberts agreed to the proposal with feigned reluctance on the condition that Maude would also act as his secretary.

May seems to have been completely unaware of what was going on behind her back. During the period when Jean Carré was giving him a hard time, Roberts found consolation in a flirtation with Maude Clarke. On 10 January 1892, Nan Prat described for Carman (whom she called 'Kelly') several visits that Roberts (the 'Old Man') paid to the home of her married sister in Windsor while she and Maude were staying there alone:

The one & only 'Old Man' dined with Maudie & me this afternoon at half past five o'clock. ... The heroine of the goldenheaded bottle & the above are as *spoony* as ever if not moreso. Don't you think I'm pretty good natured to sit quietly by (gooseberry) while they have *so* much fun & you know when I came over I put up a cozy little hammock in the corner of the sitting-room next the balcony, & didn't the wretches break it down on Friday morn. Maude landed safely on the cushions, but poor 'O.M.' I fancy got pretty badly shaken, though he didn't like to say much about it. You have really no idea, Kelly dear, what devils they are! Why that bad Old Man will come in & they will stay here in the sitting-room where I am working just as long as they can stand it – & then a brilliant idea will strike the O.M. He wants (?) 'a drink of water.' Then Maudie politely offers to go get it for him, when he hastens to assure her he would rather get it himself & the matter invariably ends in both of them paddling off down stairs where they laugh and talk gaily for a few moments and then for the space of from half to three quarters of an hour there is silence prolonged & unbroken, and *I* sit up here painting and whistling 'two is company, three is none,' etc., etc. to keep my spirits up.[10]

The Roberts children adored the 'tall and slim' Miss Clarke, who became a 'tutoress and far more' to them. Lloyd, who later admitted to being the most wayward of the offspring, always felt that she was an ally whose 'sympathies, deep down, respond bravely to the underdog.' As a secretary, Maude struggled diligently with Roberts' difficult handwriting, but, by her own admission, her behaviour sometimes took an impish turn:

I'm afraid I was frivolous. I sat at one end of the long study table, which ran beside bookshelves against the wall, while the O.M. sat at the opposite end. He plugged hard at his work. ... I used to get deadly tired; so tired that I'd do things to divert him from his work – throw him kisses – or make faces at him. I mostly made faces! This was not nice, but we understood each other pretty well.[11]

It was while Roberts was being distracted by Maude Clarke that Jean became more amenable. On 6 April 1892, when he informed Carman, 'She is very good now,' he added, 'as is the Queen of Bohemia!' Of the two women, Maude eventually held a deeper place in Roberts' affections, but the relationship was either so discreet or so innocent that May never seems to have felt threatened. In fact, she regarded Maude as one of her 'most loyal friends,' and apparently thought nothing about going off to Fredericton for a prolonged visit that summer, leaving the governess in charge. After she had been gone two weeks, Roberts commented: 'May is still in Fredericton, and here I keep the waters unruffled with some difficulty and peril.' When he left King's College permanently in 1895, Maude Clarke was uppermost in his thoughts. He had been away for only a couple of weeks when he told Carman: 'the Queen of Bohemia retaineth a charm for me that others, though perchance far younger and fairer, cannot really match! She rules!'[12]

There are hints of several other involvements of a more fleeting or a less amorous nature. One confidante named Louise, who is mentioned frequently in the letters to Carman from 1892 onward, had such a profound appreciation of Roberts' talents that she even agreed to lend him money. Although he never referred to Louise's full name, she was the only one of his women friends for whom he never used a pseudonym. Many of the allusions are obscure today, but they were obviously well known to Carman. The details that are missing in the letters had all been filled in during Roberts' occasional trips to New York, and more particularly during Carman's lengthy visits to Kingscroft.

The Roberts progeny conferred the honorary title of 'Uncle' upon Carman. Lloyd in his family chronicles has pictured Uncle Bliss as he appeared to the eyes of a child. He emerges as an enigmatic figure in a grey suit:

He stalked into our house like an etherealized Lincoln – huge, gray and quiet – made droll remarks at long intervals, now and then smiled with his eyes, and lived in the study. He seldom spoke to us four youngsters, and his drawl would begin with 'Say, Old Man,' and end with a grunt. He was a mystery to us and we liked mysteries. Our only meeting ground was the dining-table, where we watched with amazement his daily devastation of reams of buttered toast. The rest of the time, though hidden behind closed doors, we could hear him droning his verses like some great bumble-bee, now low, now loud, as inspiration wavered or gathered energy for a fresh burst of speed.[13]

In 1891, Carman apparently accepted Roberts' invitation to join him at Kingscroft about mid-September while May was visiting in Fredericton. 'I shall have a darling little dame keeping house for me,' Roberts wrote, 'and the devil's own time soothing the wrath of her whose name is writ in music! Come and watch the fun!' When Carman arrived, he was accompanied by his friend Richard Hovey, a young American poet whom he had met at Harvard. In appearance and manner, Hovey was the antithesis of Carman: 'He was broad, black and bearded; he roared in the gale of his own exuberance; he was as inevitable as the other was elusive.'[14]

Like Carman, Hovey disappeared behind the study door, where he suggested a poetry game, which Roberts later described in 'More Reminiscences of Bliss Carman':

This was the manner of it. First we would agree as to what form we were to exercise our craftmanship upon, whether a fixed form, – sonnet, quatrain, dizain, as might be chosen, – or a piece of verse of any form, or of any length up to about a hundred lines. We limited the length because we limited the time, – usually to forty-eight hours. Never less than that, because we took the game very seriously, and would not encourage the perpetration of any slap dash impromptus. These weighty points settled, we would each select three titles upon which we would like to write. Each title was written on a separate slip of paper, folded minutely, and dropped into a hat. Then some unprejudiced hand would draw one slip, and read out the title. After that it was go-as-you-please until the appointed hour, some days later, when we would meet in my study and compare the fruits of our labours.[15]

In that fashion, each of the three poets composed several poems that he later felt to be worthy of publication.

Roberts has recorded that when Hovey and Carman visited him the next summer he was hard at work on his ode for the Shelley centenary, while the others were engaged in equally serious projects which precluded any games. During the day, they virtually ignored each other. 'But in the evening,' Roberts recalled, 'we would foregather again, and produce for mutual commendation and criticism (the commendation greatly predominating), what the day's travail had brought forth.' After Carman's departure, Hovey stayed on during September while May was visiting in Fredericton. Roberts, who was enjoying the liberty of 'bachelor's hall,' wrote to Carman: 'Hovey is a jewel and makes no effort to trespass on my court so far.'[16]

In the spring of 1893, Hovey was able, through his parents, General and Mrs Charles E. Hovey of Washington, DC, to repay some of Roberts' hospitality. Mrs Hovey was always adopting her son's friends as her 'boys,' and when she learned that Roberts needed to recuperate from influenza and overwork, she insisted that he come to her home. Roberts, 'sick of slush & cold,' eagerly accepted the invitation, and left for Washington on 5 April. Carman and Richard Hovey joined him there, and Mother Hovey, the 'most generous-hearted of women,' fussed over her boys and pampered them outrageously. At a picnic arranged in their honour, Roberts gallantly lifted a young lady over a brook. Afterwards, to the special delight of his hostess, he celebrated the bumbling chivalry of the 'country lad' whose 'foolish heart' was 'a-quaking with delight' in 'The Ballad of Crossing the Brook.' 'It runs through my head so continually,' Mrs Hovey told Carman weeks later, 'that I have concocted a regular tune to it.'[17]

On his way home from Washington, Roberts stopped over in Boston, where he met E.W. Thomson, a Canadian writer who had recently given up his post with the *Globe* in Toronto to become one of the editors of *The Youth's Companion*. Thomson took him out to dinner and later acknowledged in a letter to Archibald Lampman that he found him to be 'a prepossessing person,' but felt that 'there *is* a touch of Mr Hyde' about him. 'He hadn't been talking to me two minutes,' Thomson reported disapprovingly, 'when some allusion gave him an opening to mention matters usually hidden from polite society.'[18] However, since Thomson refrained from divulging any further details, the exact nature of Roberts' disclosure remains a tantalizing mystery.

It may have been during his trip to Washington that Roberts first met Mrs Henrietta Russell, a follower of Delsartism, who had borne Hovey an illegitimate son and was then in the process of arranging a divorce from her husband. Probably it was on Roberts' invitation that Hovey and Mrs Russell spent the summer of 1893 in Windsor, arriving in June and staying on until September. They set up two tents on the Kingscroft grounds, one occupied by Hovey and the other by Mrs Russell and her friend, Mrs Gertrude Burton. Carman was unable to join them until the end of August, but Hovey's mother kept him informed about their activities: 'Mrs Russell writes me a great letter about camping out in Nova Scotia, and invites me to join.' Early in September, Mrs Hovey wrote happily to Carman: 'You, Dick and the Old Man are once more together and I am glad.'[19] On the subject of Mrs Russell, Hovey's mother was reserved, although later letters, written by her after Hovey's death in 1900, express a strong antipathy. When, in the course of the summer at

Windsor, Henrietta Russell secured her divorce, Hovey announced to Roberts in great consternation: 'My God, she means to marry me!'[20] One can only speculate on the reasons why the ready lover suddenly became a reluctant bridegroom. Perhaps he had a feeling that Henrietta's strong personality, which he found refreshing as long as he was independent, would make his life difficult as her husband. Possibly he was concerned that the marriage would be less than acceptable to his parents. As usual, however, Henrietta got her way, and in time she became Mrs Hovey.

It was not unusual for the Kingscroft premises to be used as a camping ground. Edmund Collins, for one, had pitched his tent there during the summer of 1890. Roberts' old friend had fallen upon hard times after going to New York in 1886. For a couple of years he edited the *Epoch* there, but he had become a heavy drinker following the deaths of his two children, and it is not clear whether he left the paper or was fired. During that time, also, he appears to have separated from his wife. When Carman joined *The Independent* staff, early in 1890, he shared a flat with Collins, who was then working as a freelance writer. Roberts was happy to welcome 'Dear old Kobins,' as he called him, for he had not forgotten the favours of the past. He had already expressed a measure of his gratitude by dedicating his second volume of poetry, *In Divers Tones* (1886), to Collins. But the Collins he had known had been changed by dissipation, and it was not possible to be on the same free terms with him as of old. When word came from Carman of Collins' death in New York a year and a half later, Roberts replied:

I was profoundly surprised, and to a certain extent grieved by the news of poor Collins' death. I remembered the old regard, – which had not, however, been really the same for years, though up to a year and a half ago I had not acknowledged the fact to myself. My profound distrust of him had absolutely killed my affection for him.

It is the Collins of years ago that I shall try to remember.[21]

To Roberts fell the responsibility of paying off the debts that Collins had accumulated in Windsor. Altogether, about $50 was owing; but Roberts, who had learned to be persuasive in such matters, managed to get the amount reduced by half.

The number of visitors who travelled to Windsor for the express purpose of meeting Roberts is an indication of his emergence as Canada's leading literary figure. Among those who came from afar was Douglas Sladen, a young English writer and anthologist, who arrived in the spring of 1889. After a brilliant academic record at Oxford, Sladen had become the first person to hold a chair in history at the University of Sydney. The literary labours of the four years he had remained in Australia included *A Century of Australian Song* (1888), in the Canterbury Poets series in which Roberts' anthology, *Poems of Wild Life*, appeared at about the same time. Fresh from the Antipodes, with his wife and little boy, Sladen was paying his expenses around the world with a lecture tour and other literary chores such as a proposed anthology of younger American poets. He conferred with Roberts about the preparation of the Canadian section of the book, but because the latter could not afford to donate his valuable time without substantial financial gain, it fell to young Goodridge Roberts to co-operate with the editing. The completed volume, *Younger American Poets, 1830-1890*, published in 1892, contains an appendix on younger Canadian poets with a generous inclusion of poems by Charles G.D. Roberts.

Following Sladen's visit, William Sharp, the general editor of the Canterbury Poets series, arrived from England in September. A handsome blond-bearded Scot, Sharp possessed a magnetic personality that drew people to him at once. Although only four or five years older than Roberts, he had been associated with Dante Gabriel Rossetti's circle in London, and had published a biography of Rossetti in 1882. Under his own name, Sharp produced several novels, biographies, and volumes of verse. Today he is chiefly remembered for the remarkable Celtic tales in prose and verse, written by 'Fiona Macleod,' the pseudonym with which he was identified only after his death in 1905. During his stay at Kingscroft, he read and admired a number of Roberts' sonnets. Later, he included several of them in the *Anthology of American Sonnets*, which he edited for the Canterbury Poets series.

Roberts enjoyed playing host, but May often found the succession of visitors extremely taxing. Incapable of taking part in an intellectual discussion, she felt left out when the conversation inevitably turned to topics for which she possessed neither understanding nor interest. Their guests might be distinguished and clever, but, as far as she was concerned, they simply added to her household duties. Even when they camped on the Kingscroft lawn, or took rooms in a local inn (as the Sladens did), she could not entirely escape the task of entertaining them. More mouths to feed meant a worrisome strain on the meagre family budget. Furthermore, few of the male house guests ever thought of waiting upon themselves, and their presence was particularly burdensome during the periods when there was no maid at Kingscroft. William Sharp was an exception to the rule, however; although May was overawed by his impressive bearing, she appreciated his willingness to wipe dishes and carry his own bath water.

Even in ordinary social intercourse, May was too diffident to make small talk easily with strangers. Her shyness was especially surprising since, as the daughter of George Fenety, she had grown up in a household that habitually welcomed prominent personages from all walks of life. For someone of Roberts' gregarious nature, her attitude towards company was often disconcerting, and sometimes downright embarrassing. On one occasion when John Bourinot, the chief clerk of the House of Commons, was due to call, she stormed to her room, absolutely refusing to come down. Roberts, left to greet their guest alone, excused his wife's absence by explaining: 'Mrs Roberts is extremely disappointed not to be able to meet you, but she is confined to her bed with an excruciating headache.'[22]

Nan Prat (who joined the household as Roberts' secretary for $20 a month while he was translating *Les Anciens Canadiens*) took a charitable view of May's social reluctance, calling her 'a good listener rather than a talker.' She hastened to add that 'where there were so many clever talkers to listen to,' as they sat around the fireside in the evening, 'listening was the more delightful part.' Undoubtedly, that statement was an accurate expression of Miss Prat's own attitude, but it is questionable whether the same feelings could always be attributed to May. 'There is little to tell about Mrs Roberts,' Maude Clarke wrote in 1928, 'for she was just a very quiet and retiring woman. ... Men often marry their exact opposites.' But Maude staunchly commended her for being 'most thorough in all her duties pertaining to the household.'

To all outward appearances, certainly, Kingscroft ran as smoothly as most households. According to Maude Clarke, Roberts 'was a most attentive husband & a devoted father' whose family 'adored him' even though he always 'exacted obedience.'[23] Her view has been corroborated by Lloyd Roberts, who once declared: 'I fear that we children loved our Papa as children are supposed to love God.' At a later time, Lloyd (in a thinly disguised autobiographical novel) described his father as an autocratic disciplinarian, albeit a loving one:

The professor ... was in theory a democrat, in practice a benevolent autocrat. He ruled rooftree and classroom alike with an exacting justice, all the more exacting because of his love for his subjects. Outside the house the four children raised all the commotion they pleased; within, it was 'No romping,' decorum and unswerving obedience to authority. Mama obeyed, protesting; Major, the little Boston bull, never growled back; even Lizzie, primitive and Irish, curbed tongue and tinware when the Man was home. Thus, despite minor inharmonies in kitchen, bedroom and nursery, the domestic wheels as a whole turned noiselessly and the children learned their elementary lessons in the peculiar ways of this peculiar world.

The mealtime ritual at Kingscroft always began with Papa pronouncing 'a rapid-fire grace in a dead language' while the children tried to accompany him, 'buzzing in unison like a swarm of bees.' Lloyd had a droll recollection of the proceedings:

Eggs were a luxury then as now, it seems. Whenever Papa would indulge in one, he would most carefully decapitate the shell, giving the top to each of us in turn. We children ate porridge, if it were breakfast. During dinner, if there were two courses and no Lizzie, who was rather intermittent, we would rise after the first course and scrape our plates out of the dining-room window to a large and expectant assembly of fowls. This brilliant scheme saved both waste and dishwashing, though my mother never quite approved, especially if there were guests. After each meal, unless college classes were on, the study door would be closed on Papa and Major, and the rest of the house became as silent as a church. One knew instinctively that mighty things were brewing in the book-lined room on the other side of the door, and it behooved us not to meddle therein.

On winter evenings, the children were allowed the use of the study for an hour, but immediately upon entering they had to possess themselves 'of a book and become "still as a mouse".' The happiest times were those when the family gathered around the fireplace after tea before the lamps were lighted. Roberts, reclining on the sofa with his 'chicks' snuggled around him, would sing rousing college songs, while the children would 'join with Mama in the choruses, all on the same flat.'[24] At bedtime, after their mother had tucked them in, Roberts would come to kiss the children goodnight, carefully stroking back his Louis Quinze moustache to prevent it from tickling.

One visitor who would have been welcomed to Kingscroft by both Roberts and May was Andy Straton, but an occasional note (with 'A.W. Straton, Civil Engineer' on the letterhead) continued to be their only contact with him. Although Andy still used Fredericton as his home address, he worked mostly in Maine and Massachusetts, and sometimes managed to see Carman, either in Boston or in Northampton, where

Carman's sister lived. In the spring of 1890, Carman wrote to Roberts expressing concern over Andy's declining health. Roberts replied:

I wrote to poor old Andy the same day I got your letter. I urged him energetically to come over and pitch his tent at Kingscroft, and May seconded the bid with all her might. Have heard nothing from him yet, however. Hope he will come. We'll brace him up if he does. Urge him, thou.

But the reunion at Kingscroft never took place. Andy Straton was in the advanced stages of tuberculosis, and within five months he was dead. Both Roberts and Carman felt the loss deeply. Andy had been a kindred spirit, and although he had harboured no ambitions to become a writer himself, he had been a generous admirer of the early work of his two cousins. That they missed his approbation is evident in Roberts' lament over one of Carman's later poems: 'Would that dear old Andy could see it!'[25]

A still closer tragedy struck Kingscroft when Goodridge Roberts died suddenly of pneumonia on 4 February 1892, while visiting Minnie Prat and her family in Wolfville. Before the sad tiding arrived that morning from Acadia Villa, Athelstan and Lloyd had gone off to King's Collegiate School, where they were day students. Lloyd never forgot the shock of being called from class by Lizzie, their maid, to be told: 'Your Uncle Gool is dead!' It was the children's first experience of family bereavement, and they were overwhelmed by the strange solemnity of drawn blinds and the sight of dear Papa's stricken face. It was almost beyond comprehension that they had lost 'one of the dearest uncles a child ever had,' one who answered 'a hundred questions to the minute' without getting cross.

By all accounts, Goodridge was the son whose personality was most like that of the godly rector, his father, for whom he was named. Jean Bliss, his maiden aunt, confessed to Carman: ' "Gool" was one of my pets – I love[d] him more than any of that family.'[26] To his brother Charles, Goodridge was a soul-mate – a scholar and a young writer of considerable promise. His death was one of the great blows of Roberts' life.

Mixed with Roberts' grief was the acute distress of financial worries, not that money problems were anything new. Over the last two years, nearly every letter he had written to Carman had either contained a request for the endorsation of a bank note or an allusion to a story or poem for which he hoped to be paid by *The Independent*. Usually he remained optimistic about his promissory notes. 'Shall handle 'em all right, however,' he wrote in one characteristic passage, 'if the Fates do not

shear off my thread, – in which case the Policy would handle 'em anyway.'
Maude Clarke noted that he undertook his everlasting financing 'with
great cheerfulness, but believe me it required great feats of engineering as
his tired out look testified.'[27]

Following Goodridge's death, which coincided with the financial
obligation for Edmund Collins, Roberts was compelled once again to call
upon the good graces of his father-in-law for a loan. By the middle of
November, he reported happily to Carman that his debt of $250 to Mr
Fenety had been paid. 'I was *determined* to pay it in full, to impress him with
my prompt & business-like methods!' he declared. 'Thus I can call on him
again, emergency requiring!!' However, the next letter requested Carman to co-sign a special note with him:

> This one is a mere security for *Louise*; I am borrowing cash *from her*, to relieve
> myself of other debts, & to consolidate, & so work more freely. Of course, *she*
> doesn't want any name but my own, but I have insisted on her taking thine (if thou
> wilt give it!) in case anything should happen to me. In that case, it would then
> devolve on thee to see the settlement of the claim out of my *Life Insurance* (of which
> I have six thousand). The amt of borrowing I have not yet quite resolved upon, but
> I think it will be nearly $400.00.[28]

His income was supplemented in a very modest way by his frequent
lecture tours, particularly during the first four or five years that he was at
King's. He spoke on literary topics in various Maritime centres, including
Halifax, Fredericton, Truro, Amherst, and New Glasgow. There were
three trips to Montreal, and another that took him to Lennoxville and
Quebec City. As early as December 1886, he addressed the Canadian Club
of New York on the subject of Acadian history. In 1890, he was invited to
Boston's Tremont Temple, where he spoke on 'Province Literature' to a
group of former Maritimers.

Whenever he travelled to the United States, he took a bundle of his
manuscripts, stories, and poems, which he literally peddled from one
editorial office to another. As a result of those personal contacts, many of
the editors, such as Robert Watson Gilder of *The Century*, became his close
friends. However, it was not only the tangible gains of selling his wares
and finding new markets that made his journeys worthwhile. He was
starved for the stimulation that came from associating with brilliant and
creative men. He deliberately sought to acquaint himself with as many
of the American literati as possible; and several established personages,
such as Thomas Bailey Aldrich, Oliver Wendell Holmes, and Edmund

Clarence Stedman, extended many courtesies, including the hospitality of their homes. But he had more in common with the young intellectuals of Carman's circle; and, after one particularly refreshing visit, he commented enviously upon his cousin's 'congenial'[29] associates.

While he was at King's, Roberts accepted a number of writing commissions in order to augment his income. Many of those undertakings exacted a tremendous toll of time and energy for which the financial return was pitifully inadequate. Reference has already been made to the 'Literary Chapter' of *The Dominion Annual Register*, which kept him so busy in 1886 that he scarcely had time to prepare for his classes. Shortly thereafter, he was busy with his anthology of wildlife poems for the Canterbury Poets series. His introduction to that volume contained a comment that revealed his own expectations of literature: 'Among the young poets, with all their admirable dexterity, there is a too general lack of romance, of broad human impulse, of candid delight in life.'[30]

One of his most important commissions was his translation of Philippe Aubert de Gaspé's *Les Anciens Canadiens*, for which he was paid $200 by D. Appleton and Company. In the original work, published in 1863, the author, at the age of seventy-four, had drawn upon his family's recollections of the English conquest of Quebec to produce a valuable compendium of facts, traditions, and folklore. In his translation, Roberts gave a literal rendering of the text except for the numerous habitant folk songs, which he treated much more freely. With the aid of Nan Prat, who made 'a fine little secretary,' the work was finished on 31 August 1890. In October, it came off the press bearing the title *The Canadians of Old*.

Next in importance among his various commissions were his three travel guides. The first of those, completed before he went to King's College, was the New Brunswick section of *Picturesque Canada*, for which George Monro Grant of Queen's University was the general editor. In the early months of 1891 he was hard at work on Appleton's *Canadian Guide-Book*. The latter task was long and tiring, and he complained to Carman that 'funds are especially low here just now, working on the book has kept me off the stories – and hence cashless.'[31] Eventually, he was paid $300 for his work, but he felt that the sum was poor compensation for all his time and effort. He appears to have taken more pleasure in writing *The Land of Evangeline and the Gateways Thither*, which the Dominion Atlantic Railway published in 1895 to attract more passengers.

Book reviewing was another task that took time from Roberts' creative work. He wrote generous notices of the early publications by many of his Canadian contemporaries, men such as Archibald Lampman, William

Wilfred Campbell, Frederick George Scott, and, of course, Bliss Carman. The greater number of those reviews appeared in *Progress*, a weekly journal published in Saint John and edited by May's brother-in-law, Edward Carter, who had been a classmate of Roberts at the University of New Brunswick. Roberts contributed a regular column called 'The World of Books' for which he was paid next to nothing. A slightly more profitable market was found in *The Dominion Illustrated*, which ran his column of philosophical musings and reviews, called 'Modern Instances,' for five issues beginning in February 1892.

Roberts sometimes took up his pen to address the national issues of the day. Between 1882 and 1892, he underwent a political metamorphosis that saw his early advocacy of complete independence for Canada transformed into the concept of autonomy within the British Empire. As a youth, he had been so fired by Macdonald's election slogan of 1878, 'Canada for the Canadians,' that the idea of independence had taken hold of him. At the age of twenty-three, he announced that he had become politically active and had already converted 'several opponents in Fredericton.'[32] Just a few months later, he was editing *The Week* for Goldwin Smith, who looked upon Canadian independence as utter folly. Smith was not able to change Roberts' views, but he may have influenced the modification that took place.

The chief products of Roberts' early proselytizing were three patriotic poems. The first of them, 'Canada,' written in January 1885, was followed within a few months by 'Collect for Dominion Day' and 'An Ode for the Canadian Confederacy.' Desmond Pacey has exhibited them as evidence that Roberts 'consciously essayed the role of a national poet,' but such a conclusion is slightly misleading. Pacey's phrasing suggests that Roberts aspired to be a Canadian poet laureate, but it would be nearer the truth simply to say that he was consciously promoting the cause of nationalism. 'Canada,' with its dramatic juxtaposition of rhetorical questions and exclamatory statements, was the most popular of the three poems. It made a strong appeal to his countrymen:

> How long the ignoble sloth, how long
> The trust in greatness not thine own?
> Surely the lion's brood is strong
> To front the world alone!

Although the foregoing stanza may have failed to inspire any French Canadians, if they ever read it, the contemporary impact upon English

Canadians was hardly exaggerated by W.D. Lighthall, who avowed that it 'stirs the heart of every true Canadian like a trumpet.'[33]

The inclusion of 'Canada' and its fellows in Roberts' second volume of poetry in 1886 created the impression that his 'independent' phase was a permanent stance. In reality, however, his 'Mother of Nations' (written for Queen Victoria's Golden Jubilee, but never included in any of his collections) indicated as early as 1888 that he was beginning to approve of a role within the British Empire for

> This nation that hath weighed the worth
> Of its heroic birth,
> And now in manhood shall not shame
> The strong loins whence it came.[34]

He became convinced that complete independence for Canada was unrealistic at that point in her existence. He concluded that it would inevitably lead to annexation with the United States and the ultimate loss of autonomy. It was possible, he reasoned, to devise 'a form of Imperial Federation which would so guard the autonomy of each federating nation and so strictly limit the powers of the central government as to satisfy even those who desire absolute independence,' for their interests 'would be secured by the force of the whole empire.'[35]

In the general election of 1891, he actively campaigned against the Liberal party's policy of reciprocity with the United States. Macdonald had again raised the spectre of annexation by claiming that the policy was widely supported by the American politicians, who urged 'as the chief reason for its adoption, that Unrestricted Reciprocity would be the first step in the direction of Political Union.' Privately, Roberts damned Goldwin Smith, who scoffed at Macdonald's fears, as being 'the most impertinent coxcomb that ever cursed our Canada,' and took him to task publicly in the Halifax *Critic*. A letter to Carman indicated his general involvement:

In the election I made some speeches and got in some two-edged editorials, – and verily the Maritime Provinces did us proud, – but may the Grand Trunk Railway be damned! It threw all its power against us in the contest and dished us in Ontario. I believe we shall have a majority even in Ontario, but our losses there are largely due to the G.T.R.[36]

He now shared Macdonald's vision of Canada as a partner within the

Empire. 'A British subject I was born – a British subject I will die,' the Old Chieftain had declared in his last address to the Canadian people. Roberts could find no fault with that sentiment.

The pressures of writing and classwork, combined with constant financial worries, took their toll of Roberts, despite his rugged constitution and his natural optimism. Sometimes he broke temporarily under the strain, and was forced to take a respite such as his prolonged visit with Hovey's parents. On another occasion, after he had put on an exhaustive drive to finish an article about a projected ship railway across the Isthmus of Chignecto, he confessed that he 'simply had to rest' and give his 'pumped brain a holiday.' There were times when he felt that foreign travel would be the best escape from the drudgery of his routine. At the end of January 1892, he wrote to Carman: 'All last night and all today the desire for wandering has been strong upon me.' Before the winter was over, he wrote again:

I hunger and thirst for escape. ... I feel as if a few months with thee in Japan, Italy, England, almost anywhere where the skies would be new and the environment fresh and seemly, and the routine of life a little while hidden, would make a new man of me, or make me my old self again. I'm getting vigorous again bodily, but am sick for change.

His friend Douglas Sladen had financed a trip to Japan by writing a book about the journey. Roberts, who had already published two travel guides, proposed using the same method of defraying expenses. The scheme was practical, he assured Carman, adding, 'And Italy we must have, must, must, must!'[37] As the year wore on, it was Jean Carré who became his prospective travelling companion, although he still urged Carman to accompany them. Carman's presence was desirable for several reasons, not the least of which was the matter of appearances. It might even be possible to convince the family that the whole escapade was merely an adventure of two vagabond cousins. But Carman was only lukewarm to the idea; and Roberts, as we have seen, quickly lost his nerve.

Without success, Roberts had begun a search for greener academic fields at least as early as February 1888, when he asked Edmund Clarence Stedman to recommend him for the new Chair of Political Science at the University of Toronto, which offered a salary of $2,500. In May he informed George T. Denison: 'I have withdrawn my application at Toronto, & am applying for the new Chair of English at Queen's.' But Queen's wanted someone with European training, and he was passed over for

James Cappon, a Scot, who is remembered today chiefly for the two books he wrote about the poetry of Charles G.D. Roberts. Turning his attention to Toronto again, Roberts wrote to the Canadian poet Charles Mair on 4 January 1889, asking: 'By the way, will you put in a spoke for me in my search for the Toronto Chair of English Literature? Your name is potent in Toronto.' At about the same time, he applied for a similar position at Dalhousie University, but withdrew his name after learning that 'a bit of personally hostile canvas' was being circulated against him. A couple of years later, when his disillusionment with King's was increasing, he toyed with the idea of going to Acadia University in nearby Wolfville, but decided that the move would not be a satisfactory change. 'I long for a big centre,' he explained to Carman.[38]

For a short time in 1895, it looked as if his wish for academic advancement might be granted. Edmund Clarence Stedman, an important figure in North American literary circles of the day, had recommended him for the Billings Chair of English Literature at Yale University. As a member of the corporation and president of the Yale alumni, Stedman had been asked to find a candidate 'in his prime, doing good work, likely to do better, and capable of getting hold of young men.'[39] In Stedman's opinion, Roberts met all of those requirements. Not only was he impressed with Roberts' volumes of published poetry, but after meeting the author in New York, he had formed a high regard for him as a person. However, Stedman's endorsement was not enough, and Roberts was not offered the position with its relatively munificent salary of $3,500 a year. From his letters to Carman, we learn that he was optimistic about his chances at the universities of Washington and Boston, but no firm offer ever materialized from either of those institutions.

While Roberts longed for the limelight of some more luminous intellectual sphere, he did not entirely languish in remote obscurity. Nor was he altogether a prophet without honour in his own country. In 1890 the Royal Society of Canada elected him to fill the vacancy caused by the death of William Lyall, a distinguished professor at Dalhousie University. His candidature had been proposed by William Kirby, author of *The Golden Dog*, who urged a number of his influential friends to support Roberts' nomination. At the age of thirty, Roberts became one of the youngest members of the Society. In 1893, he was elected a fellow of the Royal Society of Literature.

Financial stress prompted Roberts to enter the Dominion History Competition, which opened in July 1893, and closed on 1 July 1895. In the hope that a suitable high school text might be forthcoming, the provincial governments had jointly offered $2,000 for the winning entry. Roberts had previously written a series of historical sketches, 'Echoes from Old Acadia,' which had been so warmly received that he felt confident about attempting a complete history of the country. With Maude Clarke acting as his typist, he wrote nearly 2,000 words a day on the average, although there were times when his daily output reached as much as 3,000 words. On 4 June 1894, he reported to Carman: 'Have 50,000 words done – shall do about 80,000 more.' By keeping up the pressure, Roberts had the manuscript ready well before the deadline. He expressed his satisfaction with it to Parkin, his old schoolmaster: 'I have made a good history – clear, interesting, and of literary quality. It is the best work that I can do in prose.'[40]

The contest judges, representing the various provincial departments of education, deliberated for ten months. At one time, Roberts heard that he was among the 'final 6 out of 15 competitors'; but, in the end, he lost out to W.H.P. Clements, Judge of the Supreme Court of British Columbia. His efforts were not wasted, however, for Lamson, Wolffe & Co. of Boston brought out his history in 1897 to general acclaim in many leading newspapers and periodicals, including the London *Times*. In 1915, L.C. Page & Co. (successors to Lamson, Wolffe) brought out a second edition and arranged with the Macmillan Company of Toronto to add another chapter by another hand, although they claimed in the preface that the work had been 'revised and brought up to date by Mr Roberts.' Since that time, of course, Roberts' *History of Canada* has been superseded by works that are better, not only because they are up-to-date, but because the treatment is more balanced, for Roberts dealt with everything that happened after Confederation in a rather desultory fashion. Yet he retold some of the episodes from early times in such a colourful manner that Desmond Pacey was led to assert in 1961 that they might fittingly 'be included in school textbooks.'[41] No one has ever suggested that any portion of Clements' history deserves to be reprinted.

Although Roberts turned to prose to pay his bills, his most enduring literary achievements to the end of the Kingscroft years are to be found in his poetry. *In Divers Tones*, his next book of poems after *Orion*, appeared in 1886, but most of the contents pre-date his King's College period. Appropriately named, the new volume not only shows the poet moving slowly but surely away from classical themes, but it also includes almost the complete range that his poetry was to cover in the years ahead.

'The Tantramar Revisited,' by far the best poem in the second volume – possibly the greatest poem Roberts ever wrote – is in the elegiac mood, which Carman and Roberts both employed so eloquently that Northrop Frye remarked (a trifle too slightingly, perhaps) that they were 'much better at whimpering than banging.'[42] It owes its powerful nostalgic effect to the accumulation of evocative details: the farmhouses 'stained with time,' the mudflats 'pale with the scurf of the salt,' 'the gossiping grass.' The poetic form, similar to that of Longfellow's *Evangeline*, is perfectly suited to the mood – a feat that Roberts could not always duplicate. By contrast, 'A Song of Regret,' a nostalgic lyric in the same volume, is marred by jangling rhymes and inappropriate rhythm.

The love poems of *In Divers Tones*, precursors of Roberts' *New York Nocturnes* and *The Book of the Rose*, have been dismissed by Desmond Pacey as 'almost incredibly artificial and laboured,'[43] yet lines such as the following sound like the genuine expression of a personal dilemma:

> But, heart, be still!
> I will refrain, and break my dreams, afraid
> To stir the yearning I can not fulfil.
>
> ('In Notre Dame')

The three nationalistic poems in the volume established Roberts' reputation as a patriotic poet, although his total output of such poems would be limited to a half dozen. More characteristic of his later verse is the optimistic faith of 'The Marvellous Work.' The first of Roberts' sonnet vignettes of Maritime life also appears in this second volume, including 'The Potato Harvest' with its perfect ending: 'And day fades out like smoke.'

'Ave,' the lengthy ode (310 lines) that Roberts composed for the centenary of Shelley's birth in 1892, is Shelleyan in concept and diction without being merely imitative. The whole undertaking had been a labour of love, for he worshipped Shelley as 'chief of all those whose brows prophetic wear / The pure and sacred bays.' He liked to think of himself as being shaped by the 'impetuous stress' of the Tantramar, and thus he could identify with his idol because the spirit of Shelley seemed 'strangely akin' to the same region. 'Ave' is highly successful in many respects: the scenes of Rome and the Tantramar are vividly recreated, the diction is admirably suited to the subject, for once the rhyme is unforced, and the rhythm is appropriately dignified. Yet, although the tribute is obviously sincere, it lacks the vitality that a deeply felt emotion or conviction might have given it.

Most critics agree that in Roberts' *Songs of the Common Day* (1893) there

are more poems of a consistently high quality than in any of his other
volumes. It contains a series of thirty-seven landscape sonnets (seven of
which are reprinted from *In Divers Tones*), twenty-eight miscellaneous
poems, and 'Ave' (which had first appeared in December 1892, in a
limited edition of 200 copies). Of these three groups, it is the sonnets that
are generally thought of as representing Roberts' greatest strengths as a
poet. We have his own statement that he was attempting to

> see what beauty clings
> In common forms, and find the soul
> Of unregarded things!
>
> ('Across the fog the moon lies fair')

In keeping with his subject-matter, his diction becomes less ornate and
more suited to a faithful rendering of the Maritime scene.

The majority of the sonnets begin with a clear picture of the landscape,
followed by a relevant philosophical reflection. The homely details
depend upon a total accumulation for their impact, but there are many
isolated phrases and lines that are impressive by themselves:

> the harsh, wind-ridden, eastward hill
>
> ('The Cow Pasture')

> A barn by many seasons beaten grey
>
> ('The Oat Threshing')

> The gusts reveal / By fits the dim grey snakes of fence
>
> ('The Winter Fields')

> I hear the low wind wash the softening snow
>
> ('The Flight of the Geese')

It is commonly held that the meditative appendages which follow the
pictorial lines are too mundane, too vague, and express too blind a faith in
the beneficent powers of nature, but it is an injustice to dismiss all of the
philosophical musings as inconsequential. Roberts, like Alexander Pope,
may not have been an original thinker, and his determined optimism
seems to have gone out of fashion, but he could on occasion voice 'What
oft was thought but ne'er so well expressed':

> Not in perfection dwells the subtler power
> To pierce our mean content, but rather works
> Through incompletion, and the need that irks, –
> Not in the flower, but effort toward the flower.
>
> ('The Cow Pasture')

The public perception of the superiority of Roberts' poetry over his prose was the correct one almost to the turn of the century. Although he had been selling short stories to magazines for years and had published three novelettes in book form (*The Raid from Beauséjour and How the Carter Boys Lifted the Mortgage*, 1894; and *Reube Dare's Shad Boat*, 1895), his contemporaries quite rightly took him more seriously as a poet. Whenever he was referred to as Canada's leading literary figure (as frequently happened), it was his poetry that the speaker had in mind. In *Songs of the Great Dominion* (1889), anthologist William Douw Lighthall had declared: 'The foremost name in Canadian song at the present day is Charles George Douglas Roberts...'[44]

If for no other reason, Roberts gained his foremost position among the Canadian poets of his generation by getting a head start in publication. *Orion* pre-dated Isabella Valancy Crawford's only volume by four years; *In Divers Tones* appeared a year earlier than George Frederick Cameron's single volume and two years before the first offerings by Archibald Lampman, William Wilfred Campbell, and Frederick George Scott. In 1893, the year that marked the appearance of the first books by Bliss Carman and Duncan Campbell Scott, Roberts published his third collection, *Songs of the Common Day*. Being a forerunner, he set the standards against which the achievements of each newcomer were measured. The extent to which any other poet of his generation may have surpassed him is a matter of debate to this day.

CHAPTER FIVE

The Turning Point

1895–1897

AFTER TEN IMPOVERISHED YEARS at King's College, and many unsuccessful attempts to find a better appointment, Roberts decided to abandon the academic life, at least temporarily, to have another fling at freelancing. Having earned a small reputation in the literary world since those difficult months after he first left *The Week*, he felt that he was in a safer position to take the risk. As early as 8 January 1895, he announced to Carman: 'I shall resign here in March (in the guise, remember, of a year's leave without pay).'[1]

His decision had been precipitated by the uncertainty and turmoil in the affairs of the college, as he explained to Parkin:

The President of King's, my very dear friend Willets, is leaving here in righteous disgust at the methods of the Governors...

You are ... talked of in connection with the Presidency of King's! But I should be sorry indeed to see any friend of mine take *that* position. The Governors have made it a hell for every man who has been so unfortunate as to occupy it during the last quarter century. The pay is ridiculous, the work very heavy (including *Bursar's* work) and the finances & whole outlook of the college very bad. I myself have resigned, partly for the purpose of devoting myself altogether to writing (I have a year & a half's engagements ahead, at good rates), and partly because of my contempt for the mismanagement of affairs by the Governors. I intended resigning *last* year, but stayed on in order to help the Faculty fight their battle through with the Governors.[2]

He realized that, although he 'lived *for* poetry,' he would henceforth have to 'live *by* prose.' He told Parkin:

My present plan is to settle in Fredericton. I can live there cheaply & write without hindrance, running on to Boston & New York whenever business makes it necessary. I have a couple of romances to write, for prominent publishers – one on Louisburg, the other on lumber-camp life. And my short stories for young folks are easy work & excellent pay. I have a new volume of poems, too, almost ready – but *this* doesn't mean *money*!

As he outlined his intentions to Parkin, he could not foresee that he was embarking upon a course that would nearly end his career as a poet.[3]

After a busy summer that included a trip to Cape Breton (although he missed getting to Louisbourg) and a public auction of all the household goods that were not shipped to Fredericton, he was able to report to Carman on 25 August: 'Here we are in F'ton at last. ... We have the Rectory, while the Rectory contingent is out at Aldergarth [a backwoods farm that brother Theodore was managing] till October 1.'[4] He was waiting to move into a house that was being constructed in a secluded location on the edge of town, but it was not ready until early November, a full month after 'the Rectory contingent' had returned from Aldergarth. From Roberts' letters to Carman, it appears that he himself remained at the rectory throughout this period, although May and the children may have spent some time at Linden Hall. Living under those conditions, it was understandably difficult to settle down to a regular routine of steady writing; indeed, Roberts was probably glad of an excuse to lay his pen aside temporarily. He was hard at work again, however, soon after getting established in his new home, christened 'Edgecroft' in accordance with the family tradition of assigning fanciful names to their modest dwellings.

The fact that Roberts published four books in 1896 is an indication of how diligently he worked during the first year away from King's. At last, he had a chance to put the finishing touches upon his latest collection of poems, which he called *The Book of the Native*. Similarly, he was able to prepare a collection of his stories, all based on the idea of an inexplicable fate. For that volume, he considered two titles, *Riddles of Earth* and *Backwoods and Tide-water*, but eventually chose *Earth's Enigmas* as the most suitable expression of the common element of the stories. Many of the tales that he had written as adventure stories for boys were gathered together in *Around the Campfire*, in which he used the device of a group of campers spinning yarns to each other on successive nights. He also published his first novel, an Acadian romance called *The Forge in the Forest*, which bore a flattering dedication to his magnanimous father-in-law, George E. Fenety. *The Book of the Native*, *Earth's Enigmas*, and *The Forge in the Forest* all carried the imprint of Lamson, Wolffe & Co. of Boston. *Around the Campfire* was issued simultaneously by Thomas Y. Crowell of New York and William Briggs of Toronto. Canadian editions of *The Book of the Native* and *The Forge in the Forest* were issued by Copp, Clark and William Briggs respectively.

Because his fate as a writer depended upon the larger markets in the United States and Britain, Roberts was pinning his hopes upon favourable reviews from American and British critics. Early notices of *Earth's Enigmas* were extremely encouraging. 'We have long known Professor C.G.D. Roberts for the foremost of Canadian poets,' wrote William Morton Payne in *The Dial* (Chicago), 'and the publication of *Earth's Enigmas* now calls upon us to recognize him as a writer of a high order of imaginative prose.' Payne found the stories 'noteworthy for their artistic finish and poetic feeling, no less than for the fidelity with which they picture Canadian landscape and character.' Another favourable review appeared in *The Nation* (New York), and a belated but complimentary notice was published in *The New York Times* the following spring. All that commendation coming from the United States refuted any charges that the Canadian critics who thought that his prose was 'skillfully handled' were simply inflating the merits of a native writer. *Earth's Enigmas* was also reviewed in at least one British periodical. Frank Pinder wrote in *The Academy* (London): 'The Canadian poet and prose-writer, Prof. Charles G.D. Roberts is not as widely known in this country as he deserves to be: his work is strong, individual and distinctive.'[5]

Even *Around the Campfire*, which Roberts personally classified as juvenilia, received favourable mention in *The Dial* and *The Critic* (New York). *The Book of the Native* was not widely reviewed in the United States, but the periodicals that took notice were unanimous in their praise. *The Nation* set the general tone early in 1897 by pointing to it as a further proof that Canada was 'producing a younger group of poets who are forcing our rhymers in the United States to look to their laurels.' *The Critic* added that Roberts took the reader 'most delightfully into an atmosphere which is perhaps best described in the first two lines of the dedication, "The kindly strength of open fields, / The faith of eve, the calm of air."' *The Chap-Book* (Chicago) concluded: 'He must be a purblind reviewer who does not find many pages of serene and ennobling poetry in *The Book of the Native*.'[6]

As important as the foregoing reviews were to Roberts, it was probably the notices of *The Forge in the Forest* that he awaited with the greatest anxiety. It was his first novel, after all, and its success would help to place him in the profitable ranks with Stanley Weyman, Gilbert Parker, and other popular writers of historical romances. His hometown paper proudly declared: 'The book ought to make a reputation for its author second to none among the greatest of English fiction writers,' but the American reviews were mixed. *The New York Times*, which felt that the book was not equal to Gilbert Parker's *Seats of the Mighty*, was of the opinion that the writer was 'not by natural gift a novelist.' *The Critic* found it 'pleasantly written,' while *The Bookman* (New York) applauded its 'lyrical elation,' its 'strong human interest and dramatic movement,' and the 'primeval instinct of elemental joy that animates the whole book.' *The Nation*, on the other hand, called it 'a feeble disjointed tale,' a sentiment that was echoed in *The Chap-Book*:

For the work of an experienced and successful literary man, *The Forge in the Forest* is a curiously amateurish and inconsequent production. It is evidently a hasty attempt to take advantage of the temporarily romantic taste of the reading public; and except for occasional graces of style, and a certain delicate poetic feeling, it is a book which anyone might have written. It was not worth doing – in spite of the picturesqueness of the setting and the glimpses it gives of brilliant possibilities.

It was later reviewed in at least two British periodicals, both of which had serious reservations about it. *The Academy* thought that it read 'more like the end of a longer story than a tale complete in itself.' *The Athenaeum* commented: 'It is well-written; the episodes are exciting and well contrived; the scenery is fascinating; a better story or a firmer grip of it would be expected of Mr Weyman; and a dash of humour, if Mr Roberts could have spared it, would have made one forget that the plot was inadequate.'[7]

It is always interesting to compare the assessments by contemporary critics to the verdict that comes with the passage of time and the changes in taste and fashion. The tales in *Around the Campfire* have been all but forgotten, although it might be argued that a few of them, such as 'Bruin and the Cook,' deserve to be remembered longer. *The Forge in the Forest* has long been regarded as a crude attempt to exploit the ready market for Acadian romances that had been created by the immense popularity of Longfellow's *Evangeline*. While it is conceded that Roberts conveys a real sense of the Acadian setting, it is felt that he did not know the people as well as he knew the place: his characters, those he invented and the historical figures he recreated, do not come to life. If anything, the early reviews of *The Forge in the Forest* are seen as being too kind to its inadequacies of plot and characterization.

The mystical note, sounded occasionally in *Songs of the Common Day* but dominating *The Book of the Native*, was more acceptable when Roberts first voiced it than it is today. Modern critics complain that he merely restates the enormity of the cosmic riddles without offering any penetrating insights into them. Aside from the so-called mystical poems, *The Book of the Native* contains a handful of ballads (largely ignored today) and a group of miscellaneous lyrics. Among the latter, there are many that adequately maintain the standards he had set in his earlier descriptive pieces, but most of them are short and none of them is a sustained attempt to produce the kind of major statement that would match his sonnet sequence or 'Ave.' He was, as we have seen, turning away from poetry, although it is doubtful whether the full extent of the shift had yet dawned upon him. Since *Songs of the Common Day* had appeared, he had been busy – overworked, indeed – with two major prose productions, his comprehensive *History of Canada* and *The Forge in the Forest*. With those ambitious undertakings in hand, poetry became more of an incidental diversion, not something upon which he was expending the full energy of his creative powers. The direction in which he eventually was to move with the greatest success is foreshadowed in *Earth's Enigmas*, whose initial raves still have considerable support.

Roberts' excitement over the publication of four new books was not enough to conceal the fact that the move to Fredericton was not as good an idea in practice as it had seemed in theory. Life in the quiet little city was too uneventful and he still found himself yearning for the stimulation of a larger centre. He seems to have realized, fairly soon, that an occasional business trip to Boston or New York was not going to be enough to satisfy him. He was like a migratory bird, resting en route in Fredericton, ready to take flight as soon as an opportunity beckoned elsewhere. A reluctance to settle permanently in Fredericton may have been one of the factors in his decision not to apply for the position in classics that became vacant at the University of New Brunswick.

He was nearing forty, and, in spite of the esteem he had won in his own country, he seems to have had a deep sense of unfulfilment. For almost twenty years he had been regarded as a promising young writer, but his reputation outside Canada was not yet established. He was conscious, also, that Fredericton was far removed from the literary mainstream. It kept him isolated from his markets and allowed too little contact with the creative minds of his own generation. His camaraderie with his congenial cousin Fred Bliss and the latter's poet-friend (and drinking companion) Frank Sherman was hardly a substitute for the intellectual give-and-take he had sampled in the company of Carman's New York associates. In addition, he still longed to travel, to 'taste the life of many lands,'[8] but there was little likelihood that his family responsibilities would permit such a luxury in the foreseeable future. That he had married and settled down too soon to have a youthful fling may have been another reason why he was growing increasingly restive with the approach of middle age.

Whatever the causes of his boredom may have been, idleness was not one of them. Indeed, he used his work as an excuse for not wielding his pen in support of the Conservative party during the Canadian general election of 1896. The truth of the matter was that recent political events had convinced him that the Conservatives had become corrupted by being in office too long. However, he did not wish to be too outspoken on the subject, especially since the local Conservative candidate was his former classics professor, George Eulas Foster. Furthermore, the incumbent prime minister was Sir Charles Tupper, who had been his family's physician during the Westcock years. At about the age of seven, young Charles Roberts had been taken to Amherst, across the Nova Scotian border, to have Dr Tupper pull a troublesome tooth. Once in the office, however, the tooth having stopped aching, he had absolutely refused to have it pulled. The frustrated doctor had tried to force his mouth open, but had only succeeded in getting his finger bitten.[9] In the 1896 election, an older version of the rebellious patient bit the same hand metaphorically by casting a vote against the Conservatives, but he probably took meagre satisfaction from the ensuing defeat of the party.

Adding to Roberts' general discontent was the painful realization that he was not making ends meet as a freelance writer after all. The time he had spent completing *The Forge in the Forest* had kept him from the shorter prose pieces that brought in the ready cash. If he were lucky, there might eventually be some significant royalties from his books; in the meantime, he was falling so far behind that it was not uncommon for his creditors to come pounding on his door demanding payment. So far, he had succeeded in mollifying most of them with his unique blend of charm and deviousness, but, as his debts continued to mount, the encounters were growing more and more perilous. How much longer, he may have wondered, could he stave off the inevitable reckoning merely by inviting an unpaid tradesman into the study to offer him nothing more substantial than 'a nip of brandy and a promissory note?'[10]

Just when the future seemed darkest, he received a welcome proposal from Frank Bellamy, a friend he had made on the staff of *The Youth's Companion*. Bellamy had recently been appointed managing editor of *The*

Illustrated American, a New York weekly, and wanted Roberts to be his assistant. The offer was accepted without hesitation. It was more than just a solution to pressing financial problems: it was an escape from isolation and restriction. Roberts was not repudiating Canada – he would wear his Canadianism like a badge – but he wanted to be at the centre of the literary scene. And there was no doubt about it, New York was becoming the literary capital of North America. It had most of the leading publishers of books and periodicals, and it was drawing writers from all over the continent in the same way that Paris attracted the artists of Europe.

May and the children were to remain in Fredericton until Roberts sent for them. The separation would only be temporary, he assured everyone, and he undoubtedly believed what he was saying. However, he was unable to fix a date for the family to join him – that would depend upon circumstances. May was troubled by this indefinite arrangement, and wondered aloud as to what 'circumstances' could possibly postpone their reunion for very long.[11] She may not have completely understood her husband's reasons for wanting to live in New York, but she agreed that it would be better than being 'stuck' (her word) in Windsor or Fredericton. It would be unfair, she felt, if she and the children were left behind for any undue length of time. The last thing she wanted was to be 'stuck' with all the household responsibilities.

Because he would soon have the additional expense of renting accommodation in New York, Roberts was forced to move his family to a smaller, cheaper house shortly before his departure. It was a tiny cottage, wedged between two other dwellings, with a narrow, dingy alley on either side. The parlour, which faced the street, never got the sun; and the rear view from the kitchen was blocked by the backs of two large barns. Not only was the cottage dark and damp, but it was pervaded by a sewer-like smell that was as depressing as it was offensive. The family went through the usual ritual of naming their new home; but, although it was formally christened 'Cosycroft,' it was always known as 'Dark House.' The latter name was appropriate in more than the literal sense, for everyone was unhappy in the cottage's cramped, musty quarters, and later events indicate that its unwholesome atmosphere may have had tragic effects upon the health of the children.

At the time of the move to 'Dark House,' the Roberts' children ranged in age from eight to fourteen. Athelstan, the eldest, was a handsome, sturdy lad who was already carrying on the Roberts' tradition of scholarship. None of the other children was studious, although each had inherited to some degree the father's literary instincts. Twelve-year-old Lloyd was the one who was always getting into mischief ('He is heedless, headstrong – not like the others,' his father had once said of him). Edith, the only daughter, even at the age of ten was very much like her mother in temperament. The youngest son, Douglas (or 'Duddy'), was 'a sweet winning child,' according to Jean Bliss, his great-aunt. Their father was very fond of all his 'chicks,' as he called them, and it greatly relieved his mind to know that their mother would have the aid of two sets of relatives in looking after them during his absence. May did not find that thought particularly comforting, and before Roberts left for New York on 2 February 1897, she had finally extracted a promise that he would send for her and the children before the advent of another winter.[12]

CHAPTER SIX

Assailing Manhattan

1897–1898

IT HAD BEEN FIFTEEN YEARS since Roberts had seen New York for the first time. During his frequent visits since then, he had witnessed its growth into the eighth wonder of the world – the city of skyscrapers. 'Where will it all end?' people were asking as lower Broadway became dotted with taller and taller buildings. For the moment, the answer was eighteen storeys, the height of a newly completed structure at 66 Broadway. Business and commerce were gradually creeping north-wards on Manhattan, although the majority of the big establishments were still located south of 23rd Street. Much of Fifth Avenue was still sacred to the mansions of the Vanderbilts, the Astors, and other members of the fabled Four Hundred, but even there changes were under way. At 33rd Street (on the site where the Empire State Building now stands), Roberts could see the workmen putting finishing touches on the Waldorf-Astoria, the world's most magnificent hotel, due to open in November. Horse cars were still in common use, but electric trolleys were coming in, and cable cars were operating on Broadway and Lexington Avenue. The population was burgeoning, and immigrants from all over the world gave ethnic colouring to various parts of the city. Like Roberts, the newcomers had gravitated to New York to improve their fortunes.

Bliss Carman was back in New York City after a few years' stint in various editorial positions in Boston. He had recently returned from a trip to England and France to live in a boarding house on East 58th Street. Roberts joined him there, and the two cousins remained together until Carman left in the summer for Haines Falls in the Catskills, where he was drawn into the company of a Connecticut doctor's wife, Mary Perry King.

Carman and Mrs King were brought together by their interest in the Delsartian theories of Henrietta Russell Hovey, but their relationship soon deepened into a close attachment that lasted for over thirty years. Between Mrs King and Roberts there was a growing antipathy, for each came to resent the influence that the other had over Carman.

The offices of *The Illustrated American* were located on the north side of East 23rd Street, between 1st Avenue and the East River, approximately two miles from Roberts' boarding-house. They were certainly within walking distance for a vigorous man who, on occasion, had hiked forty miles in a day. The chances are that, when time and weather permitted, he often went to work and returned home on foot, not only to save a few pennies, but to keep in shape.

The Illustrated American was a 32-page weekly which sold for ten cents a copy. In addition to its contributed articles on current affairs and other topics of general interest, it also published stories and poems and reviewed the latest books. Along with many other editorial duties, Roberts was expected to write feature articles regularly and edit the book columns. His six articles commemorating the Diamond Jubilee of Queen Victoria are examples of the decidedly British bias of much of his writing for the periodical. Luckily, it was a time of special interest in British affairs, although some objectors agreed with the New York *Sun*, which fulminated: 'Every American who subscribes to the proposed preposterous tribute to Queen Victoria should be a marked man.'[1] The routine work of publishing the weekly was exhausting, and Roberts was back in the all-too-familiar position of not having enough time for his creative work. Without the chance to augment his inadequate salary appreciably, there was no immediate hope of being able to keep a family of six in New York City.

Two of Roberts' colleagues on *The Illustrated American*, Frank (Francis) Bellamy and Albert White Vorse, remained his friends long after all three of them had severed their connection with the weekly. Bellamy, who was about five years older than Roberts, had been ordained a Baptist minister. However, his interest in the social and educational responsibilities of the church became increasingly incompatible with the rigid Baptist doctrines of his day. When he eventually came to the conclusion that his talents should be employed elsewhere, he was persuaded by the owner of *The Youth's Companion* (who happened to be one of his parishioners) to join his staff. For the rest of his life, he held various editorial posts. Wherever he went, he loyally continued to publish the work of Charles G.D. Roberts. His own writings were mostly of an ephemeral nature, but in 1892, in connection with the celebrations for the 400th anniversary of Columbus' discovery of America, he composed the following statement: 'I pledge allegiance to my flag – and to the Republic for which it stands – one Nation indivisible – with liberty and justice for all.' This pledge, with minor revisions, continued in popular usage and was finally given official congressional sanction in 1945. Albert Vorse (who had been on the Peary Relief Expedition) was Roberts' assistant on the paper and a boon companion outside of office hours.

Richard and Henrietta Hovey, who had returned to New York the previous October, had taken rooms in Carnegie Hall Studios. A short time later, Bliss Carman deliberately selected a nearby boarding-house, where he was still staying when Roberts joined him. Although the Hoveys' living quarters were downtown in Chelsea Square, they maintained their studio rooms as a place to teach, give readings, and hold receptions. Because they believed that human beings, not furnishings, should be the chief ornaments of any room, the only accessories were a couch, some ornate chairs, and an oriental screen. But most of the men and women who visited the rooms were indeed decorative, often flamboyant, both in dress and personality. Carman, tall and lanky, with his long mane of copper-coloured hair, was always a striking-looking guest, although he had not yet taken to wearing excessive jewellery and other eccentricities of dress that he affected later. When Roberts began to frequent the Hoveys' studio, it was his infectious high spirits, not his appearance, that made him stand out in the various gatherings.

Roberts had been in New York for only a few weeks when Richard Le Gallienne arrived from England on a lecture tour. In both appearance and intellect, Le Gallienne was a perfect adornment for the Hoveys' studio. He was a rather short man, although slight and well-proportioned; his face, framed by flowing dark hair, was arrestingly handsome. His brilliant conversation, with its felicitous turns of phrase, indicated a keen mind that revelled in its mastery of the English language. Still in his early thirties, he had gained attention with several volumes of poetry and his novel, *Quest of the Golden Girl*, of which he commented ruefully: 'The publisher got all the gold and poor Richard got the girls.'[2] His fascinating appeal to women was so well known that *The Chap-Book* unfairly credited the success of the American lecture engagement to his famous charm rather than his literary gifts. Indirectly, the tour would lead to romance, and his new friend Roberts would somewhat unwillingly play the part of Cupid, but that turn of events was still two years away.

It was Le Gallienne who used the term 'Romantic '90s' to characterize the last decade of the nineteenth century. As he saw it, the representative writers and artists of the period were trying 'to escape from the deadening enthraldom of materialism and outworn conventions, and to live life significantly – keenly and beautifully, personally and, if need be, daringly...'[3] That was certainly the philosophy of the artistic circles in which Roberts was now moving, and he embraced it with some peril. It could lead to a way of life that was not compatible with the only kind of domesticity that his wife understood.

Spring and summer came and went while May and the children waited in vain for the elusive 'circumstances' that would take them to New York before the coming of winter. Since the necessities of life could not be obtained on credit in the great American metropolis, Roberts would be unable to maintain a family there as long as it took most of his earnings to pay for his single room and lunch counter meals. His letters home were full of optimism for the future: although he was having a hard struggle right now, he was making valuable contacts in the publishing world and the outlook was very promising. Those messages soon rang hollow to May unless (as happened all too seldom) they were accompanied by some money to pay the bills. 'Not a cent!'[4] she would exclaim bitterly each time she opened a cashless letter. Then, rhetorically, she would ask the children what their father thought they were going to live on. As summer passed into autumn, she became apprehensive when he still said nothing about sending for them. It began to look as if they were going to be 'stuck' alone in Fredericton for the winter after all, and she fumed aloud over her husband's folly in giving up the security of his professorship at King's.

Then tragedy struck. Athelstan came down with typhoid fever, which possibly had its origin in the bad drainage that befouled the air of Dark House. That illness was followed by meningitis, which progressed so rapidly that the doctors had already begun to despair before May sent for Roberts, who never forgave her for not notifying him sooner. By the time the distraught father arrived, Athelstan had lapsed into unconsciousness from which he never rallied. Three days later, on 16 October, he was dead. Fate had dealt Roberts the most devastating blow of his entire life: the untimely death of his gifted eldest son.[5]

The day after the funeral, Roberts returned to New York. The next issue of *The Illustrated American* had to be prepared and the associate editor could not neglect his duties any longer, no matter how great his personal grief nor how much his family needed the strength of his presence. On the eve of his departure, and long into the night, May reiterated her many fears about spending the winter in Fredericton.

Roberts told her that she was being unreasonable. She must understand that his only hope of establishing a solid reputation lay in New York. If she would only be patient until his new novel was on the market – his publisher had high hopes for its success – he would undoubtedly be in a position to send for her and the children. In the meantime, unfortunately, such a move was absolutely out of the question. He, too, was making sacrifices: he was living in the least expensive accommodations, scrimping on clothes and food and sending home every spare penny. When he chided May for not taking a long-range view of the matter, he may have been doing her an injustice. Perhaps she sensed something that he had not yet admitted, even to himself: the longer he was away, the more addicted he was becoming to his new mode of living. However, as he boarded the afternoon train, it seems unlikely that he had any thought of abandoning his family. On the other hand, as much as he loved the children and recognized his obligations to May, he was probably not overjoyed at the prospect of a reunion with them in New York.[6]

Before he left Fredericton, Roberts told the children that he would be home again for Christmas, but as the holiday season drew near, he felt obliged to break his promise. Several considerations may have contributed to that decision. When all the funeral expenses were added to his other unpaid bills, he was likely too much in debt to afford the train fare. He was behind in his schedule for his new novel, and he was undoubtedly trying to find some extra time to catch up. He may also have heeded the wishes of an unidentified woman who was the inspiration for his latest love poems. Probably none of the many possible reasons would have been enough by itself to make him disappoint his family, but, taken together, the arguments against the visit changed his mind.

The depleted family tried to carry on as usual. On Christmas morning, May made a valiant attempt to observe all the customary rituals. She was up at dawn to stoke the furnace, light the lamps, and bundle the presents upon her bed, where they would be opened. The Roberts children always hung up large pillowcases or burlap bags instead of mere stockings, but without Athelstan and their father, the fun of emptying them was gone. Matters improved somewhat when they went to the rectory later in the day for Christmas dinner. Their two boisterous young uncles, Will and Thede, had just arrived from New York to add to the merriment.

During the summer, Roberts had found a place for his brother Will on the staff of *The Illustrated American*. Will had already shown his literary inclinations by writing poetry, some of which had been published in various magazines. However, at the age of twenty-three, he had no clear prospects of a career. Over a year earlier, shortly before graduating from the University of New Brunswick, he had quit his course and, according to the Fredericton *Reporter*, departed for the southern United States 'for the benefit of his health.' The *Reporter* also stated that his friends from the university 'gave him a rousing send off at the railway station,' but it remained silent on the nature of his illness. From another source, we learn that within the year 'he completely regained his strength.' His beginnings at *The Illustrated American* were humble, and the only written contributions that bore his name were a couple of full-page poems, appropriately illustrated. After a few months, he moved to *The Literary Digest* where he remained for the rest of his working life, rising to become managing editor, a position he held for thirty years. Of the three brothers, he was by far the least peripatetic in the course of his career, and much the least prolific in his writing. As his editorial duties increased, even his occasional poems ceased to appear. His most ambitious undertaking was the organization of the Garden Tower Corporation in 1917 to take over a contract for the purchase of Madison Square Gardens for $2,400,000; but, because the title was not clear, he was unable to complete the deal. He also served for a time as professor of politics at New York University.[7]

As a writer, Thede Roberts had almost as precocious a beginning as his eldest brother. Before he was twenty years old, he had already published several poems and short stories. He matriculated into the University of New Brunswick, but did not have the patience to complete his course. He was chafing to follow Will to New York, and in November obtained a position on *The Independent*. Probably it was brother Charles who helped him get the appointment, though being a cousin of Bliss Carman, a former associate editor, may also have been a factor. Thede had the misfortune to be in the literary shadow of Charles G.D. Roberts and Bliss Carman all his life. Over the years he published scores of poems and short stories in addition to some thirty novels of adventure and historical romance, but literary critics usually dismissed him as a minor figure in the tradition that boasted Charles G.D. Roberts and Bliss Carman among its leading members. His novels were never widely successful, and his short stories included many pot-boilers, but his best poetry was distinctive and owed nothing to the influence of his eldest brother or his famous cousin. In his later years he became rather sensitive about his comparative lack of recognition, and sometimes seemed to take a special delight in debunking the reputation of his more famous brother. It has been said that he was his mother's favourite child, which may have been because he was the baby of the family, or possibly because he was the most like her in temperament.

Two of his own children achieved some success in the artistic world: his daughter Dorothy as a poet, and his son Goodridge as a painter.

Throughout the latter part of 1897, the Reverend Canon Roberts had been in such poor health that his parishioners urged him to seek the warm sunshine of Florida to recuperate. The Cathedral congregation and St Ann's parish presented him with a total of $312 to speed him on his way. He decided to visit his sons in New York en route, and it was arranged that May would accompany him (possibly he paid her fare) on that part of the journey. For several days they became guests at the boarding-house where all three of the canon's sons were then staying. The Fredericton *Reporter* commented that 'such congenial company could not fail to prove beneficial to the father...'8 Unfortunately, there is no record to tell us how much May saw of her husband's new milieu or what her impressions were of it. The visit had to be brief because her three children had been left in the care of their Grandmother Roberts. That worthy lady was also to spend a few days in New York at a later date. There is nothing to show that May ever made a return visit.

In mid-January, after being an assistant editor for a little less than a year, Roberts resigned from *The Illustrated American*. The Fredericton *Reporter* explained that he wished to 'devote himself to completing the novel, to be called *A Sister to Evangeline*, which he now has well under way.'9 Concurrently with the novel, which was another Acadian romance, he was writing a series of short stories, set in Acadia and employing some of the same characters who had been introduced in *The Forge and the Forest* or would appear in the new novel. It was the sale of those stories that enabled him to survive without *The Illustrated American*, which suffered several vicissitudes following his resignation. In less than a fortnight the editorial offices were destroyed by fire; the next issue, which was being set up for the press, was a mass of molten lead. Furthermore, all the manuscripts, photographs, drawings, and advertising copy had gone up in smoke. However, Bellamy moved quickly into new quarters, put the issue together again, and got it out on time. It was his last major task as editor, for within a few weeks he joined Silver, Burdett and Company, the book publisher. With the departure of Roberts and Bellamy, *The Illustrated American* lost its literary character and became more strictly a news magazine.

The reviews of *A Forge in the Forest* began appearing when Roberts was in the midst of writing his second novel. Far from being deterred by the mixed reception, he plunged with apparent optimism into the task of completing *A Sister to Evangeline*. As he worked, however, he must have been fully aware that he was going through a crucial period in both his professional pursuits and his personal life. Once again he was taking a chance on being able to survive by his freelance writing, and he was counting heavily upon the success of the novel-in-progress. Meanwhile, his emotions were divided between his devotion to his family and the strong attraction of a new life that could not include them because it revolved around a lovely woman who gave inspiration to his pen. Years later, he inscribed the following comment in a friend's copy of *A Sister to Evangeline*: 'This story was written out of one of the deepest experiences of my life and at a time of crisis which explains and I hope excuses the over-tense lyricism.'[10]

The identity of that woman who had such a profound influence upon Roberts' life remains a mystery. Although he spoke about her quite freely in later years, he seems to have been curiously reluctant to reveal her name. Even Miss Pomeroy, the confidante of his old age, did not know it. 'If it pleases him never to tell me,' said Miss Pomeroy in reply to some questions raised by Roberts' publisher and benefactor, Lorne Pierce, 'I have no desire to know.' Earlier, Pierce had asked Roberts if the love poetry in *The Book of the Rose* (1903) was autobiographical. 'Yes,' Roberts had acknowledged, 'I was intensely in love. The lady is also in *New York Nocturnes* and in *A Sister to Evangeline*.' His answer raises the tantalizing question of how closely this woman served as the model for Yvonne de Lamourie, the heroine of *A Sister to Evangeline*. Was Roberts describing his own inamorata when he pictured the wit and beauty of Yvonne, her broad forehead, her finely chiselled nose and firm chin, her deep hazel-green eyes, and her thick dark hair?[11]

Another fascinating question arises: What did May Roberts think about the love poems her husband was writing? Did she accept an explanation that this was the kind of poetry that sold easily in the magazines, and that poets often sang of imaginary lovers just to satisfy the demand? Even some critics have implied that he may have been writing love poems merely because they were currently fashionable; but, as we have seen, Roberts himself confirmed that the woman to whom they were addressed did, in fact, exist. Taken at face value, Roberts' love poems suggest that the affair brought him comfort and tranquility such as he had never found in his marriage. Indeed, the dedicatory poem in *New York Nocturnes and Other Poems* (1898) expresses this assuaging influence in terms that ought to have aroused May's suspicions. If there was a darker side to his involvement, it was not the kind of fare that the popular periodicals were offering to their public. They had no space for the anguish and self-approach of a man torn between love and loyalty.

It is not known how long the affair lasted, but it may have been still flourishing when eighteen-year-old Lloyd went to live with his father in 1903. At that time, Roberts found plausible reasons why the rest of his family still could not join him: it would cost too much, May would be lonely and unhappy in the big city, and his long hours of exacting work would keep them apart. But Lloyd had not been in New York very long before he 'saw the truth and saw that it was inevitable.' It was only out of sympathy for May, he realized, that his father 'refrained from declaring the circumstances, which would have clinched the argument and killed the last shred of her hope for a return to things-as-they-once-were.' Roberts had long ago ceased to love his wife. As their years of separation lengthened, he was finally acknowledging that he could never live with her again. Nothing was changed even when his love affair in New York was ended by 'circumstances over which they had no control' (as Miss Pomeroy explained cryptically to Lorne Pierce). His estrangement from May had not arisen because there was another woman in his life.[12]

Roberts had two new books in print before 1898 was over: *New York Nocturnes and Other Poems* and *A Sister to Evangeline*. The poetry was favourably received, although most of the critics (then as now) preferred the poems that dealt more with nature and less with love. The reception for *A Sister to Evangeline* was much warmer than the one accorded *The Forge in the Forest* although ultimately it would be rated as only a slight improvement upon its predecessor. *The New York Times*, for example, which had earlier questioned Roberts' potential as a novelist, now declared that he had written one of the best novels of the season. Good reviews, a modest flow of royalties, and a ready market for his poems and short stories gave him reason to feel that his literary star was rising.

The writing of *A Sister to Evangeline* had actually been completed in Fredericton, where Roberts spent a couple of weeks in August 1898. Upon his return to New York, he and his brother Will went to live at 105 East 17th Street. Thede had left them in May when *The Independent* sent him to Cuba as a war correspondent. Along with other members of the press, Thede fretted at the prolonged delay in Tampa before they were allowed to cross to Cuba. Shortly after their ship finally left Florida, he became seriously ill with a fever, and by the time he arrived in Santiago he was too sick to go to the front. His last dispatch to *The Independent* was dated 'In Cuban Waters,' 6 July 1898: 'Health unimproved and cash too low to carry one through the campaign, the boys advised me to get aboard the first ship for Tampa. I did so, and am still here.'[13] Thus ended, through the bad luck that dogged him so often, the first major adventure in the eventful life of Theodore Goodridge Roberts. While he was languishing in sick bay, the by-lines of many other correspondents were becoming famous as their reports filled the pages of American newspapers and journals. Brother Charles got into the act by celebrating the battle of Manila Bay in a lengthy poem which emphasized the significance of America's British heritage.

After an unhappy winter in Dark House, May and the children moved into half of a house which had the advantages of being a little brighter and, most important of all, odourless. For some time afterwards, Edith and Lloyd were in the grip of a mysterious ailment that was not enough to confine them to their beds but kept them weak and listless. Douglas, alone, escaped its debilitating clutch. Lloyd eventually recovered without any obvious after-effects, but Edith was left with a weakness that led to severe curvature of the spine. The children's illnesses were not helped by their daily diet of bread and molasses and canned salmon or beans. May was an indefatigable worker as long as she was dusting and cleaning, but her energy always flagged when it came time to cook meals. To be fair to her, however, it must be said that the diet also reflected her valiant struggle not to extend her credit with the butcher and the grocer whenever she could avoid it. She was already so humiliated over her indebtedness to them that sometimes she even 'blushed when she was sipping her tea, remembering that it was not hers but the grocer's, whose guest she was as surely as though she had been sitting at his table.' Lloyd recalled rather reproachfully that while his father

wrote drama and romance by day, in his little green studio in Bohemia, dined in an 'atmosphere' as thick as one of his own Fundy fogs, bandied compliment and criticism with true metropolitan fervor, and watched his sun rise slowly but grandly over the tallest sky-scrapers, the family played more humble drama with canned salmon and credit toward the consummation of his hopes.[14]

Charles G.D. Roberts was by then something of a celebrity in Fredericton, but fame without fortune can sometimes be an inconvenience. His creditors mistakenly assumed that a successful writer could afford to pay his bills. Consequently, they were ready to pounce whenever the word got around that he was in town again. The most memorable incident occurred during his Christmas homecoming in 1898. One day when all the family were at the table in the basement dining room of the rectory, Nan Powers came down to say that Charlie was wanted at the door.

Roberts went up to be met by an embarrassed sheriff's deputy who stammered that he had been sent to escort the professor to jail. Roberts calmly donned his black fedora and set off with his knobby walking stick, but the officer drew back and offered to walk behind for the sake of appearances. His companion laughingly assured him that appearances did not matter, and they walked side by side in full view of the curious neighbours, who were always gossiping (or so May believed) about the irregularities of the Roberts' domestic affairs. At the city hall, the grey-haired sheriff greeted his 'guest' hospitably, took him to a third floor cell, and motioned him inside. He closed the door for a moment, to satisfy the letter of the law, then opened it again, remarking drily that the 'prisoner' had served his time. 'Opera bouffe?' Lloyd Roberts asked as he pondered over the incident nearly fifty years later. 'Perhaps,' he admitted. 'But such things could and did happen a few generations back in the Loyalist towns and ports in the lands along the sea.'[15]

The publication of *Wild Animals I Have Known* by Ernest Thompson Seton in October 1898, was to have an important influence upon Roberts. Becoming an instant best-seller, the book created a vogue for the type of realistic animal story that Roberts had been writing a few years earlier. Roberts and Seton were the same age, and although the latter had been born in England, he too had grown up in Canada before going to the United States. It is one of the curiosities of literary history, therefore, that the realistic animal story appears to have been developed concurrently by two Canadians who were exact contemporaries. Opinions differ as to which of them should be given credit for originating the new story form. Although Seton published his first piece about wild life as early as 1883, all of his writings prior to 1894 either read more like the journals of a naturalist or else, as Seton himself admitted, employ 'the archaic method of making animals talk.' During that period he had certainly not written any animal fiction in the realistic manner of Roberts' 'Do Seek Their Meat from God,' which first appeared in the December issue of *Harper's Monthly*, 1892. Earlier, Roberts' story had been rejected by an editor who pronounced it 'neither fish, flesh, fowl nor good red herring.' Even *Harper's* were so sceptical that they offered him only half of what he was normally paid for stories of similar length. When two more of his animal stories met with practically the same reception, Roberts felt that he had no choice but to abandon the form. Seton's success, however, was enough to convince him to return to a genre that was compatible with his background and interests.[16]

Seton and Roberts had become friends shortly after the latter's arrival in New York. At that time, the tall, bushy-haired Seton was best known as an illustrator. When he read 'Do Seek Their Meat from God' in *Earth's Enigmas* he rushed to Roberts saying: 'That's just what I want! I've sold some wild life illustrations to Scribner's and they want letterpress for them.'[17] When Roberts advised him to illustrate his own material, Seton acted upon his suggestion, and the result was *Wild Animals I Have Known,* charmingly decorated with the marginal drawings that became characteristic of his books. It is perhaps a matter of regret to collectors of Canadiana, however, that posterity was deprived of a volume of animal stories written by Charles G.D. Roberts and illustrated by Ernest Thompson Seton.

The first edition (2,000 copies) of *Wild Animals I Have Known* was sold out within three weeks, and the book went on to become an international best-seller, establishing Seton's fame and fortune. Suddenly, animal stories were in demand, and Roberts began receiving requests from the same editors who had rejected his submissions only a few years earlier. He was quick to take advantage of the ready market, but he generously gave Seton the credit for making it possible, saying: 'It is he who is chiefly responsible for the vogue of the modern Animal Story.'[18]

Seton's engaging but sentimental stories, superbly illustrated by his own drawings, were obviously the work of a painstaking naturalist, but the popularity of his writings cannot be attributed to their intrinsic merits alone. He had the good luck to hit the market at just the right moment. There had already been some enormously successful books about domesticated animals (e.g., *Black Beauty, Beautiful Joe*), but those tales, generally advocating a more humane treatment of animals, were not aimed at outdoor enthusiasts, as were the stories by Seton and Roberts. The growth of the large urban centres, particularly in the United States, had been so rapid and so recent that many city-dwellers were not long removed from the country. Nostalgia for a wilderness that was becoming increasingly inaccessible had touched a great many people, from office clerks to Theodore Roosevelt (soon to be president). Nor is it surprising that those readers supported the sympathetic attitude taken by Seton and Roberts towards the endangered creatures of the wild. Darwin's theory of evolution had undoubtedly led to a wider acceptance of the idea of the kinship of man and beast. Nevertheless, to a large extent it was a yearning for the passing frontier that created an interest in natural science.

Perhaps the cult of the armchair naturalist accounts for the greater popularity of Seton over Roberts, despite the fact that literary critics are generally agreed that Roberts was the better writer. Even Seton appears to have acknowledged Roberts' superiority in that respect. He once told an audience that a young admirer had expressed the wish that Seton would write more like Charles G.D. Roberts in *The Heart of the Ancient Wood.* 'I would if I could,' Seton admitted frankly, 'but I can't.'[19] Furthermore, when Seton came to write his autobiography, he called it *Trail of an Artist-Naturalist,* which suggests that he did not think of himself foremost as a writer. However, he had the satisfaction of knowing that he was the most successful nature writer of all time. He was the experienced guide for whom all the novices in woodcraft were looking. He wrote as a teacher, often in the first person, and there was no doubt in the minds of most of his readers that they were being instructed by an expert. Roberts, aware of his limitations as a naturalist, did not impose himself upon his readers in that way. Accordingly, although his stories are usually as authentic as those of Seton, and may in fact be better art, they were less satisfactory in meeting the demands of the amateur naturalists of the day.

Roberts was a good story-teller, having mastered all the techniques for building suspense and creating atmosphere. Occasionally the effects are too melodramatic, but that usually happens when human characters intrude upon the world of the beasts. The backgrounds are sketched in prose that is more eloquently descriptive than much of his landscape poetry. Being freed from the strictures of rhyme and line length, he could indulge in his forte for complexities of syntax to create greater subtleties of shading and nuance. Nor was his story-telling restricted to the traditional plot with beginning, middle, and end. Some of his nature pieces fall into the classification of sketch (or 'anecdote of observation,' as Roberts called it); at other times he wrote animal biographies.

For several years, Seton had an apartment in a new studio building on the corner of 6th Avenue and 40th Street above the roar of the city and the roll of the elevated cars. Friends often dropped in during the afternoons to chat while he was drawing. Roberts was one of those who frequently spent an hour or two with him while he worked at his easel in front of a huge window overlooking Bryant Park. When Roberts first began his visits, Seton was newly married to Grace Gallatin, a charming and cultured woman who aspired to be a writer. Grace's social poise and intellectual interests were in sharp contrast to the capacities of poor May Roberts. Furthermore, unlike May, she was an independent woman who would never be content merely to live in her husband's shadow. However, her eventual rift with the strong-willed Seton was still a long way off, and Roberts must have envied the stimulating domestic atmosphere of his friend's apartment. Aside from the congenial company, the studio was a fascinating place for anyone with a love for the out-of-doors. Seton's superb drawings and paintings of wild life, wolves and bears and caribou, looked down from the walls. Equally engrossing were the personal journals stacked on the crowded bookshelves beside the carefully arranged and classified volumes of wild animal photographs. As Roberts began once again to write his realistic animal stories, he undoubtedly found inspiration in Seton's studio. It is also highly probable that he took advantage of Seton's research and relied upon his friend's expertise as a naturalist.

Another studio where Roberts felt very much at home was that of Roland Hinton Perry, the young sculptor, who was already famous for his work in the Library of Congress, including the fountain of Neptune for the main approach. In 1895, Perry had married his beautiful cousin, Irma Hinton, whose sister Cleo, another noted beauty, was also a sculptor. Roberts was greatly attracted to the lovely sisters, and there is even a possibility that Irma Perry may have been the mysterious woman of his love poems. Many years later he confided to Lorne Pierce that she had been an 'old flame,'[20] and time would prove that her marriage had indeed been vulnerable. However, the fact that he appears to have retained Roland Perry's friendship seems to indicate that the affair may never have gone beyond a mild flirtation.

It was natural that such brilliant and charming people as the Perrys would attract some of the most interesting members of New York's artistic community. Among the frequent visitors were Oliver Herford, the humorist; Ethelbert Nevin, the composer; and Hildegarde Hawthorne, the journalist-granddaughter of Nathaniel Hawthorne. A later member of the same set was Mary Fanton, a young journalist specializing in art who became Mrs William Carman Roberts in 1906.

It is a tribute to the force of Roberts' personality, even more than to his literary attainments, that he was a welcome member of any gathering. His wide interests, quick wit, and contagious enthusiasms made him a delightful companion. Having a nature that was utterly devoid of envy and petty jealousy, he took genuine pleasure in any of the artistic successes of his friends. His popularity was marked by his prompt election to the Authors' Club of America. He was present when the National Institute of Arts and Letters was founded one bitterly cold night in February 1898. The building was unheated and everyone was thoroughly chilled, but there was such a warm response to Roberts, who 'took an active part in the proceedings,'[21] that the rules were bent to admit him as the only non-American member.

CHAPTER SEVEN

The Upswing

1899–1907

THE APPROACH OF 1899 saw the beginning of a modest improvement in Roberts' finances. If he had not exactly conquered the literary world of New York, at least he was finding an increasingly profitable market for his wares, particularly his Acadian romances. So far, however, his sales in England had been negligible. Now that he could afford the trip, it seemed a shrewd business move to go over to establish personal contact with the British editors and publishers. 'I am going to take the English market for my *Sister to Evangeline* & my forthcoming *Collected Poems*,' he announced to his old mentor, George Parkin. He gratefully accepted Parkin's offer to supply letters of introduction to several important Englishmen. Earlier, he had stressed that he was 'particularly anxious' for a letter to Canada's high commissioner in London, Lord Strathcona.

In April, Roberts paid a quick visit to Fredericton for 'a glimpse of the folks at home before sailing for England.'[1] When he returned to New York, he took along his fourteen-year-old son, Lloyd, to accompany him overseas. They were joined by Will Roberts, and the three New Brunswickers left New York harbour, 4 May, on board the Atlantic transport ship, *Menominee*. Father, son, and brother were all boyishly excited, but much of Roberts' exhilaration was due to the presence on board of Irma Perry, who was travelling with her sister, Cleo Huneker. Shortly after their arrival in London, the Roberts trio settled in a boarding-house in the Earl's Court district of the city, not far from Kensington Gardens.

Roberts was very pleased with the contacts he made over the next few months. In August, he wrote to Carman that he had 'got pretty solid with

Editors without seeming to seek them.' An important connection was made with *The Windsor Magazine*, which became an unfailing market for his animal stories for two decades. Arrangements were made for publication of his Acadian stories under the title *By the Marshes of Minas*; in general, he felt that he had 'effectively paved the way for success'[2] for his books. There was not much new work to show the editors because his busy social schedule kept him from maintaining the normal productivity of his pen. He completed only one short story, a nature poem, and a few articles, but he began a book that would firmly establish his reputation as a writer of animal fiction. One day as he sat in Kensington Gardens, dreaming about his boyhood haunts near his beloved Westcock, the idea came to him for a novel about a child, with a special affinity for animals, growing up in the backwoods of New Brunswick. He began the story at once, using 'The Folk of the Ancient Wood' as his working title. When he mentioned the project to his friend Richard Le Gallienne, the latter protested that 'Folk' should be changed to 'Heart'; and thus the novel made its appearance a year later as *The Heart of the Ancient Wood*.

Le Gallienne was the first of Roberts' literary acquaintances to greet him upon his arrival in England. After Roberts introduced him to Irma Perry, Le Gallienne soon became so enamoured of her that he begged Roberts 'to give him a chance.'[3] The romance flourished; within a few years, Irma and Richard divorced their respective spouses and married each other – and lived happily ever after, it appears. Roberts was also welcomed by William Sharp and Douglas Sladen, who amply repaid the hospitality that he had once extended to them in Windsor, Nova Scotia. It was through Sladen that he met George Washington Stevens, a celebrated correspondent for *The Daily Mail*, who took him into his household as one of the family. He also met and dined with Anthony Hope, who was still basking in the recent success of *The Prisoner of Zenda*. W.J. Locke, destined for fame as a prolific and popular novelist, also dined with him. Several visits to 'The Pines' at Putney Hill, where Theodore Watts-Dutton tended an ailing Swinburne, were undertaken in the spirit of a pilgrimage. Swinburne was one of the 'masters' whose sensuous lines Roberts had first heard as a schoolboy in George Parkin's classes. The famous poet was only in his early sixties, but youthful dissipation had left him a burned-out shell. Only when his eyes occasionally lighted with momentary animation was it possible to believe that the little man with the large, balding forehead was the author of the passionate verses that had once caused him to be denounced in the British House of Commons.

In addition to his literary encounters, Roberts also had a taste of high society, as he noted to Carman, 'from Princess Louise at Kensington Palace on down – !' The Marquis of Lorne, Princess Louise's husband, still retained an interest in Canada from the days when he had been there as Governor General. Moreover, because he had a literary bent and fancied himself as a poet, he found Roberts an extremely congenial companion, and invited him to Kensington Palace several times – twice to private family breakfasts. During one of those latter occasions, the Prince of Wales (soon to be Edward vii) happened by and stayed to dine informally with them. Usually, the Marquis would walk back to Roberts' lodgings at 8 Templeton Place to continue the discussions of literature in general and Canadian affairs in particular.[4]

Because he had favourably reviewed *One Hour and the Next* by the Duchess of Sutherland, Roberts was invited to an 'At Home' given by the Duchess shortly after his arrival. During the party, he met the Duchess' sister, the beautiful Countess of Warwick, and made himself so agreeable that he was later invited to Warwick Castle. Further excursions into the upper levels of society are glimpsed in a letter written to his wife on 19 July 1899:

Lloyd is ever so well. He is out in the country visiting the Count de Soissons. There he plays tennis and rides the pony. It is a lovely country place, about thirty miles from London. He comes in on Saturday to go to a grand Garden Party at Lord Strathcona's. Dear old Lord Strathcona took a fancy to him. He'll be the only boy there; but I'm going to let him go, because he'll have to settle down so hard at school when he gets back to Fredericton this fall. I took Lloyd out to visit the famous 'Burnham Beeches,' said to be the loveliest beech woods in England. We have lots just as lovely in Canada; but it is nice to see the holly growing wild among the trees, – and here is a leaf of it I picked for you![5]

The frame of mind in which May Roberts received her holly leaf is not known. The chances are that she thought it was a poor substitute for something practical – such as money. As usual, her absent spouse seemed to be having far too good a time while she was 'stuck' at home with the responsibilities. He was never around to deal with family emergencies. In the late spring, for example, Douglas had fallen into the Saint John River while playing on some logs near the railway bridge. He might have been drowned if a companion had not been successful in fishing him out. If the accident had been fatal, she would have had to cope with the tragedy without the support of her husband.

Roberts admitted to Carman, although he did not tell his wife, that he had been 'chiefly dissipating in London.' But the visits to his friends' country places also meant more play than work. He often stayed with his new-found friend George Stevens and his wife at Merton Abbey. On one occasion, Mrs Stevens held a garden party in his honour to which she invited such interesting people as Thackeray's daughter and young Winston Churchill. During August, he and Lloyd were the Stevens' guests while they were renting Aughill Castle in the Lake District. 'The folks here are extremely nice,' he wrote to Carman, ' – G.W. Stevens & party, – & the country, the high heathery moors, the wild streams (becks), the miraculously clean & quaint stone villages, the tonic air, would delight your soul.'[6] Later in the season, when Roberts and Lloyd were attending a house party at Merton Abbey, Stevens was suddenly called away by his paper to report on the Dreyfus case at Rennes. It was to be the last time Roberts would ever see him. A promising friendship was abruptly ended when Stevens died within the year while covering the Boer War in South Africa.

Originally, Roberts had intended to return to Fredericton in time for Lloyd to begin the fall term at school, but business and pleasure conspired to detain him. He had a fairly clear conscience over the matter of his son's education, however, having hired a tutor (incidentally a chess expert) to keep Lloyd up in his studies. Unfortunately, he was too busy to supervise the lessons, and never discovered until long afterwards that tutor and pupil had spent most of their time playing chess. He had not yet reached any decision about living in England permanently, although there were rumours in several Canadian papers that he would not be coming back. The Fredericton *Reporter* implied that such a possibility existed and further strengthened the argument adding: 'Professor Roberts is assured by his publishers that he can make very much more money in London than on this side of the water.' He confessed privately that one of his reasons for not remaining in England was due to 'a certain lady having decided not to come over!' but, unfortunately, there are no clues to her identity. Father and son finally sailed for Halifax, Nova Scotia, at the end of November, while Will remained behind to complete some work for *The Literary Digest*. Leaving Lloyd in Fredericton, Roberts continued on to Boston and New York, where he spent several weeks before rejoining his family for Christmas.[7]

The war in South Africa had been in progress since September, and the majority of English-speaking Canadians, particularly in a Loyalist city such as Fredericton, were outraged that so far the Canadian government had sent only one contingent of a thousand men to the aid of the Mother

Country. It was well known that Laurier, the French-Canadian prime minister, was inclined to the view of Goldwin Smith and others who seriously questioned the justness of the British cause. Roberts was too much a product of his background to listen to such heresy, and his fighting blood was stirred by the thought of serving his country in the face of danger and death. With what his hometown paper proudly hailed as 'his characteristic push,' he sent a telegram to Frederick Borden, the minister of militia and defence, begging to be placed for service with the Canadian forces in South Africa. *The Reporter* commented approvingly that Canada was full of such men who 'would gladly give their services to the Queen if they would be accepted.' A few months later, the government reluctantly dispatched a second contingent, but the forty-year-old Roberts, who had not served in the militia since his college days, was not called upon to honour his pledge.

While Roberts was in England, May's father had died, leaving an estate of about $100,000. In his will, after providing for his widow and the three children of a son who had predeceased him, Fenety had left the residue of his estate to be divided equally among his four surviving sons and three daughters. The sons' shares were to be paid to them at once, but the daughters' shares were to be held in trust and the interest arising therefrom was 'to be paid annually to each for her sole and separate use.' The ensuing income was not enough to make May independent of her husband's support, but it probably helped to give her a greater feeling of security. Moreover, since her father had effectively put the principal out of Roberts' reach, there was no chance of its being used to finance any of the latter's enterprises.[8]

Upon his return to New York, Roberts took a furnished fourth-floor flat from Albert Bigelow Paine at 22 West Ninth Street, where Fifth Avenue begins. The studio of his friend Roland Hinton Perry was just around the corner on Tenth Street. Washington Square, which was only a two-minute walk away, was the centre of a district that was fast becoming a haven for writers and other artists. The encroaching tenements to the south had turned many of the once elegant homes into rooming-houses that were now occupied mostly by struggling hopefuls in the artistic world. It was a community that began spontaneously and then developed more self-consciously as it gained a reputation as an American Bohemia. Twenty years earlier, Henry James had remarked upon the area's 'established repose which is not of frequent occurrence in other parts of the long, shrill city.' Despite the changes in its fortunes, it had not entirely lost its 'look of having had something of a social history.'[9] Roberts undoubtedly relished the aura of former greatness that formed a subdued background to his grinding existence as a writer. Bliss Carman, who also found the surroundings to his liking, moved in with his cousin.

Although Carman was a shy, retiring man, he had a genius for lasting friendships. Richard Hovey, however, remained the closest of Carman's intimate group, whose other members were Frank Edge Kavanagh of the New York municipal service and Tom Meteyard, the artist who had done the designs for the 'Vagabondia' books by Carman and Hovey. Roberts was drawn into that circle, long before he took up residence in New York, and was acknowledged as one of the five 'birds of a feather' whom Hovey had celebrated in his famous 'Stein Song':

> For it's always fair weather
> When good fellows get together
> With a stein on the table and a good song ringing clear.

As we have seen, Hovey had been an occasional guest at Kingscroft during the Windsor years. At a later date, Kavanagh spent a summer holiday camping with Roberts and his sons in the wilds of New Brunswick. Roberts always regretted Henrietta Hovey's overly possessive manner towards her husband, and may have been right in thinking that she resented the conviviality that Hovey enjoyed with his friends. In spite of her possible objections, however, the relationships continued until Hovey was fatally stricken by a blood clot on 24 February 1900, following surgery.

Around the time of Hovey's death, Roberts' Acadian stories, *By the Marshes of Minas*, appeared under the imprint of Silver, Burdett and Company, with which Frank Bellamy was then associated. Roberts was profiting from the good fortune of having a faithful friend in the publishing business. Within a few months of publication of the Acadian collection, Silver, Burdett brought out *The Heart of the Ancient Wood*, which had been serialized in *Lippincott's Magazine* in April. The company later published Roberts' *Collected Poems* (1901) and an edition of *Alastor and Adonais* (1902) which contained Roberts' essay on the pastoral elegy.

Canadian and British editions of *The Heart of the Ancient Wood* came out shortly after its appearance in the United States. Overall, it met with greater approval than *By the Marshes of Minas*, whose pictorial 'prettiness' several critics found 'cloying' in a work that was generally 'lacking in life and probability.' Even the *New York Daily Tribune* reviewer, who felt that *The Heart of the Ancient Wood* was not the product of genius, conceded that

'Mr Roberts' story shows much talent and is calculated to give a great deal of pleasure.' The Canadian reviewers were effusive in their praise. 'Only the heart of a poet could have dictated the writing of this book,' rhapsodized *The Globe* (Toronto), 'only the hand of a master craftsman given it form.' If *The Globe*'s enthusiasm might be considered suspect on nationalistic grounds, the same cannot be said of *The Times* (London) which lauded Roberts in similar terms: 'He is a poet at heart, and handles his fantastic and somewhat difficult theme with a skill and success that deserve unstinted praise.' One British reviewer, who got off to a bad start by declaring that the story was set somewhere in the United States, 'probably in Maine,' came closer to the mark when he suggested that the most engrossing parts of the novel were those that were 'devoted to studies of beast and birds in a wild state.' The general consensus that Roberts' forte was the realistic animal story undoubtedly convinced the erstwhile poet and novelist that he was right in taking advantage of the vogue created by Ernest Thompson Seton.[10]

By now, Roberts was writing animal stories in earnest, not to the complete exclusion of other prose, but more and more to the exclusion of his poetry. He found a ready market in *Outing*, a monthly magazine that had recently been purchased by his sports-minded friend Caspar Whitney. Like Roberts, Whitney was an athletic man of forty whose love of the out-of-doors was almost as strong as his love of literature. Roberts never forgot Whitney's generosity as an editor – nor the fact that he had an extremely attractive wife! Soon, however, Roberts' animal stories were appearing regularly in other periodicals such as *Youth's Companion*, *Frank Leslie's Monthly Magazine*, *The Metropolitan*, and *McClure's*. In Britain, his chief outlet became *The Windsor Magazine*, which accepted his stories almost on a monthly basis, usually printing them after they had already been published in American magazines. Fortunately, he no longer tried to sell his stories himself, but put them in the hands of a literary agent who was able to double the price.

Since Seton's stories owed much of their appeal to his own superb illustrations, Roberts had been hoping to find an artist who could depict animals with similar skill. One day, a young man of about twenty-seven appeared in the studio, saying that he had read some of Roberts' work and would like to become his illustrator. He produced a portfolio of such excellent animal drawings that Roberts knew at once that the young artist, who introduced himself as Charles Livingston Bull, was the right person to interpret his animal creations. He took his discovery to meet several of his editors, who immediately engaged Bull to work on Roberts' stories.[11]

Soon, the popular artist was also illustrating such successful works as Jack London's *The Call of the Wild* (1902), but he continued for many years to be known chiefly as 'Roberts' illustrator.'

An indication of Roberts' growing reputation may be found in the increasing number of occasions when he was the guest of honour of the Canadian Club and similar organizations in various centres throughout New England and eastern Canada. Instead of a formal address at those functions, he usually 'gave a quiet little talk, at times philosophic, at times poetic, at times humorous, but always entertaining.'[12] As a rule, his subject was Canadianism.

'I felt it to be as much a duty as a pleasure,' he told the Canadian Club of Toronto, 'to obey your call and come over to show that I am a Canadian first, last, and always, in every way that I know how to be.' Alluding to the five years he had spent in New York, he maintained, 'Residence under another flag, rather than mitigating, only makes me more proud of my birthright and more determined not to forfeit it.' Fredericton, New Brunswick, was his permanent address, he explained; his New York address was liable to change at any moment. Turning to the subject of writing, he boasted that 'Canada has accomplished more in literature than any other young country in history.' After paying tribute to Lampman, Carman, Campbell, and the two Scotts, he gave Ernest Thompson Seton credit for popularizing the realistic animal story. He insisted, however, that Seton had merely created the fad, not the form. 'Young though I may seem,' he laughed, 'I am the father of the animal story.' He referred to his three animal stories that pre-dated Seton's work, pointing out that he had received only $14, $20, and $25 for them, and had been advised by one editor to stick to poetry. Although he admitted that he was now following the fashion, he denied that he was turning out pot-boilers. He declared that his animal stories grew out of the same emotional urge as his poetry, and that he took meticulous care in writing them.[13]

Roberts had two new books ready for publication in 1902: a novel called *Barbara Ladd* and a collection of his animal stories with the significant title *The Kindred of the Wild*. Both books bore the imprint of L.C. Page and Company, successors to Lamson, Wolffe, his earlier publisher. L.C. Page remained his American publisher for many years, although the association eventually proved to be extremely unsatisfactory from Roberts' point of view. They made a great success of *Barbara Ladd*, however, selling 80,000 copies in the United States. Perhaps the fact that it was set in New England during the American War of Independence was a large factor in its popularity. Most critics damned it with praise as faint as the following comment: 'Mr Roberts' tale is no worse than the majority of Revolutionary romances.'[14] The story had its roots in Roberts' own boyhood, and the Connecticut village of which he wrote was almost identical to Westcock: the same type of environment, the same breed of people, the same set of attitudes. The heroine of the story, Barbara Ladd, an impulsive and emotional young woman, was modelled after Jean Carré, who designed the cover of the book. The former lovers were still friends, although it is clear from Roberts' severely objective appraisal of Barbara that his infatuation with the original was over.

In *The Kindred of the Wild*, Roberts had collected the animal stories that he had been publishing in magazines over the last couple of years. To introduce them, he wrote an essay which traced the development of the animal story down to the type of psychological romance constructed on the framework of natural science that he and Seton were writing. Adding greatly to the attractiveness of the collection were fifty-one full-page illustrations by Charles Livingston Bull. Since this was Roberts' first complete book of animal stories – *Earth's Enigmas* had contained only three such stories – it is interesting to note that the critics were almost unanimous in their enthusiastic approval. The reviewer in *The Nation* wrote:

the reader of Prof. Roberts's book, as he proceeds, cannot avoid the conviction that it is a masterpiece of its kind. An earlier volume by the same hand, *The Heart of the Ancient Wood*, showed a most intimate and appreciative acquaintance with the habits and motives of the animal life of the woods. This one, which describes the life histories of various wild animals, does so with extraordinary fidelity and breadth of knowledge. The writer makes it evident that he knows whereof he writes, and writes from the fulness of his knowledge and interest for an audience which can detect such errors of fact and flights of egotistic fancy as embellish the popular narratives of a certain favourite author on wild life and natural history.

It seems probable that the unnamed 'favourite author' was not Seton but William J. Long, an American clergyman, junior to Roberts by about seven years, who had written some very popular tales based upon his rather questionable knowledge of natural science. The Toronto *Globe* regretted that *The Kindred of the Wild* did not prove to be a continuous story like his 'matchless *The Heart of the Ancient Wood*,' but felt that the new book was further proof that no other writer excelled Roberts in his knowledge of woodcraft. Only a few critics suggested, as did the reviewer in *The Athenaeum*, that whenever Roberts introduces human interests and sentiments, 'he fails, lapsing into sentimentality.' *The Kindred of the Wild* never had the financial success of *Barbara Ladd*, but it had the greatest critical acclaim of any of Roberts' books up to that time. One Boston bookseller took a humorous view of it, however, suggesting that 'probably Roberts was writing about his wild life in Canada to divert attention from his wild life in New York.'[15]

The most important attention that *The Kindred of the Wild* received was in 'Real and Sham Natural History,' an article by John Burroughs which appeared in the March issue of *The Atlantic Monthly*, 1903. Burroughs, who had taken an early retirement from the business world and retreated to a farm on the Hudson River, was a highly respected naturalist whose observations had been carefully recorded in several popular volumes. Recently, he had become alarmed over the proliferation of nature stories, which he considered to be based more upon fancy than fact. He had four particular books in mind: Roberts' *The Kindred of the Wild*, William Davenport Hulbert's *Forest Neighbours*, Seton's *Wild Animals I Have Known*, and the Reverend William J. Long's *School of the Woods*. Seton and Long were accused of seeking 'to profit by the popular love for the sensational and the improbable, Mr Long, in this respect, quite throwing Mr Thompson Seton in the shade.' Hulbert and Roberts, in Burrough's opinion, were more reliable in their portrayal of wild life. Although he felt that the porcupine's behaviour in Roberts' 'In Panoply of Spears' had no foundation in fact, he expressed his overall admiration for *The Kindred of the Wild*, despite his reservations over the reasoning ability that the author ascribed to his animals:

In Mr Charles G.D. Roberts's *Kindred of the Wild* one finds much to admire and commend, and but little to take exception to. The volume is in many ways the most brilliant collection of animal stories that has appeared. It reaches a high order of literary merit. Many of the descriptive passages in it of winter in the Canadian woods are of great beauty. The story called 'A Treason of Nature,' describing the betrayal and death of a bull moose by hunters who imitated the call of a cow moose, is most striking and effective. True it is that all the animals whose lives are portrayed – the bear, the panther, the lynx, the hare, the moose, and others – are simply human beings disguised as animals; they think, feel, plan, suffer as we do; in fact, exhibit almost the entire human psychology. But in other respects they follow closely the facts of natural history, and the reader is not deceived; he knows where he stands. Of course it is mainly guesswork how far our psychology applies to the lower animals. That they experience many of our emotions there can be no doubt, but that they have intellectual and reasoning processes like our own, except in a very rudimentary form, admits of grave doubt. But I need not go into that vexed subject here. They are certainly in any broad generalization our kin, and Mr Roberts's book is well named and well done.[16]

Although Burroughs' censure of *The Kindred of the Wild* had been extremely mild, the famous naturalist's opinion carried so much weight with the readers of his own day that Roberts felt constrained to respond in a prefatory note in his next collection of stories, *The Watchers of the Trails* (1904):

A very distinguished author – to whom all contemporary writers on nature are indebted, and from whom it is only with the utmost diffidence that I venture to dissent at all – has gently called me to account on the charge of ascribing to my animals human motives and the mental processes of man. The fact is, however, that the fault is one which I have been at particular pains to guard against. The psychological processes of the animals are so simple, so obvious, in comparison with those of man, their actions flow so directly from their springs of impulse, that it is, as a rule, an easy matter to infer the motives which are at any one moment impelling them. In my desire to avoid alike the melodramatic, the visionary, and the sentimental, I have studied to keep well within the safe limits of inference.[17]

It is highly likely that Seton, who had greater reason to be outraged, discussed the Burroughs article with his friend Roberts. Seton had left New York for the spacious country home called 'Wyndygoul,' which he had built on a hundred-acre retreat in Connecticut. Roberts was a frequent visitor and it was there that he completed 'The Freedom of the Black-Faced Ram,' the opening story of *The Watchers of the Trails*, which bears the dedication: 'To my fellow of the wild, Ernest Thompson Seton.' At Wyndygoul, Seton finally had the space to house his nature collections: his thousands of photographs, his thousand animal skins and two thousand bird skins – all collected and skinned by his own hand – hundreds of his own detailed drawings done from life, and his 5,000-book library. In those surroundings, Roberts must have found it ironic that the owner's knowledge of wild life should ever be called into question, but like many another of Seton's acquaintances, he was inclined to be overawed by the man's industry and self-confidence – even Burroughs later succumbed in the face of those qualities. Had Roberts been able to be more objective, he might indeed have wondered whether Seton sometimes went too far in humanizing his animals.

During March 1903, Roberts visited his young poet friend, Frank

Sherman, the head of the Merchants' Bank of Canada in Havana. Ever since 1895, when Roberts resigned his professorship at King's to live in Fredericton, he had regarded the tall, distinguished-looking Sherman as a kindred spirit. Lately, the younger man had been too active in banking circles to devote much of his time to poetry, but one glance at his familiar face was enough to convince Roberts that the 'wistful eyes of the poet rather than the banker' were still his most distinctive feature. Among Sherman's clients in Havana was Sir William Van Horne, who had just built another railroad – this one in Cuba. The genial Van Horne at once invited Roberts to join him on a train tour that he had arranged for a group of visiting capitalists. From one of Van Horne's private coaches, Roberts had a splendid introduction to the country before resuming his visit with Sherman.

Years later, Roberts fondly recalled the happy hours he had spent in Sherman's company.

Heavily engrossed though he was in banking affairs, out of hours he threw them off completely. Our concern, our conversation was, to paraphrase Horace, about libros, venerem, vinum [the last being Sherman's unfortunate weakness]. Over our fragrant 'green Havanas' and the potent golden distillage of Bacardi rum, we discussed everybody's poetry except our own, – for in regard to his poetry he was always extremely reticent. Sometimes we would drive out to the lovely silver-sanded bathing beach on the Marianao, which was protected from the sharks of those infested seas by a broad shelving bar of white sand which the man-eaters feared to cross. I had misgivings lest some shark more individual and exploratory, and more voracious, than his fellows might venture in over the bar; but I pretended to be content with Sherman's assurance that this was, as he casually phrased it, 'rather improbable.' And the swimming there was so delightful that I almost forgot the remote but uncomfortable possibility of sharks.[18]

Roberts may have found it difficult to justify his Cuban holiday to his wife. Trips to Europe might be explained as necessary in terms of overseas markets, but she probably regarded his Caribbean jaunt as an inexcusable extravagance when he still could not afford – or so he said – to move his family to New York. She would never be reconciled to her role as a grass widow. To make matters worse, she refused to allow herself any diversions that might have taken her mind off her troubles. She had no social activities, for how could she face the sewing circle, or even mingle with her close neighbours, when she felt sure that they were gossiping that she had been deserted. Whenever she visited Linden Hall, she put on a brave front to convince her family that she would soon be reunited with her husband, but the excuses and the explanations wore thin with the passing of time. At the rectory, there was no need to keep up appearances, and there she complained bitterly about her circumstances. Poor Canon Roberts shook his head sadly, and confessed that his greatest worry was over what was to become of his eldest son's family.[19]

Unfortunately, as Lloyd remembered bitterly, it was the Roberts children who 'had to atone for their parents' incompatibility.' They were the ones who bore the brunt of May's daily outbursts. Some days were worse than others, depending upon the mail: 'No-letter days had better never been born; chequeless days were like clouds before rain; cheque-letter days were but the passing showers to a summer drought.' The children had learned long ago that their mother would not be soothed by their feeble attempts at comfort, nor would she listen to any defence of their father. They devised their own ways of coping: Lloyd would either look for his two best friends or escape to the rectory and 'take his chance' of finding his grandmother 'in an amiable mood'; Edith 'seconded without amendment everything her mother said and felt'; Douglas, blessed with an imperturbable nature, could 'shake the dust of tragedy from his feet' almost as soon as he left the house.[20]

As a rule, Roberts returned to Fredericton twice a year – in midsummer and at Christmas. Sometimes he cut his visits short, explaining that he simply had to leave sooner than expected. 'Good Lord, how I miss you chicks!' he would exclaim and there was never any doubt about his sincerity. Often he would be home long enough in the summer for one of those family camping trips to Savage Island that involved the whole Roberts clan and various followers. One of the best times would be in the evening with stories and songs around a campfire on the beach. As the last embers were flickering, long after darkness had settled down over the river, Canon Roberts would finally end the singing by leading them in the benediction hymn 'Forever with the Lord.' All eyes would turn to the patriarchal clergyman as he stood in the shadows with his arms lifted in blessing. His eldest son would watch him with deep affection and possibly a twinge of envy. In his heart, Roberts must have feared even then that he would forfeit his chance to succeed his father as head of the various branches of the family. In later years, beneath his worldly bravado, it was apparent to his close friends that 'he was greatly humiliated and disappointed' that, unlike his father, he headed no household that could serve as a central meeting place for the far-flung members of the Roberts clan.[21]

In 1903, when Lloyd was eighteen years old, Roberts 'reluctantly surrendered his expectation of ever making his son a scholar after the manner of his fathers,'[22] and sent for him to come to New York. Lloyd had always led his class in the subjects he liked, but he rebelled against those that did not interest him. Consequently, his English teacher thought that he was a budding genius while most of his other teachers thought he was an idler. For several years he had been begging to live with his father, but Roberts hesitated until he was finally convinced that such a move would be in Lloyd's best interests. If his son were determined to be a writer, he reasoned, perhaps it would be best after all to allow him to begin his apprenticeship where he could keep a watchful eye upon him. He secured a position for him, albeit a humble beginning, as an office boy at *McClure's*.

For many months, Lloyd had been living at the rectory, being 'clothed and fed' by his grandparents while May and the two younger children had 'been transferred from house-keeping privileges to boarding-house inhibitions.' Lloyd had grown to love and revere his grandfather, and the wrench of parting took the edge off his excitement over New York. He also had qualms over joining his father when he knew that his mother had been told that she and the others could not go – not yet. After a few days in New York, he realized that his father no longer had any intention of ever living permanently again with May. It was not in Roberts' nature to be unkind, but in Lloyd's view he lacked the fortitude to make a final break which, in the long run, might have caused his wife less grief. As courageous as he was in meeting many of life's challenges, Roberts went to great lengths to avoid painful human confrontations. 'The real Charles,' Lloyd declared in retrospect, ' – what a strong, weak, lovable, remarkable character!'[23]

It was cramped quarters, living on the top floor of 22 West Ninth Street. The space had been divided into two small suites, one occupied by Roberts and the other by Frank Verbeck, an artist who specialized in comic animals. Now and then a friend would stay with Roberts, taking advantage of his hospitality for an indefinite period, but mostly it was his cousin Bliss who shared his cluttered studio-bedroom. With Lloyd's arrival, Carman moved in with Verbeck, vacating the lounge upon which he had been sleeping. The younger Roberts, who had an uncomfortable first night in his new environment, rose early complaining of bites. His father was apologetic: 'Unfortunately these old residential blocks are infested with bugs. One can clean them out temporarily, but they always return. It's time we burned some more sulphur candles.'

New York had other disappointments in store bedsides bedbugs, and Lloyd came to call it 'that Mecca of all the mental misfits of North American life,'[24] but in the beginning he was exhilarated by the Bohemian atmosphere of Washington Square. His daily companions were a long-haired vagabond poet, a bearded artist whose baggy clothes were always besmeared with paint, and a clean-shaven writer (whom he now called *Pater* instead of *Papa*) whose chief affectation was a broad black ribbon dangling from his eyeglasses. It was heady company for an impressionable young lad, but Lloyd soon discovered that artistic temperaments can have healthy appetites even when they are almost too preoccupied to notice what they are eating. Therefore, he undertook to prepare breakfast daily for his three elders, offering them eggs, fruit, coffee, rolls, and butter for the bargain price of twenty-five cents per customer. Whenever a question arose about the quality of the fare, especially the freshness of the eggs, it could be squelched by a threat to raise the prices.

Inspiration thrived on his menu, Lloyd pointed out later, for this 'was the age of many of the Pipes of Pan [Carman], of the Rose poems and of full-page Bruin escapades.' However, an examination of the facts show that most of Roberts' love poems with the symbolic use of the rose had been written previously, for *The Book of the Rose* was published by L.C. Page early in 1903. The book actually contains a greater portion of poems that do not use the 'rather tiresome figure' of the rose, but nothing about it excited much critical attention. *The New York Times* chose to ignore it completely.[25]

Roberts himself does not seem to have been particularly pleased with another book he published in 1903. Called *Exploration and Discoveries*, it appeared as Volume XIV of a history of the nineteenth century, edited by Justin McCarthy, the Irish historian. As early as April 1899, he had written to Parkin that he had 'a fine contract for it';[26] and, during his trip to England that year, he had done much of his research in the British Museum. The finished product, consisting of thirty-one good-sized chapters, obviously represents a lot of hard work, but he was strangely reticent about it in later years. His 'official' biography, written by Elsie Pomeroy under his direction, makes no mention of it whatever.

In the early summer of 1904, the editor of Lippincott's, who had accepted Roberts' story 'A Prisoner of Mademoiselle,' suggested that the romantic tale should be expanded into a full-length novel. Since the studio at 22 West Ninth Street was now more crowded than ever – brother Will having moved in with them – Roberts hit upon the idea of a working holiday in continental Europe. Sailing from New York to Cherbourg, he went to Amsterdam, where he settled down for several weeks of work. The writing did not come easily, however, and he worried himself into such a nervous state over it that he suffered from severe indigestion – aggravated no doubt by the rich Dutch cuisine. Putting the novel aside, he set out again, slowly making his way down southern France through Dijon and Lyons to the Mediterranean port of Sète (Cette). Turning westward, he reached the valley of Luchon in the shadow of the Pyrenees, where he found the ideal spot to resume his work. With his good digestion completely restored, he remained in the valley until the novel was finished. After continuing up the western coast of France, crossing the Loire valley, and pausing briefly in Paris, he sailed for home to deliver the manuscript of *A Prisoner of Mademoiselle* into the waiting hands of his publisher. Miss Pomeroy once referred to it as 'the least important'[27] of his novels; since she usually deferred to Roberts' literary judgment, it seems safe to infer that the book was not one of the author's own favourites either.

He was probably able to take more satisfaction from his next two books of animal stories: *The Watchers of the Trails* (1904) and *Red Fox* (1905). The former had already appeared, piece by piece, in various journals, but in their collected form some of the stories were rediscovered to be 'extraordinarily good.' Some of *Red Fox*, which is an episodic novel of animal life, was first printed in *Outing* by Caspar Whitney, who had recently done Roberts another good turn by taking on Lloyd as his assistant editor. *The Athenaeum* (London) hailed *Red Fox* as a literary landmark: 'We have reached a stage – remote indeed from the day of *Black Beauty* – at which the psychology of such life is treated with the same close analysis as is applied to human character.' Four years later, when Seton published a similar book, *The Biography of a Silver Fox*, *The New York Times* commented that 'Mr Roberts' chief advantage over Mr Seton, aside from priority of publication, is that his is the better, more vivid, and more dramatic story.'[28]

Roberts' return from Europe marked the end of the ménage at 22 West Ninth Street, where the five top-floor tenants had been co-existing 'on the whole with surprising harmony.' Verbeck went his separate way, while the three Robertses took a larger studio on the top floor at 226 Fifth Avenue. Carman, who was becoming increasingly dependent upon the strong-willed Mrs King and her easy-going husband, did not join his cousins. Roberts began to feel that Mrs King's influence was having a deleterious effect upon Carman's poetry, and he could never forgive her determination to separate his kinsman from all his old associations. Lloyd, who had never known the same bonds of comradeship with Carman, and for whom the rift was consequently less painful, was able to take a more tolerant view. 'Personally,' he said, 'I feel some allowance should be made for Carman's now-failing health and his need of mothering rather than romancing, of three square meals rather than studio "atmosphere".'[29]

The third great blow of Roberts' life struck on 11 October 1905. For the past two or three years, Canon Roberts had been in such indifferent health that he had found great difficulty in shaking off even a common cold. A few days prior to Thanksgiving, he caught a severe chill, but insisted upon taking the Harvest Home service at St Ann's on Sunday. By the time he reached home, pneumonia had set in, and his condition deteriorated so quickly that Charles and Will were summoned from New York at once. They reached home in time to be with the rest of the family at the end. Canon Roberts retained consciousness almost to the last, and when his curate softly sang 'Forever with the Lord' at his bedside, he was able to repeat the words with him before sinking into a slumber from which he never roused. The eulogies that followed his death far exceeded the customary tributes that one might expect to a beloved pastor. 'Canon Roberts might not have been a perfect man,' wrote one newspaper correspondent, 'but what imperfections were his, were not known to the people of this world.' His eldest son, to the day of his own death, grieved for him a 'the wisest, kindest, most wholly admirable man I shall ever know.'[30]

Shortly after his father's death, Roberts began planning a novel in which one of the leading characters was a thinly disguised version of Canon Roberts. Set in Westcock at the time of the author's boyhood, the story was to be called, appropriately, *The Heart that Knows*. During the ensuing winter, he again visited Sherman in Havana, but he spent most of his time in the neighbouring city of Matanxas in a quiet little hotel where he could work on his novel without distraction. One evening, however, he accompanied Sherman to a masquerade ball where they 'made the acquaintance of a pair of slender and flower-like girls, gracefully and scantily costumed and heavily masked.' When the music began, one of the seductive creatures introduced Roberts to the Cuban *valson* and stayed with him throughout four or five dances until she was whisked off by a possessive young cavalier in scarlet. After the enchantress had gone, Roberts discovered that his gold matchsafe and gold watch – the only gold watch he ever owned – had disappeared with her. Later, when he confessed to Sherman that he had been robbed, the astute banker sheepishly admitted that his partner had lifted his purse and cigarette case.[31]

The Heart that Knows vies with *The Heart of the Ancient Wood* for the distinction of being Roberts' best novel. It is not as unified as the earlier work, shifting as it does between realism and melodrama, but it is more ambitious than his backwood fable, and shows what he was capable of doing when he concentrated upon the life he knew instead of copying the cliches of the popular adventure story. It went unnoticed by most of the influential periodicals, but one noteworthy exception was *The Literary Digest*, which carried an extremely favourable notice that might well have been written by a staff member called William Carman Roberts. Most of the critics had come to look upon the animal story as Roberts' forte, and it was that aspect of his work that chiefly gained their attention. Even the revised edition of his *Collected Poems*, which L.C. Page brought out in 1907, did not interest as many reviewers as his latest collection of animal stories, *The Haunters of the Silences*, which appeared in the same year.

While Roberts was at King's College, he had written to Carman about his great desire to see Italy, but his dream did not come true until March 1907. After stopping briefly in London and Paris, he spent a week in Rome before going on to Naples, where he remained for the next two months. Taking a couple of rooms on the top floor of the ancient Palazzo di Don'Anna, he settled down in front of an open lattice overlooking the Bay of Naples, to write about the backwoods of New Brunswick. Early in May he was joined by Lloyd, with whom he explored the surrounding area, including Sorrento where they visited the villa of Marion Crawford, the American novelist. At the beginning of June, father and son left Naples, passing through Florence and Milan on their way to Paris, where Lloyd remained while Roberts returned to New York by way of London.

Roberts arrived back in the United States to be greeted by the furor caused by an article in the June issue of *Everybody's Magazine* in which President Theodore Roosevelt accused Roberts, Seton, William J. Long, and Jack London of being 'nature fakirs.' The initial article was introduced by the following 'Editor's Note':

It is about time to call a halt upon misrepresentative nature studies. Utterly preposterous details of wild life are placed before school children in the guise of truth. Wholly false beliefs have been almost standardized. Only by an authoritative protest can the fraud be exposed. At this juncture it is fitting that the President should come forward. From every point of view he is the person in the United States best equipped for the task, and we are fortunate in being able to fire the first gun, so to speak, with a charge of Mr Roosevelt's vigorous, clear-cut, earnest English.[32]

Roberts must have been amused to remember that the same magazine, which now applauded the president so self-righteously, had, within recent months, published two of his animal stories: 'The Terror of the Sea Caves' and 'In the Deep of the Snow.' The president's second article, which appeared in the September issue, was immediately followed in October by Roberts' story 'In Blackwater Pot,' which, although it does not feature wild animals, is one of the author's most melodramatic stories of the backwoods. A further irony occurred only a year later when *Everybody's* carried 'From the Teeth of the Tide,' which one critic has called 'one of Roberts' more vulnerable animal stories.'[33]

Roosevelt, whom Edmund Clarence Stedman dubbed 'our President Nimrod,'[34] fancied himself to be the world's authority on the big game animals in North America. As such, he felt well qualified to distinguish fact from fiction. He also had a gift for memorable phrases, and his term 'nature fakirs' (which became 'nature fakers') caught on with the journalists. They bandied it about for weeks until it was fixed in the minds of the public, and Roberts et al. were stuck with the label forever. Actually, Roosevelt's harshest criticisms were directed at Long and London. Seton – with whom the president was personally acquainted – received qualified praise, as did Roberts:

Some of the writers who at times offend, at other time do excellent work. Mr Thompson Seton has made interesting observations of fact, and much of his fiction has a real value. But he should make it clear that it *is* fiction, and not fact.

Many of the nature stories of Charles G.D. Roberts are avowedly fairy tales, and no one is deceived by them. When such is the case, we all owe a debt to Mr Roberts, for he is a charming writer and he loves the wilderness. But even Mr Roberts fails to consult possibilities in some of his stories.[35]

Roosevelt went on to demonstrate that the battle between a lynx and eight wolves in Roberts' 'On the Night Trail' was totally unrealistic. Unfortunately for the president, he was thinking about the small Rocky Mountain lynx pitted against timber wolves, while Roberts was actually writing about the powerful Canadian lynx and small eastern brush wolves. Shortly after the controversy began, Roberts was entertained at the White House, where Roosevelt took down a well-thumbed copy of the former's *Collected Poems* from the library shelves. The president might consider himself

Roberts' superior in nature studies, but his egotism did not extend to poetry.

Following in the footsteps of his father and grandfather, Roberts had received the honorary degree of Doctor of Laws (along with Bliss Carman) at the 1906 convocation of the University of New Brunswick. Also in the tradition of his father, he took charge of a large family celebration on Savage Island during two weeks in August 1907. The reunion was a gala occasion, and it took on greater significance in retrospect, for it was the last time that Roberts was surrounded by all his family. Lloyd, who had returned to New York from Paris in July, arrived with his fiancée, Hope Balmain. Will and his wife, Mary Fanton Roberts (then editor of *The Craftsman*), also came from New York, as did Roberts' friend Bronson Howard, the American dramatist. All the Fredericton members of his clan were present: May, Edith, Douglas, his mother and Nan, brother Thede and his wife, and his sister Nain and her family. Various in-laws and other friends were added to the party until it became such a remarkable social event that it was written up in the *Daily Telegraph*, Saint John. The reporter stressed that the tiny island did, indeed, hold more than its due proportion of literary folk, for the professional writers numbered seven, six of whom belonged to the same family.[36]

Games and water sports were the order of the day, and at night there was the old ritual of stories and songs around the campfire, ending as always with the singing of 'Forever with the Lord.' The family of Canon Roberts seemed as united as ever, but this would be the last grand-scale reunion. There would be other gatherings, but they would grow steadily smaller as the children and grandchildren scattered far and wide, and returned less and less frequently to Fredericton. Ironically, the eldest son, his father's natural successor as head of the family, was the first to defect. Within three months, Charles G.D. Roberts sailed again for Europe. He remained there for nearly eighteen years.

CHAPTER EIGHT

European Interlude

1907–1912

IT WAS UNDERSTOOD BY Roberts' family that his fourth trip overseas would be just another of those brief excursions that combined work with travel. He planned to spend the winter in France, but there was no mention of a prolonged absence. In a short while, so everyone believed, he would be back in New York, where he was just a few hours away from Fredericton.

His private intentions are unknown beyond the fact that he was looking for a change. He soon would be forty-eight years old, and, although he was still strong and vigorous, he felt that time was running out on him. His father's death appears to have shocked him into a realization of his own mortality: 'Till now, with startled eyes, I see / The portents of Eternity' ('Under the Pillars of the Sky'). He wanted to put new meaning into his life and he believed that France could offer the fulfilment he was seeking. In other words, he had fallen in love again; and the object of his affections was an American woman, Mrs L. Morris (whose first name is unknown), who had an apartment in Paris.

It may have been difficult to convince his wife that another European jaunt was necessary – after all it was his second visit within the year – but he could always use the argument that change and fresh experience gave him the stimulus he needed as a writer. Besides, he could live more cheaply on the European continent than in New York, and London was not far away if he needed to see a British publisher in person. He could also point out that it was the turn of his younger son to go abroad with him. Douglas, who was nineteen, was no more of an academic than Lloyd, and he would have to settle down soon to earn a living. It would do him good to see a bit of the world first.

In a sense it did not matter whether or not Roberts had May's approval. She was not a very perceptive woman, but even so she must have begun to realize that there was no longer any hope of saving their marriage. There was no need for them to pretend to each other that their separation was not permanent. Yet her fierce pride still drove her to conceal the truth from her family and neighbours. To acknowledge that Roberts had walked out on her would have been more painful than the actual desertion. She preferred to continue the charade of a loyal wife waiting to take her rightful place by her husband's side. Whatever reasons Roberts gave for going abroad were meant to aid her pitiful efforts to keep up appearances.

Accompanied by Douglas, Roberts sailed from New York in November 1907 and went directly to Paris, where he remained for the next two months, not far from the enchanting Mrs Morris. Within a short time of their arrival, father and son settled in the Montparnasse district at 5 rue Stanislas. Both revelled in the Bohemian atmosphere of that area, which had long been the haunt of artists, musicians, and writers from all over Europe. It was still largely unknown to North Americans, however, and nearly two decades would pass before it would be discovered by Ernest Hemingway and his generation.

The great attraction of Montparnasse was to be found in its crowded restaurants. They were the meeting places – almost the unofficial headquarters – of convivial students, aspiring artists, and other kindred souls. The prevailing attitude towards life struck Roberts and young Douglas as being remarkably high-spirited and unconventional. Not far from rue Stanislas was the famous rue de la Gaîté, almost side by side with the Cimetière de Montparnasse. The lively cabarets and dance-halls of the former were not really such incongruous neighbours of the tombs of Guy de Maupassant and other luminaries whose names had given lustre to the Latin Quarter.

With his usual zest, Roberts entered wholeheartedly into the spirit of his new surroundings. As a former teacher of French, he had a basic knowledge of the language and could carry on a conversation with only a minimum of difficulty. Sometimes the talk may have turned to a discussion of the arts, but if his associates espoused any avant garde ideas, he was not influenced by them. Despite his enjoyment of Montparnasse society, he did not neglect his writing and he continued to produce animal stories in the style to which his readers had grown accustomed. Douglas, who was left on his own while his father was working, explored the city and attended an occasional lecture given in English at the Sorbonne.

By February, Roberts had worked so diligently – and so profitably –

that he felt justified in taking a holiday. He decided that the time had come for Douglas to see the French Riviera. The fact that they stayed as long as two months in the resort town of Hyères raises the possibility that Mrs Morris may have been vacationing there as well. Much of the time appears to have been spent hiking across the hills and along the seashore. Chief among their nightly entertainments were the frequent dances held at the main hotel. Roberts, who had a passion for dancing, remembered those evenings with a special fondness for the rest of his life. The big event of the season, however, was the annual Battle of the Flowers, in which he and Douglas participated with typical Roberts gusto.

Early in April, father and son returned to Paris for a couple of months before going over to England for the summer. They stayed in Bushey, just outside London, with their artist-friends, the Hadleys. Mrs Hadley, who had lived in Windsor, Nova Scotia, before her marriage, was a former intimate of the Kingscroft circle. At the end of August they journeyed to Dieppe, where they remained together until the beginning of November when Roberts returned to Paris, leaving Douglas behind. Taking a couple of rooms at 33 rue de Londres, near the Gare Saint Lazare, he found himself within easy walking distance of Montmartre and its alluring cafés and dance-halls. Douglas rejoined him in December, and it is more than likely that the two exiles celebrated Christmas in the company of Mrs Morris.

The date is uncertain, but sometime before February 1909, Mrs Morris left Paris for the Loire Valley town of Pontlevoy to live at the local convent where her children were being educated. She pointed out to Roberts – who had suddenly lost his preference for large centres – that the quiet little town would be an ideal retreat for a writer. When he went down around the beginning of February to investigate for himself, he was fortunate in finding a quaint stone cottage to rent for the modest sum of a hundred francs à month. The owner, a wizened old lady named Madame Bédard, had been bequeathed the cottage by her former mistress, a countess of the Old Régime. Not only was it completely furnished, but many of the pieces were valuable antiques that had come from the countess. In addition to the comfortable quarters, Roberts also had the luxury of a peasant cook who came in three times a day to prepare meals for him and Douglas.

Prior to his move to Pontlevoy, Roberts had been plagued by an attack of nerves that had prevented him from settling down to any steady writing. While he was fretting over his inability to work, he read a biography of Balzac and *In Tune with the Infinite* by the American writer,

Ralph Waldo Trine. He found inspiration in those two volumes, and the latter, in particular, had a marked effect upon his recovery. He had been in Pontlevoy only a few days when he completed a lengthy story called 'The Ladder,' which was published almost immediately in *Collier's*. Many years later, he included the story in his final volume of animal lore, *Eyes of the Wilderness*.

Life at Pontlevoy soon fell into a regular routine in which every morning was devoted to writing. After rising at eight o'clock, Roberts would eat a light breakfast before taking a stroll in the tiny garden to admire Madame Bédard's prize roses (which bloomed ten months out of the year) and spy on the nightingales that nested in the overhanging trees from the adjoining estate of the Marquise de Cuy. Often, he would meet Madame Bédard herself, who came daily at an early hour to tend her flowers and her small flock of chickens. After half an hour or so, he would go inside to write until lunch was ready at one o'clock. Douglas followed a similar routine, but, although he produced several poems and short stories during that period, his apprenticeship did not lead to a career in writing.

The afternoon schedule was more irregular. Sometimes Roberts took time off for social calls in the town, or went to visit one of the nearby châteaux in the country. Whenever he was in a hurry to finish something, he might work right through until tea time. At four-thirty, however, his pen would be resolutely laid aside for the day, and friends were welcome to drop by unannounced. Not infrequently, the Canadian author's tiny dining room would be filled with an assortment of nationalities: several Americans (including Mrs Morris), probably a French baron, possibly a Spanish nobleman or two, and almost certainly a local priest. If there were no guests, the simple tea usually would be followed by a long walk into the sunset across the flat, open countryside.

Several times a week, Roberts took French lessons at Pontlevoy's famous Benedictine college, which had been founded in 1034 on the site of a former fortress. The sessions were usually conducted informally while he and his teacher, an old abbé, strolled through the gardens under the shadow of the ancient walls. About once a week, Roberts returned to the college in the evening, but not for instruction. Just before the gates closed at eight o'clock, he would arrive with several other outsiders for a night of poker. It was not uncommon for the games to last until four o'clock in the morning, 'at which time those who did not live at the college would have to make their exit over the high stone walls, being very careful not to tumble into the deep waters that surrounded part of the walls.'[1]

Like the Frenchmen around him, Roberts was thrilled when Louis Blériot made aviation history on 25 July 1909 by completing the first flight across the English Channel in a heavier-than-air machine. It was the most recent of the many aeronautical advances that had stirred his sense of adventure over the last five years. Now that there were really no new regions to discover on earth, it was wonderful to think that man was on the brink of exploring the skies. Therefore, nothing could keep him away from Paris in October when the Aeroplane Exhibition was held at the Grand Palais. Even more exciting were the demonstrations, known as Aviation Fortnight, which were taking place at Juvisy Aerodrome, thirty miles from the city.

Roberts arrived in Paris during the first week of October to discover that the whole city 'had gone quite mad over flying.' Even nature seemed delirious, he mused, as he walked down the Champs Elysées to the Exhibition, for some of the trees along the avenue were shedding their leaves prematurely, while the horse-chestnuts were bursting into bloom as if it were spring. Inside the Grand Palais, in the bewildering array of balloons, dirigibles, and aeroplanes, he found Blériot's famous little monoplane occupying the place of honour in the centre of the main hall. Ranged around it were other celebrated machines, including the white and blue biplane of the Wright brothers. Roberts felt that the display was ample evidence of man's greatest achievement since the finding of fire.

He chose to go to Juvisy on opening day, 7 October, which had been declared a public holiday. When he and Mrs Morris set out in the late morning, they virtually had to fight their way on board one of the crowded trains in the aerodrome. By the time they arrived, every seat in the pavillion was taken, but they succeeded in finding chairs to place in front of the railing near the starting line, and were able to congratulate themselves on having the best seats of all for the flying demonstrations. It was a crowd-pleasing show, with one of the most successful flights being that of a Wright plane, which stayed in the air for twenty-nine minutes. The most spectacular event, however, was staged at the end of the day by a pilot named Louis Paulhan in a big Voisin plane, which circled the aerodrome until it reached the breathtaking height of 200 feet and then vanished dramatically over the woods, into the sunset. The crowd waited in nervous suspense for several minutes before the Voisin reappeared:

Black, massive, incomprehensible, high against the mystic sky came the great machine, a portent and a promise, whose full significance the world then hardly dared to guess at. The crowd seemed to feel, all at once, that aspect of the Event. They had begun to cheer at the first sight of its return; but as it drew upon them out of the sunset they fell silent as if at command. At last, as it swept humming over their heads, and they saw young Paulhan gaily and most humanly waving his hand at them, the spell lifted, and their shouts rent the air.[2]

Before returning to Pontlevoy, Roberts went over to London on a business trip. While he was there, he visited Thede, who was living in Abingdon, near Reading, with his wife and family. At thirty-two, Theodore Roberts was a prolific writer whose work was appearing in British and American periodicals as often as that of his eldest brother. He was just beginning his seventh novel since 1900, and Charles suggested that Pontlevoy would provide the ideal conditions for completing it. The little town could offer quiet surroundings, inexpensive lodgings, and congenial company. Deciding to follow his brother's advice, Thede moved his family into the Hôtel de l'Ecole de Pontlevoy in February 1910; thereafter, they 'invariably burst in'[3] upon Madame Bédard's tenants at tea time. When the light but leisurely meal was over, the Roberts men would frequently adjourn, along with anyone else who cared to join them, to a nearby sports field that had been rented from a local farmer. The activities varied according to the number of players available, but every game was played very competitively whether it was cricket, baseball, or tag.

As early as August 1909, the London *Bookman* reported that Roberts had 'made a beginning ... on an aeroplane romance (largely of military and political adventure) which he is naming *The Runners of the Air*.'[4] That announcement marked the start of the novel which would be retitled *A Balkan Prince*, but the work must have proceeded slowly, for chapters three to nine are given over to detailed accounts of the exhibition and demonstrations in Paris and Juvisy, over a year later. Probably its progress was interrupted by the necessity of writing animal stories to meet his expenses. For a story that approached 4,000 words, he could expect to receive about $300. *The Windsor Magazine* continued to be one of his regular markets, but the American periodicals were so unpredictable that he sometimes complained about America leaving him 'so badly and so inexplicably in the lurch.' Once, in the summer of 1910, he 'was compelled by most bitter stress & distress' to beg Edward Bok, the editor of *Ladies' Home Journal*, to send him $300 immediately by cable. At about the same time, he announced that 'Last Bull' would be 'the last animal story which I expect to write for six months or more.'[5] Presumably he hoped to devote all his time to his novel, but economic necessities again intervened, and *A Balkan Prince* was further delayed while he spun his backwoods yarns to pay the bills.

Some of Roberts' anxieties over money arose from an altercation with his American publisher, L.C. Page. In 1908, after publishing another collection of his stories, *The House in the Water*, Page was greatly incensed when Roberts granted the rights to the English edition to Ward, Lock and Company. Accusing him of acting illegally, Page refused to pay him any further royalties whatever. Since Page held the American rights to most of his books to that date, the financial loss was substantial – especially since many of his titles continued to be reprinted. Page was noted for its irregular dealings with its authors, but unfortunately Roberts could never afford to follow the example of L.M. Montgomery, who spent $15,000 before winning a nine-year court case against the company. In 1909, his next volume of stories, *Kings in Exile* and *The Backwoodsmen*, appeared in the United States under the imprint of the Macmillan Company, which remained his American distributor. Ward, Lock continued to be his British publisher (controlling the Canadian and Australian rights as well) until 1918.

In addition to the Roberts brothers, another writer had recently joined the English-speaking colony at Pontlevoy. Roy Norton, an American engineer turned novelist, had moved there with his wife to complete his sixth book, *The Plunderer*. Although he was a prolific and popular writer whose work appeared in seven languages, his hastily-written adventure stories are all but forgotten today. As an individual he was much more interesting than his books, and Roberts was undoubtedly intrigued by the exciting life this colourful American had led. In 1901, for example, he and Rex Beach (an author whom Norton took for a model) had crossed Alaska from Nome to the Arctic Ocean by dog team, becoming the first white men to perform that feat.

As much as Roberts enjoyed his North American circle, he did not keep apart from the French community. He 'was always very friendly with the peasants and consequently was very popular with them.' As for the châteaux life of the Old Régime, he fitted in naturally and easily, 'in contrast to the rich Americans who were trying by all means to break into the circle of the so-called exclusive set.'[6] He was invited to the big social events, such as the boar hunt and the stag hunt, but he accepted for the hospitality, not the sport. On a number of occasions, he followed the hunt on a rented bicycle. He found the French machines to be light and particularly well built, and they became his favourite mode of transportation. Accompanied by Douglas, he enjoyed many long rides along the Loire, sometimes going as far as Blois or Tours.

In the summer of 1910, Douglas Roberts' thoughts were turning homeward to New Brunswick. He had spent nearly three years as a tourist, and, at the age of twenty-two, he must have felt a trifle uncomfortable over his complete dependence upon his father's charity. His travels abroad may have been as valuable in many ways as a university education; unfortunately, they did not qualify him for any trade or profession. He still had no prospects of earning a living, nor would he be likely to find any as long as he remained in Europe. Deciding, therefore, that the time had come to end his odyssey, he sailed for home at the beginning of August. His father saw him off at Le Havre, but whatever twinges of conscience or homesickness the elder Roberts may have felt at that time, they were not enough to draw him back to Fredericton.

Douglas was home in Canada for almost a year before securing a civil service post that took him to Ottawa, where he remained for the rest of his life – following the kind of career that his father had almost chosen nearly thirty years earlier. His mother and Edith accompanied him to Ottawa, and it seems to have been at that point that May finally abandoned any hope of a reunion with her husband. Perhaps she was able to face the truth a little easier in Ottawa, away from her family and friends, who – she felt sure – considered her position a scandal. Public sympathy appears to have been on her side, however, even among her in-laws. Jean Bliss, Roberts' aunt, wrote to Carman from Massachusetts: 'I never hear C.G.D.R. mentioned; is he in the family black books?'[7] The indications are that he was.

Roberts' mother, ever impatient with human frailties, would certainly not have approved of her son's desertion of his wife, even though he still contributed to her support. By Emma Roberts' standards, incompatibility was irrelevant. A husband and wife should remain together, for better or worse, until death parted them. Always one to speak her mind, it would not be surprising if she admonished her eldest child to act his age. She could even remind him that he was a grandfather, for Lloyd, who had married Hope Balmain in 1908, now had a baby daughter named Patricia. It was just as well that Emma could not foresee that little Patsy would be a young woman before she ever met her roving grandparent.

In less than two months after the departure of Douglas from Pontlevoy, Roberts went to live in Munich. Madame Bédard, who had always been overwhelmed by the charm of her Canadian tenant, wept copiously as she bade him good-bye. He cited his congenital restlessness as the main reason for the change, but there may have been another factor that was even more compelling. It so happened that Mrs Morris and her children moved to Munich at about that time, but it is not clear whether Roberts was following her or whether she was following him. When the Nortons also removed to the Bavarian capital, the intimates of Roberts' Pontlevoy circle were reunited except for Thede, who shortly returned with his family to Fredericton.

Soon after his arrival in Munich, Roberts found inexpensive but roomy quarters on the top floor of a building on Viktoria Strasse, a considerable distance north of the central Marienplatz. Apparently the flat was difficult to rent because it was rumoured to be haunted by the spirit of a twelve-year-old girl who had committed suicide there. At first Roberts took the idea of a ghost lightly, but he soon found himself waking at night, imagining that a small hand was stroking his face. The feeling was so real, and so unsettling, that he resorted to various methods of discouraging the mysterious intrusion. He finally discovered that a light on the floor in the doorway was enough to keep his slumbers from being disturbed.

After he was settled in his spacious lodgings – solitary, too, if one can discount the unseen company of a supernatural presence – Roberts began to long for Carman and the lost intimacy of their relationship. He wrote an enthusiastic letter to his cousin, extolling the amenities of Munich, and offering to share his flat with him, rent-free, for as long as Carman might wish to stay. It seems reasonable to suspect that there was another motive for the gesture, in addition to Roberts' genuine desire to see his favourite kinsman again. More than likely, it was an attempt to get Carman out of the clutches of Mary Perry King. The ruse might have worked if Mrs King had not intercepted and destroyed the letter (as Roberts later learned) without allowing Carman to see it. Each cousin was baffled by the other's apparent silence. 'Roberts is a devil of a correspondent,' Carman complained to a friend. 'Has been in Europe for three years now, and I have had only two letters from him in that time, who am as his twin!'[8]

No one could replace Carman in his cousin's affections, but Roberts did not lack for congenial company. Along with Mrs Morris and the Nortons, he was soon swept into the busy social life of the English-speaking community that revolved around the British consulate in Munich. But, as was characteristic of Roberts, he quickly made friends among the native Germans in the city. Among the closest of his new acquaintances was Professor Franz Wirnhier of the Royal Bavarian Art Gallery, who paid him the compliment of painting his portrait – twice. The pleasure of sitting for the artist was greatly enhanced by the presence of Professor Wirnhier's three beautiful daughters.

As much as he liked many individual Germans, Roberts could not help feeling uncomfortable about the excessive nationalism that had taken hold of the country. Even in Munich, the heart of Bavarian culture where Prussian aggressiveness was denounced as ill-mannered, German superiority was expounded with surprising fervour. The talk of war was commonplace among the Bavarian officers whom Roberts met; during his amiable arguments with them, he was never able to shatter their conviction that the German army was invincible. As further steins of beer were emptied during those debates, both sides must have been titillated by the possibility that the drinking partner of the moment might be the enemy of the future. However, although Roberts and his beer-hall companions sensed an inevitable clash between Kaiser Wilhelm's Germany and Great Britain, they could not foresee the catastrophic events that would have their birth in Munich. In just over a year, an unsuccessful painter from Austria slipped into the city, where he remained to spin his mad dreams of aggression after World War I. The fulfilment of Adolf Hitler's fantasies would surpass in horror the conflict that Roberts and his associates saw approaching. In the wake of that future holocaust, one-third of central Munich, as Roberts had known it, would be laid in ruins.

As far as Roberts' work was concerned, it made very little difference to his subject-matter or style whether he was living in New York, Paris, Pontlevoy, or Munich. Wherever he went, he continued to turn out nature stories in a manner that remained unchanged. Strangely enough, the writing of those stories came more easily when he was far removed from the scenes he was describing. As in his poetry, he was usually at his best when the nostalgic mood was upon him and he was recollecting the lasting impressions that could not be dimmed by time or distance. After publication of *The Book of the Rose*, his exercises in nostalgia became increasingly restricted to prose, not necessarily because the poetic vein was worked out but because he was not content to starve in a garret.

The list of stories that Roberts wrote during his first year in Munich is sufficiently lengthy to prove that he kept busy with his pen, but a glance at his social activities shows that his life was not all work and no play. Nor did he consort only with earnest military types, the British consular circle, and the intellectual community of the city. Wherever he came across innocent merriment, Roberts was almost certain to be one of the most active participants. He entered into the spirit of the city's annual carnival, for example, with the exuberance of a college boy. At the concluding costume ball, he came close to captivating the dancing partner of Wagner's son, Siegfried, but withdrew in deference to her escort, who gratefully invited him to share a bottle of wine.[9]

With the return of spring, he was once again seized by wanderlust. This time it was northern Italy that beckoned him. Encumbered only by a rucksack, he set off for a brief holiday on the shores of Lake Garda. After a few days at Riva, on the northern extremity, he took a boat to the southern resort town of Gardone Riviera. Several days later, as he stood on the wharf, waiting for a boat back to Riva, he happened to spot a tram bound for Milan and Brescia. Yielding to a sudden impulse, he rushed aboard for a brief visit to each of those cities.

Shortly after his arrival in Brescia from Milan, he had an experience that must have flattered his ego as a writer. While he was eating lunch in an attractive little hotel, the proprietor's daughter, who had overheard him speaking in English to the waiter, informed him that she was taking lessons daily from an English professor. The ensuing conversation was so engaging that, when she asked him how long he was staying, he decided upon the spot to remain there for a few days. Beaming with pleasure, the winsome signorina brought the register for him to sign.

'Is that *your* name?' she exclaimed in excitement as soon as she read his signature. 'Are you the writer?'[10]

When an astonished Roberts acknowledged his identity, she ran to the next room to bring back an old issue of *The Windsor Magazine* which contained his story 'The Glutton of the Great Snow.' That story, she explained, happened to be the one she was currently studying with her English teacher. Then she proudly introduced him to her parents, who were delighted to have another 'celebrity' as their guest. The previous year, so they informed him, they had been favoured by the presence of Puccini. Nearly a week later, when Roberts reluctantly departed for Munich, they would accept only a token payment for his room and board.

Back in his haunted flat, Roberts settled down once more to his work, but with the arrival of summer came new diversions. Not far to the southwest of Munich, stretches a long, boot-shaped lake called the Starnbergersee, which had become a popular retreat for the English residents of the city. They flocked to the resorts along its northern extremities, the chief of which was Starnberg, rising from the lakeshore on graceful terraces. To someone like Roberts, who had revelled in picnics and swimming parties ever since his boyhood, the frequent excursions to the Starnbergersee were a never-ending joy. To add to his pleasure on those outings, he could always count upon the scintillating companionship of Mrs Morris.

With the approach of winter, business with his publishers called Roberts to London, where he soon became a member of an exclusive little group who dubbed themselves the 'Arts and Dramatic Club' and held lively dances every Saturday night. Not being able to tear himself away before Christmas, he rented a flat on Chancery Lane, just off Fleet Street. It may have been more than just the spirited clubmen, however, who enticed him to linger in the city. It is possible that Mrs Morris had moved there at that time, for it is known that she took residence in London sometime before the outbreak of World War I; and it was already apparent that, for some reason, Roberts was losing his interest in Munich.

Sometime in January 1912, he returned briefly to Munich, travelling via Hamburg to visit the Zoological Gardens and Museum of Hagenbeck. He had a special interest in the museum, for he was starting work on the first two chapters of a new novel, *In the Morning of Time*. The writing was delayed, however, for he remained in Munich only long enough to close up his haunted flat and put his affairs in order before setting off upon an extended tour of Italy. Once that journey was ended, his next destination would be London, which he had decided to make his home – at least for the time being.

Going directly to Rome, Roberts remained there for a few days before continuing on to Capri, en route to Sicily, the birthplace of Theocritus, the Alexandrian Greek poet for whom he felt a special affinity. The ancient bard's sensitivity to nature and his acceptance of the closeness of man and beast were among the qualities to which Roberts was particularly responsive. With a volume of Theocritus' *Idylls* in hand, he explored the pastoral settings of the poems, encountering the marvel of almond trees in full blossom in February and being assailed by the pungent emanations of cypress groves. For several weeks, he lingered in Taormina, a hill-town overlooking the Ionian Sea, which many travellers have acclaimed as one of the most beautiful spots in the world. From the cavea of the time-battered Teatro Greco there is a matchless view that ranges from the expanse of sea and coastline to the snow-capped majesty of Mount Etna in the background. Recalling that scene many years later, in his poem 'Taormina,' Roberts hinted at a romantic attachment to an unidentified companion.

Leaving Sicily, Roberts returned to Capri to disport for more than a month with the international set who wintered on the island. Renting an apartment on the via Sopramonte, overlooking the town, he gave himself up to the various diversions of that popular resort, although, as was his custom, he tried to maintain a schedule of writing during the mornings. It was only a short walk to the ruins of the Villa Iovis, a former palace of the Emperor Tiberius, who had chosen the location for its panoramic view of the island. Undoubtedly, Roberts and his friends admired the old despot's aesthetic judgment, for the site was one of their favourite picnic spots. There was almost a constant round of swimming parties, house parties, and dances. If all else failed, one could always join the cosmopolitan crowd who gathered nightly at the Café Hidigeigei in the centre of the town.

CHAPTER NINE

Mother England

1912–1925

For they who battle with England
Must war with a Mother's sons.

ALTHOUGH THE FOREGOING LINES are taken from Theodore Roberts' war poem 'The Reckoning,' they accurately express the sentiments of Charles G.D. Roberts. Probably the growing threat of war was not the main consideration that drew him back to England in 1912, but it was in his patriotic nature to rally to the side of the Mother Country. He arrived in London at the end of April, mindful perhaps of Browning's famous wish to be in England 'Now that April's there.' He, too, would celebrate the English spring one day, borrowing his title from Shakespeare: 'The Sweet o' the Year.' However, as he took up residence in London, neither his love of England nor his delight in the season may have been enough to make him forget his estrangement from Canada.

For one thing, there was distressing news from his family. May, Edith, and Douglas were managing all right in Ottawa, but Fate had dealt Lloyd a cruel blow. His wife, Hope, had died less than a year after they had moved to Nelson, British Columbia, where he had been appointed to the staff of the daily newspaper. In Fredericton, Roberts' sister Nain MacDonald and her family found themselves in circumstances that led them to join Lloyd in Nelson, a move they all came to regret. Taking Annie Powers with her,

Emma Roberts followed her daughter westward as soon as her eldest son sent the money for the fares.

Up to that point, no matter where he was living, Roberts had always thought of Fredericton as home. With his mother's departure, he could no longer regard it in that way, for the last of his immediate family was gone, and there was no prospect that he would ever live there again. For the rest of his life, 'home' would be wherever he chanced to hang his hat. At the moment, it happened to be in a rented flat at No. 8 Sergeant's Inn, The Temple. He lived there quietly, enjoying the company of a select group of friends. His circle consisted mostly of aspiring writers, painters, and musicians, few of whom ever achieved even a small measure of renown.

His best friend in London was Henry Simpson, whose acquaintance he had made during a previous visit. By profession, Simpson was a bank manager, and it may have been in that capacity that Roberts – who still found it necessary to ingratiate himself with bankers – first came to meet him. But Simpson's real love was poetry, and he diligently cultivated the friendship of like-minded people. He himself was the writer of some conventionally romantic verse, which occasionally found its way into the popular magazines but usually failed to gain any attention from the high-brow press or the critics. Around 1907, he formed a coterie called The Poets' Club for which he served as the perennial president. A couple of years later, he published a little volume called *A Fairy Flute*, which even his friends soon forgot, although they hailed its author as a memorable 'Figure in the life of artistic London.'[1] Roberts considered Simpson a delightful companion, and on their frequent excursions to the country took great pleasure in teaching the Englishman how to handle a canoe.

His intimates also included several Canadians who, like himself, had taken up residence in London. The friendship of longest standing was that with George Parkin, who had gone to London in 1902 to take charge of the Rhodes Scholarship Trust. They often met as fellow members of the Authors' Club, and Roberts was an occasional guest of the Parkins at 'The Cottage,' Goring-on-Thames. Parkin was still an active advocate of imperial federation, an idea that Roberts accepted in principle while rejecting Parkin's theory of a federal or imperial government. They did not disagree openly over the matter, however, for Roberts never quite outgrew his deferential regard for his former headmaster.

One of the best-known Canadians in London at that time was Sir Gilbert Parker, a popular novelist and a member of the British House of Commons. Coming from the backwoods of Ontario, he had risen to prominence by dint of his own efforts and with some assistance from his American wife, who was reputed to have a large yearly income from her father's estate. Seeing Parker striding along Pall Mall, immaculately groomed and self-confident, it was difficult to believe that he had once been a struggling author whose career Bliss Carman had helped to launch by publishing his early work in *The Independent*. Several of his novels, especially *The Seats of the Mighty* and *The Right of Way*, had sold widely, and a deluxe edition of his complete works had recently been published simultaneously in England and the United States. Roberts must have been struck by the vast difference in their fortunes whenever he visited Parker's palatial residence – as he frequently did – at 20 Carlton House Terrace. During the liberal distribution of honours to mark the coronation of Edward VII in 1902, Parker had received a knighthood in recognition of his contribution to Canadian literature. Roberts, who would have made a worthier recipient in terms of his impact upon the Canadian literary scene, had to wait over thirty years to receive the same accolade.

On the whole, Roberts found London a congenial city, but he came to loathe the damp, debilitating cold of its winter. Late in 1912, falling prey to the unhealthy climate, he suffered from such a prolonged illness that his doctor advised him to spend a month or two in Torquay, ever the favourite winter refuge of Englishmen who do not wish to go abroad. Washed by the Gulf Stream on the south, the resort is sheltered on every other side by its seven protective hills. After the chilling fogs of London, Roberts enjoyed basking in the sun of Torquay's beautiful Princess Gardens. Sitting there among the palm trees one balmy day in January, he wrote 'On the Road,' his first new poem in three years. It came to him suddenly as he scanned the steep highway that led over the nearest hill. In his typically optimistic vein, he concluded: 'So I breast me the rise with full hope, well assured I shall see / Some new prospect of joy, some brave venture a-tiptoe for me.'

His outbursts of poetry had become so infrequent that it took another six years before he had accumulated enough work for even a slender volume. His prose, on the other hand, had begun appearing at the rate of two books a year. With the exception of *A Balkan Prince*, they were all collections of his magazine fiction, stories of the backwoods. In 1911, his two collections were slightly padded by the inclusion of a couple of the same stories in both volumes. The next year, he carried out this practice even more flagrantly in *The Feet of the Furtive* by including seven stories that had been printed in one or the other of the two previous works.

All of those books were published in the United States by the Macmillan Company and in Britain by Ward, Lock and Company, which handled the Australian and Canadian distribution. *Babes of the Wild*, which Ward, Lock brought out in 1912, was released the next year by Macmillan as *Children of the Wild*. *Hoof and Claw* (1913) followed the established publication pattern, but *A Balkan Prince* (also 1913) was published solely by Everett and Company of London. The latter work, which had been in the making ever since Roberts' Pontlevoy days, concluded with events that had taken place in the Balkans only a few months before its publication. The public's lukewarm reception of it seems to have finally convinced Roberts to abandon the traditional novel form. As one reviewer put it to him: 'So many people might have written *A Balkan Prince*, so few can write the animal stories.'[2]

Meanwhile, Lloyd Roberts indicated his readiness to don the poet's mantle which his father had all but put aside. The elder Roberts, in paternalistic pride, pronounced Lloyd 'a true poet,' although he cautioned him to widen his 'aesthetic and intellectual sympathies.' He was able to persuade a London publisher to issue a small edition of his son's poems by agreeing to accept the financial responsibility for any loss on the venture. The little volume appeared in the early spring of 1914 under the title *England Over Seas*. It did not have a very wide sale, notwithstanding the declaration of one anthologist that a first collection of poems by the son of Charles G.D. Roberts 'was a matter of national interest.' Nevertheless, it seemed like a promising advance in Lloyd's literary career.[3]

The publication of *England Over Seas* coincided with Lloyd's marriage to Leila White of New York State and his appointment as a propagandist for the Department of the Interior in Ottawa. The four members of Roberts' immediate family, reunited in Canada's capital city, became the nucleus around which the clan began to rebuild. Emma Roberts was the next to join them, arriving to stay with Lloyd for a time as affairs in Nelson grew worse and worse. Both Nain and her husband, Arch MacDonald, were plagued by ill health, finances were at the poverty level, and their two young sons undertook odd jobs to help support the family. The marriage deteriorated to the point that Will Roberts and Lloyd sent Nain the money to leave Arch and go to Ottawa, accompanied by the boys and Annie Powers. On 22 February 1915, Jean Bliss reported to Carman that his Aunt Emma was 'very thankful' to have Nain in Ottawa with her, 'away from Arch.'[4]

Time and distance separated Roberts from those vicissitudes of his clan. In the nearly seven years that he had been overseas, his only direct family contacts had been with Douglas and Thede back in Pontlevoy. He was overjoyed, therefore, to have a visit from Will and Mary Roberts in the spring of 1914. It was a working holiday for Will as an editor of *The Literary Digest* as well as for his wife, Mary Fanton Roberts, who was on the lookout for material for *The Craftsman*, of which she was the managing editor. Roberts accompanied them to Paris, where the highlight of the trip was a visit to Isadora Duncan's dancing school at Bellevue on the outskirts of the city.

Returning to England (with some souvenir snapshots of Isadora Duncan's attractive young dancers in their scanty Greek tunics) Roberts settled down for a relaxed holiday with his friend, Horace Boot, on a Thames houseboat below Henley. The threat of war with Germany had been hanging over the nation for many months, but, by mid-July, Lloyd George, Chancellor of the Exchequer, voiced the feeling of His Majesty's government that the international situation was improving. The outbreak of hostilities seemed too remote to disturb the carefree life on the houseboat or the daily tennis games and lively week-end parties. Within two weeks of Lloyd George's assurance, however, the tranquility of the summer was shattered by the declaration of war.

In the beginning, nearly everyone believed that the war would be over before autumn. After a few weeks, when it became apparent that the end was nowhere in sight, Roberts felt that he could no longer resist the call to arms. Going up to London in late September, he lied about his age and joined the Legion of Frontiersmen. Shortly thereafter, his squadron was transferred to Swaythling Camp, near Southampton, where he spent nearly two months as an ordinary trooper, drilling, riding, and training horses. In a letter to George Parkin, he boasted: 'The hard – very hard – work, with the wet & exposure (we are sleeping on the ground under canvas) has knocked out many of the softer men of the squadron, but I was never fitter in my life, & find I can more than hold my own with the youngsters.'[5]

After spending a month as a private, Roberts began to feel that he was fitted for something more important. Encouraged by some of his friends, one of whom was Sir Gilbert Parker, he wrote to the War Secretary requesting a commission. In listing his qualifications, he stated: 'I am exceedingly fit physically, accustomed to the roughest out-door life, exploration and big game shooting; and I know French together with a smattering of German.'[6] In addition to Parker, his references included two other highly placed friends: George R. Parkin and George H. Perley, the High Commissioner for Canada. In the end, it was largely through the influence of another Canadian friend, Lieutenant-Colonel Hamer Greenwood (later Viscount Greenwood), that he got his commission as first lieutenant on 9 December 1914, and was gazetted to the 16th Battalion of the King's (Liverpool) Regiment.

Giving up his flat in Sergeant's Inn, Roberts arrived in Liverpool, just as his battalion was being sent to West Kirby, Cheshire, for training. It was there, on Christmas Day, that the men came close to rioting over an unexpected delay in the serving of dinner, but Roberts took over at the request of his frantic captain and restored order. Shortly afterwards, upon the recommendation of his approving colonel, he was promoted to the rank of captain and sent to the military school at Southport to train as an instructor. After completing his course with distinction, he was sent to various camps throughout England, Wales, and Ireland for the next year and a half to instruct young officers. He had the dubious fortune of arriving at the Curragh, the famous military post in County Kildare, in time for the short-lived but bloody Easter Rebellion of 1916. Although he had asked for a transfer to the Canadian Overseas Forces as early as spring of 1915, his request was not granted until the autumn of 1916. When the transfer finally came through, he was attached to the Canadian War Records Office in London and promoted to the rank of major.

Joining him in London was his brother Theodore, who had recently returned from active duty in France. When Thede's family arrived from Folkestone in Kent, where they had been staying, ten-year-old Dorothy formed a lasting impression of her Uncle Charlie, who met them at Charing Cross Station. She never forgot his spruce appearance, accented by his greyish bristle of a moustache, nor his demonstrative affectionate manner that was as firm as it was dynamic. She did not see him again during the several months her family remained in London, for he spent practically all the winter of 1916-17 in France. Although she remembered attending a Christmas party at Mrs Morris' luxurious London home, she had the feeling in retrospect that Mrs Morris' life 'was no longer connected with Uncle Charlie's.'[7]

Roberts saw the Western Front for the first time in December 1916, when he was attached to the Canadian Corps as a Special Press Correspondent. The battles of the Somme were already over, and the two enemy lines were entrenched in the frozen Flanders mud for the winter. His headquarters was behind the lines in the shell-torn city of Albert, not far from Courcelette and Ancre Heights, where the Canadians had finally driven back the Germans from the Somme. The shelling and the bombing had not ceased, but Roberts refused to take refuge in the makeshift shelter in the cramped wine cellar of the battered house in which he was billeted. As much as he abhorred war, he was greatly exhilarated by the ever-present threat of danger. 'Those were the days,' he recalled, 'when those who did not die, *lived*.'[8] For nearly all the rest of the war, he spent long periods of time in France, although his frequent recalls to London for consultation made it worth his while to maintain his flat at 27 Charing Cross Road.

In the autumn of 1917, he was moved to Ranchicourt for a while before being stationed at Camblain l'Abbé, a post that was frequently under bombardment. The tents in which all of the staff were billeted were protected from the bursting shells by six-foot piles of sandbags. When the enemy airplanes flew over at night (as they frequently did), the occupants of the tents were supposed to take cover in a nearby dug-out. Like most of the men, however, Roberts placed his trust in the enemy's poor marksmanship and always elected to remain in his comfortable blankets. Luck was on the side of the Canadians, and sleepy shouts of derision filled the air as the attackers repeatedly failed to score a direct hit.

It was at Camblain l'Abbé that he completed most of Volume III of the series *Canada in Flanders*. Two previous volumes, telling the story from the mobilization of the 1st Canadian Division at Valcartier in August 1914 to the attack on Vimy Ridge in June 1916, had been written by Lord Beaverbrook. When the 'pressure of other duties' became too great for Beaverbrook to continue the history, he decided 'to hand over the story of the Somme to the practised pen of Major Charles G.D. Roberts.' Here was the writer, Beaverbrook asserted, who possessed 'the imagination which can convey to the future the agonies and heroisms of the past, and the chiselled style [for] shaping the rough outlines of the records into a clear-cut and enduring narrative.'[9]

Being a war correspondent and official historian left Roberts little time to write any fiction or poetry. *The Secret Trails* (1916) is a collection of his animal stories that were written before he signed up for military service. Later during the war, he wrote a story called 'The Eagle' and nearly completed a novelette 'Jim, the Backwoods Police Dog.' At the end of 1918, those tales appeared in his collection, *The Ledge on Bald Face*, which he supplemented with three pieces from *The Secret Trails*. As for his poetry, only three items issued from his pen during the war years. Two of them, 'To Shakespeare, 1916' and 'Cambrai and Marne,' were prompted by patriotism – which was seldom his best source of poetic inspiration. The third poem, 'Going Over,' records a poignant moment on the Somme when the reality of going over the parapet becomes less palpable than the soldier's dream of home.

In the spring of 1918, he was recalled to the War Records Office in London, where he remained until long after the armistice was signed. Plans were afoot for an exhibition of Canadian war photographs to tour the country, and he had been selected to give the opening address whenever the collection arrived in a new centre. In the intervals he continued his regular duties in the Records Office. He also found time to resume the writing of *In the Morning of Time*, his series of stories about prehistoric life, which had been in abeyance ever since his departure from Munich.

He was opening an exhibition at Stoke-on-Trent when the war ended. Upon his return to London the next day, he found the city still in a tumult of celebration. Not being able to resist the exuberance, he was soon charging through the crowds in Trafalgar Square and Piccadilly Circus, arm in arm with a British colonel and an Australian private. The revelry continued throughout the night, but the mood of jubilation soon vanished in the cold reality of the days that followed. An exhausted nation, faced with the grim process of recovery, quickly fell prey to cynicism. A new era was about to begin – one that would repudiate the dauntless optimism expressed by Roberts in 'The Summons,' the first of his post-war poems.

The war had been over for more than a year before Roberts completed his work for the War Records and was demobilized. During that period, he published *New Poems* and *In the Morning of Time*. The new volume of poetry, his first in sixteen years, was a slim harvest of twenty-four poems ranging from eight to forty-eight lines. Since it did not have any North American distribution, it was reviewed mostly in English journals. Although nearly all of our Canadian literary historians have labelled it 'disappointing,' the British critics generally looked upon it approvingly at the time of its publication. *The Times* (London) commended the poet for possessing 'a polished taste, a finely trained ear and an exact command of phrase.'

In the Morning of Time was hailed by *The New York Times* as a story that 'will hold the reader from the first to the last page.' Even *The Spectator*, which complained about the excessive violence, conceded that 'it is a stimulating tale and refreshingly original.' It was Roberts' last lengthy work of fiction, and it seems to have been among his personal favourites. 'This is one of my *very best* prose books,' he said of it in 1937, after he had finished writing any fiction at all. 'Perhaps *the* best,' he added. Certainly it is a tour de force of the imagination, recreating prehistoric times from the age of the reptiles to the exploits of early man.[10]

Although *In the Morning of Time* is a highly original work, it has several literary precedents, and Roberts was undoubtedly aware of them. The one that he is most likely to have read is Jack London's *Before Adam* (1906), a story about the people of the mid-Pleistocene epoch, with drawings by Roberts' own illustrator, Charles Livingston Bull. London acknowledged his indebtedness to an earlier novel, *The Story of Ab* (1897) by Stanley Waterloo, but his work bears a closer resemblance to H.G. Wells' 'A Story of the Stone Age,' included in *Tales of Time and Space* (1899). If Roberts had indeed examined any of those three predecessors, he was careful not to imitate them. Placed beside the pictorial vividness of *In The Morning of Time*, with its carefully researched details, the stories by Waterloo, Wells, and London seem quaint and unscientific.

In 1921, J.M. Dent & Sons issued a selection called *Some Animal Stories* gathered from Roberts' previous collections. It proved so popular that a companion volume, *More Animal Stories*, was published the following year. Although both books appeared in Dent's inexpensive King's Treasury series, their sales were so consistently high that they became the author's most dependable source of income for many years. Dent subsequently published new editions of *The Heart of the Ancient Wood*, *The Forge in the Forest*, and *A Sister to Evangeline* (renamed *Lovers in Acadie*). *In the Morning of Time* also appeared in their King's Treasury series. In addition to the foregoing reprints, Dent published two new collections of Roberts' animal stories: *Wisdom of the Wilderness* (1922) and *They that Walk in the Wild* (1924). The critical reception of those last two works granted Roberts 'a place in the front ranks of those who make a speciality of interpreting wild life.'[11]

Two of Roberts' cousins, who had served in the army during the war, Major Lionel Hannington and Colonel Cameron Bliss, remained in England after being demobilized. Both men were among his closest friends, not only because they were kinsmen and fellow New Brunswickers, but also because their tastes and interests were similar to his own. When Hannington's first son was born, Roberts was one of the godfathers. Bliss, who was not hampered by domestic ties, intermittently shared Roberts' London quarters. In fact, the apartment at 27 Charing Cross Road was such a favourite haven for Roberts' friends that the rightful tenant was sometimes forced to seek a secluded room down at Brighton in order to get any writing done.

For several months during the winter of 1919-20, Roberts quit the chilling dampness of London for the balmier climate of St Helier on the Island of Jersey. Cameron Bliss was also wintering there, having converted an abandoned Martello tower into fairly comfortable living quarters. Roberts, however, chose conventional accommodations at a hotel in the centre of the town. Later, he was joined by his friend Edward Platt, the novelist, who had often stayed with him in London. Better known by his pseudonym, Paul Trent, Platt was an adventurous Englishman, in his late forties, who had travelled widely in America, Europe, and Africa. After publishing his first novel in 1907, he had begun turning out entertaining yarns at such an amazing rate that he was well on his way to becoming the most prolific writer in the country. He was a good companion, but, because he adhered to a rigid writing schedule, he did not distract Roberts, who resolutely set aside a major portion of each day for work.

Towards the end of the following December, Roberts set out for North Africa, accompanied once again by Cameron Bliss. After spending a few days in Paris, the cousins arrived in Algiers on New Year's Day, 1921, and found the city so much in their liking that they remained there for about two months. Early in March, they moved inland to Biskra, the popular North African winter resort, where they lingered until the end of May. Before leaving the African continent, they spent over a week in Tunis, with its famous souks, or bazaars, where they encountered 'the musks and attars of the East.' The homeward journey took them to Rome, which they explored at their leisure before continuing to Venice, where Bliss remained for several weeks after Roberts reluctantly returned to London via Geneva.

Over six months had elapsed by the time he was back again in his flat on Charing Cross Road. The interval had been the most exotic holiday of his life, enriched by the newly formed friendships with the Kaid of Larba (who entertained Roberts at his spacious villa south of Algiers) and Prince Ben Ganem (who frequently invited the two New Brunswickers to his palace in Biskra). Although, as usual, Roberts had kept busy with his pen, the North African interlude did not furnish him with any material for his writing, unless one counts a brief reference to Tunis in his poem 'The Vagrant of Time,' completed in 1926. Typically, in the bustling seaport of Algiers, he had devoted his time to 'The Little Homeless One,' his story about a 'snow-shoe' rabbit in the wilds of New Brunswick.

Late in 1921, he became a founding member of the Canadian Club in London, which had been organized largely through the efforts of F.C. Wade, the agent-general for British Columbia. Several prominent

Canadians in the city were justifiably sceptical about the enduring success of such a club. The fact that it flourished at first was mainly attributable to the enthusiasm of Wade and the presidency of Lionel Hannington. Wade was a man of forceful views who wielded a tireless pen in support of his province and his country. His forthright manner was highly irritating to the Canadian High Commissioner, Peter Larkin, but it was a characteristic that Roberts found very engaging. As a deep friendship developed between the two men, Roberts became a frequent and welcome guest of the Wade family. He was soon equally devoted to Wade's wife Edith and to the daughter, Margery, who assisted her father in his duties. The close relationship with those two women continued even after Wade's death from a heart attack on 9 November 1924. As Roberts grieved for his lost friend, he was undoubtedly mindful of the fact that he and Wade had been the same age.

Wade's death was Roberts' fourth bereavement within the short span of three years. The tragic series began with the sudden passing of his old mentor, George Parkin (only recently created *Sir* George), on 25 June 1922. Parkin had seemed much younger than his seventy-six years. Almost to the end, he was striding off on his long walks with the youthful energy that had been so evident to Roberts and Carman in their collegiate days. The next blow came in the same year with the death of his beloved sister Nain on 9 November. In temperament and looks, she had resembled her eldest brother so closely that, as a child, she had been dubbed 'Charlie-in-petticoats.' Never in robust health, she had persevered valiantly against illness and poverty to win considerable recognition for her graceful writing and her leadership in the women's suffrage movement. On 27 February 1923, less than four months after Nain's death, Emma Roberts died at the advanced age of eighty-seven. Outspoken – and often sharp-tongued – she had always exulted in the accomplishments of her children even while she remained their severest critic. At her death, she was eulogized in the press as a 'Mother of Poets.'[12]

In the midst of those breaks with the past, Roberts received two welcome visits from old friends. Frank Verbeck, whose presence was a happy reminder of Washington Square, spent a few days with him in London. Verbeck was on his way to Cornwall to join the artists' colony at St Ives, and it was there that Roberts later enjoyed a brief holiday with him. Another visitor, the Reverend Robert Norwood, once Roberts' favourite student at King's College, brought back even older associations. Norwood, who had recently dedicated a book of poems to Roberts, insisted upon treating his former professor to a holiday at Llandudno in Wales.

It was the visits from various members of his family, however, that made Roberts feel most deeply the loneliness of his self-imposed exile. Edith, who arrived in the summer of 1921 to spend four months with her father, repeatedly raised the question of his return to Canada. He was tempted to go back, but he worried about cutting himself off from the British literary contacts, and there was always the troublesome problem of how to go home without facing his wife. During Bliss Carman's brief trip to England in the spring of 1924, Roberts heard at first hand about his cousin's highly successful reading tours across Canada. Later in the same year, Douglas visited his father and suggested that Roberts, also, might find a Canadian reading tour extremely successful. It was an alluring possibility, especially since there had been a post-war slump in the demand for animal stories, and Roberts was falling deeper into debt.

A few months later, Lloyd cabled a definite proposal. Leila, Lloyd's wife, would be willing to arrange a tour for Roberts, making all the bookings and negotiating the fees, if he would agree to come. Roberts accepted the offer, feeling that such an undertaking, aside from its probable financial gain, would be a good way to test the feasibility of taking up permanent residence in Canada. If, after the tour, it seemed unwise to remain, he would go back to London, probably with a heavier purse if not with a lighter heart.

Because the tour agenda took shape more quickly than he had anticipated, he had only a few days to put his affairs in order before embarking for America on the *Berengaria* to keep an engagement at the Jarvis Collegiate Institute in Toronto on 5 February 1925. One embarrassing complication arose when some of his English creditors threatened to prevent his departure 'until he gave them securities.'[13] He arrived in New York the day before his first reading with time for only a hurried visit in a taxicab with Will and Mary Roberts, who had been on the pier to greet him. After travelling all night by train, he was met in Toronto by Lloyd and Leila (who had come down from their home in Ottawa) and was taken off to the Queen's Hotel to be interviewed and photographed again and again. There was no time for rest as a steady stream of old acquaintances and other well-wishers kept calling all day to express their pleasure that a wandering minstrel had returned at last. Overwhelmed by his reception, Roberts was convinced almost from the start that he should remain in Canada.

CHAPTER TEN

The Homecoming

1925–1927

'E VERYONE IS HERE!'[1] exulted *Saturday Night* columnist W.A. Deacon in the note that he passed along the front row of the Jarvis Collegiate auditorium to Lorne Pierce, editor of Ryerson Press. Being dedicated to the promotion of Canadian literature, both men were jubilant that the patrons of the arts in Toronto had turned out in full force to hear Charles G.D. Roberts. A glance at the audience was almost like taking the roll call of the most prominent people in the city's literary, educational, and social circles. Furthermore, with every seat taken at a dollar per ticket, Roberts' reading tour was off to a good start financially.

The early arrivals included Elsie Pomeroy, a sparrow-like spinster in her late thirties, who taught at King Edward Public School in Toronto. Neither Deacon nor Pierce had met Miss Pomeroy yet, but the time would come when they would recognize her as one of the country's most ardent supporters of Canadian literature. As a little girl in public school, she had been 'thrilled by the patriotic poem, "O Child of Nations, giant-limbed".' Ever since, Charles G.D. Roberts had remained one of her favourite authors. While on a teaching exchange in London, England, one winter after the war, she had searched out his address; and, on several occasions, she had walked past 27 Charing Cross Road. She never caught sight of her hero, but the thought of his possible proximity was enough to satisfy her.[2]

Miss Pomeroy was surprised to see such a young-looking man when Roberts walked out on the stage. She knew that he was sixty-five years old, but he could have passed for a man twenty years younger. Even his iron-grey hair did not make him venerable enough to be the almost legendary 'Father of Canadian Literature,' as he had been called by his admirers. Still slim and athletic looking, he carried himself with square-shouldered erectness that befitted the name Major Roberts. He was almost dapper in his dress (although slightly threadbare under close scrutiny) and his beribboned eyeglasses added further to the elegant air of his overall appearance. Rugged of feature, his face was stern in repose, but it lighted with customary friendliness at the opening applause and grew animated as he began to speak.

For his first recital, he chose to read rather extensively from *The Book of the Rose* and *New Poems*. Although he drew hearty applause, some of his listeners felt that 'his selections were hardly representative of his best work.' However, unlike Carman, he had a good platform presence and a well-modulated, expressive voice, which made even the unfamiliar poems easier for an audience to grasp. There was nothing formal in his presentation, which he interrupted from time to time by taking the audience into his confidence and chatting easily to them about himself and his work. He took particular pains to assure them that his long absence from Canada had not made him any less Canadian. 'Perhaps,' he ventured, 'it has confirmed in me the rather strenuous Canadianism which I might boast has always been mine.' It was those intervals of amiable conversation, more than his poetry, that revealed the grace and charm of his lively personality. At the close, he was kept busy shaking hands and signing autographs for upwards of an hour before John W. Garvin, the indefatigable anthologist, succeeded in whisking him away to a private reception. Miss Pomeroy made no effort to meet him – she preferred to view her heroes from a suitable distance where there was less danger of being disenchanted by their human inperfections.[3]

During the next few weeks, Roberts gave a succession of readings in all the cities and many of the principal towns in southern Ontario. His engagement in Ottawa reunited him briefly with his three children. It was there, also, that he first met his seventeen-year-old granddaughter, Patsy, whom he called 'Sister to the wild rose.' Over fifty years later, that same granddaughter wrote:

All I can remember about the winter of 1925, apart from my current boy friend whom I married three years later, and my passion for skiing, was being introduced to my grandfather, then Doctor Charles G.D. Roberts, dean of Canadian literature. We scrutinized each other solemnly, then stamped a seal of mutual approval with a firm kiss. While 'Pater' was not a tall man he gave a rather commanding impression of power, standing squarely on both feet, hands in pockets with thumbs on the outside, head tilted back to let the cigarette smoke curl upward past the deeply penetrating gaze – eyeglasses leashed by the ample black ribbon looping from one lens. I remember only that he arrived after a recital in Toronto and stayed but a short time in Ottawa where he was invited to speak at a Canadian Club luncheon and for the first time met the Rt Hon. Mackenzie King, Prime Minister. He also gave a recital that evening and left soon after...

May Roberts did not attend the recital, nor did he go to visit her. Because he greatly dreaded an encounter with his long-deserted wife, he was quick to accept the advice of his sons that it was better not to see her.

The tour continued to be successful, but the schedule was exhausting. As early as 14 February, he wrote to Lloyd from Detroit:

I've run down here for a *complete* rest, – where I know no one. ... I chose this hotel by accident purely, because I liked its looks – but I have been *seized* upon by the proprietor, – who saw my name on the register & happened to be an admirer of my stuff, & the whole establishment is falling on my neck, in a way to warm my heart. He was determined I should *radio* to the town tonight! But I *resolutely refused*; for I must rest my tongue! It is getting stiff, so it stumbles over the big words.

A week later, he escaped to New York, hoping for a quiet visit with Will and Mary, but they had so many things they wanted him to do, so many people they wanted him to meet, that he found himself 'still in a whirl.'[4]

At the end of March, he undertook his first journey across western Canada, reading in packed halls, being entertained by local dignitaries, and receiving hearty plaudits from the daily press. It appears, however, that some of his listeners took a dim view of the love poems he read from *The Book of the Rose*, and that some of the people who hosted him were scandalized by his casual flirtations with various young women. After a stag party held for him by some professors at the University of Saskatchewan, he startled the company by asking – probably in jest, but in questionable taste – if they could complete their hospitality by providing him 'with a woman for the night.'[5] He lingered longest in Vancouver where he was the guest of Edith Wade, who had returned home with her daughter Margery shortly after her husband's death. He was soon adopted by the Vancouver Poetry Society, which had been flourishing for nearly ten years under the firm control of its founder, Dr Ernest P. Fewster. Chief among its members, besides Fewster himself, were Annie Charlotte Dalton, A.M. Stephen, Lionel Haweis, and A.M. Pound, although Tom MacInnes was also a member and Isabel Ecclestone

MacKay was an occasional guest. In 1922, the Society had made Bliss Carman the Honorary President. Although they had no left-over titles to bestow upon Roberts, they fluttered around their celebrated visitor like moths attracted to a light. In fact, Pound held Roberts in such high esteem that he had determined to write his biography even before he had met him. The two men had many conferences about the project; unfortunately, Pound died before the writing actually began.

Retracing his steps across the continent, Roberts was back in Toronto by the end of May. He rented a suite in the Ernescliffe Apartments on Wellesley Street, apparently with the intention of making Toronto his permanent home, although he had not dispelled the general impression that he would be returning to England before the autumn. It was good for ticket sales if the public thought they would not soon have another opportunity to see and hear him because of his imminent departure. When the Poetry Society booked his program at Toronto's Victoria College for 16 June, they billed it as his *final* reading in Canada. However, encouraged by the warm response of his audiences in Ontario and the West, he was, in fact, already planning an autumn tour of Quebec and the Maritimes.

Everywhere he travelled, Roberts heard himself praised in terms that fairly made his head spin. In truth, however, many of the tributes were as uninformed as they were uncritical. The Canadian press, perhaps unwittingly, tended to exaggerate the extent of his international reputation, and the general public unreservedly acclaimed him as the greatest man of letters the country had produced. Any unfavourable reaction was usually directed against the mutual admiration that he and Carman were displaying so openly for each other. The aging Canadian poet, Charles Mair, sniffed that 'two cousins trekking about from platform to platform and proclaiming each other the greatest living lyrists is a novel but not inspiring sight.' A younger poet, Wilson MacDonald of Toronto, publicly ridiculed Roberts' 'extravagant claims' for Carman. 'That the poetry of Bliss Carman can compare with the work of Masefield,' scoffed MacDonald, 'is a jest for the gods.' Meanwhile, out in Vancouver, dissatisfaction with Roberts was being expressed in private by historian R.G. MacBeth and by a future poet named Earle Birney. MacBeth complained in a letter to his friend Mair that Roberts had nothing worthwhile to say – 'just a few stories about "Bliss" and himself and a few stale jokes,' while young Birney, a student at the University of British Columbia, was filled with undergraduate disdain for what he viewed as 'cliché emotions and conventional thoughts' in Roberts' poetry.[6]

The actual reunion with Carman did not take place until the beginning of August 1925, when they were both invited to read at the Canadian Chautauqua held at Epworth Inn, an island hotel on Lake Rousseau, Muskoka, Ontario. Founded in the early 1920s, the Chautauqua, or Muskoka Assembly as it was more commonly called, conducted a daily program from mid-June to mid-September for the purpose of 'interpreting the best in Canadian thought and idealism.' During the first week in August, designated as 'Poetry Week,' Canadian poets were engaged to lecture and read their work. Carman had attended for the first time in the summer of 1924.

The cousins arrived together from Toronto in close comradeship once more as if the long years of separation had never occurred. In spirit they were almost like boys again on one of their old-time summer expeditions. The large, wooded island was an ideal retreat for such avowed nature lovers, and they could indulge in their passion for canoeing to their hearts' content. Much of the time, however, they were surrounded by a cluster of admirers – predominantly female and not altogether unattractive. Both cousins were susceptible to a pretty face, but Roberts was more likely to invite flirtatious advances – and far readier to return them. According to Mrs Constance Davies Woodrow, herself one of his conquests, Roberts beguiled a whole bevy of bewitching damsels at the Muskoka Assembly. 'I know that,' she disclosed, 'because I took a tell-tale picture of him with two on his right hand and seven on his left.'[7]

Sharing the limelight with Roberts and Carman was Wilson MacDonald, an elfin-faced poet, twenty years their junior, who warbled self-consciously about keeping 'faith with Beauty.' He, too, had discovered the modest rewards of public readings and was methodically touring the country from one end to the other. Blessed with a voice that did justice to his strong rhythms and his florid imagery, he was becoming a popular figure on the lecture circuit. At the end of each reading, he always managed to sell a fair number of his books by arranging to have all the exits blocked except the one where he stood ready to sign autographs. Being a neighbour in the Ernescliffe Apartments, he had developed a close relationship with Roberts which passed for friendship but was barely able to withstand the strain that his jealous temperament often placed upon it.

The success of the 1925 'Poetry Week' may be deduced from the following paragraph written by Rufus H. Hathaway, who was present for the events:

Memorable as were the individual readings given by Bliss Carman and Major Roberts, none of them all will be remembered as will a joint reading which the poet-cousins gave on the veranda of the cottage of the President of the Canadian Chautauqua Association, Rev. C.S. Applegath, just before their departure to take the afternoon boat for Muskoka Wharf. Mr Carman to return to his summer home at Haines Falls, in the Catskills, and Major Roberts to return to Toronto. It was the first time that they ever took part in such an event, and the occasion was made even more important by the fact that Wilson MacDonald also participated. It is hardly necessary to say that the fifty or more persons who sat on the veranda or stood or sat about the ground in front, appreciated the unique event to the full.

During August and part of September, Roberts shared his third-floor front apartment with Tom MacInnes, usually considered a west coast poet although he had been born and educated in Ontario. He had not been back to Toronto since graduating from Osgoode Hall and being called to the bar in 1893. His colourful career, which had taken him from the Klondike to China, had been punctuated by the publication of five volumes of vigorous verse. Roberts was delighted with the whimsical charm and irrepressible gusto of the man and his poetry. As the ever-watchful Constance Woodrow observed, his living and working arrangement with MacInnes was a model of order and compatability:

I have discovered that Dr Roberts is more than a poet, a soldier and a doctor of laws. He is a splendid housekeeper. He could put many a housewife to shame. There is a place for everything and everything in its place. You would never guess from the appearance of his desk that he is a poet, for every letter, every book, every ashtray is in apple-pie order. The rest of the living-room is in perfect harmony with the desk. As for the kitchen – well, you could sit cross-legged and eat off the floor; it is so clean. The dish-towels hang in a neat row on a little clothesline, and never a dirty dish can you see anywhere. Even the refrigerator is a model of neatness! To return to the living-room, it is the cosiest place you could ever wish for on a winter's night. There is a very large bay window, through which the sun streams in the afternoon. The desk is set in the alcove and there is always a volume of somebody's poems within reach. The long, broad mantel is Dr Roberts' art gallery, but it would never do to tell you whose pictures are arranged along it so beautifully. Here he likes to sit and read to himself or to his friends, or to smoke by the hour. Most of what I have said of Dr Roberts is also true of Tom MacInnes, for they share everything, including the neatness, no doubt. When they both want to work at the same time, Tom MacInnes takes possession of the table in the dining-room, which is then spread with a litter of papers. They might be poems; I don't know.[8]

By early autumn, Roberts was on the recital-lecture trail again. After a stop-over in Montreal, he launched his tour of the Maritimes in Halifax on 6 October 1925. 'I have come home,' he told his audience on that occasion, reminding them that although he had been born and educated in New Brunswick, he had spent a decade of his life in Nova Scotia. 'I am deeply moved,' he said, 'to observe that tonight this large audience extends to me a warm welcome to the homeland in which I first won a name and did much of my best work...'

Disturbed by the significance that was still being attached to his long residence abroad, he tried again to dispel the notion that in leaving Canada he had abandoned his country:

I went abroad to look for a wider market for my literary wares. And this step was highly reasonable. For a man who must live by his pen naturally must seek the widest possible market, the largest audience. ... Bliss Carman and I are not any the less Canadian because we went abroad. For he went abroad *for* Canada, to give, if possible, Canada a significant place in the literary world, and to increase and enhance her literature in the world. Carman is now, as I know and have seen, a more conscious and ardent Canadian than ever before. ... And I – well, I have retained while abroad everything Canadian in me, even my Canadian accent.[9]

While he remained in Halifax, he was the guest of Dr Henry F. Munro, superintendent of education for Nova Scotia. Even after his tour took him to other centres, he regarded the Munro home as his base and returned there intermittently. At first, the Munros were pleased to entertain him, but eventually they began to fear that he might spend the winter. As politely as possible, they indicated that, for all his personal charm, he had outstayed his welcome. On future visits to Halifax, he nearly always stayed with Andy Merkel, the Atlantic superintendent of the Canadian Press. Their mutual friend, Robert Norwood, had written to Roberts prior to the tour: 'Andrew knows the ropes and has it in his power to give you some pleasant relaxation, which you will need after your strenuous hours .. so do not fail to get in touch with him at once.'[10] Roberts soon came to regard Merkel as a close friend and was pleased to discover that he had known his wife Florence when she was a little girl in Windsor, Nova Scotia.

During the ensuing weeks, until just before Christmas, he spoke in nearly every large centre in the Maritime provinces. The most emotional event of the tour took place when a capacity crowd jammed Fredericton's Opera House to welcome him back to the city of his forefathers. All the familiar faces in the audience, boyhood friends and relatives, happily brought back the old days, but they also served as a sorrowful reminder that the ranks were thinned. He was so overcome by the flood of memory that several moments elapsed before he could control his voice to speak.

In Fredericton, he stayed with Thede and his family. Dorothy Roberts, Thede's nineteen-year-old daughter, was struck by the difference in temperament between her uncle and Bliss Carman, who had been their guest a year or so earlier. She had been particularly distressed that Carman, who once sang about 'the joys of the road,' apparently did not share her love of roaming about the countryside. In contrast, her dynamic uncle, who called her 'Gypsy' and seemed to understand her restlessness, loved to wander about his old haunts.[11] One chilly Sunday morning he arrived at St Ann's, his father's former church, just as the choir was proceeding up the centre aisle from a trap door in the basement. He intended to slip quietly into a back seat, but his glasses were misted by the sudden warmth, blinding him to the opening in the floor, and he fell with a crash down the basement steps. Before anyone could help him, he jumped up and announced that he was all right.

Throughout the rest of the tour he did not experience any other mishaps, but his agenda was strenuous and tiring. 'Living in suitcases & having no fixed abode, no writing table, proves most distracting,' he wrote to Lorne Pierce, '& this continual platform work takes it out of one.' But he was able to report favourably upon the financial success of the undertaking, assuring Pierce that he had been able to meet the $500 bank note that the latter had signed for him.

Almost from their first meeting, Roberts had become dependent upon the serious young editor of Ryerson Press. It was Pierce who helped Leila Roberts arrange the western tour through the contacts he made while travelling in the West for his publishing company. It was soon understood that he could always be counted upon for a loan of ten dollars or so whenever an emergency arose. Convinced of the enduring quality of Roberts' work, he had recently extolled it unreservedly in a series of articles for the *New Outlook*, a publication of the newly formed United Church of Canada. Most important of all, perhaps, he had hurried into print a collection of Roberts' poems, called *The Sweet o' the Year*, to inaugurate a series of chap-books by Canadian poets. Except for the title poem which first appeared in the May issue of *To-Day*, 1920, all of the other eight selections were reprinted from *New Poems*.

Pierce, who was an ordained Methodist minister, had gone from the pulpit to publishing at the age of thirty when he accepted the editorship of the Methodist Church's publishing house, Ryerson Press, in 1920. He immediately dedicated himself to the advancement of Canadian literature so zealously that his lists of Canadian titles often revealed more about his good will than his discrimination. He established himself as a patron as well as a publisher by providing a gold medal to be awarded annually by the Royal Society of Canada in recognition of cumulative achievement in imaginative or critical literature. This award, known as the Lorne Pierce Medal, was offered for the first time in 1926. The first recipient, chosen upon the recommendation of Pierce himself, was Charles G.D. Roberts. 'Lord, old man,' Roberts acknowledged to Pierce, 'but I'm proud of that honour!'[12]

Pierce's diary reveals that he remained susceptible to Roberts' charm even after he came to deplore his reputation as a 'ladies' man.' Pierce marvelled at Roberts' skill in causing people 'to think the very best of themselves when he addresses them,' but found it 'difficult to associate the man with the loveliest of his poetry.' The strait-laced editor tended to take gossip about Roberts at face value without allowing for exaggeration and outright fabrication. Many of the stories he heard had some basis in fact, but he was slow to realize that more often than not they were part of a mythology that Roberts was deliberately creating to delude himself about the encroachment of old age. It was unfortunate that Roberts misjudged the depth of Pierce's urbanity and unwittingly jarred the latter's Methodist principles with his mildly risqué sense of humour. When Roberts jokingly suggested that Wilson MacDonald's ailments could be cured by taking either a wife or a mistress, Pierce was filled with revulsion: 'Such ideas come out of the pit. A cad W.M. has often been, but he has been clean. Thank God.'

The first hint of scandal that reached Pierce's ears came from the Muskoka Assembly where, according to his informant, the lasciviousness of Carman and Roberts had been 'too disgustingly apparent.' For the most part, Pierce heard about Roberts' alleged sexual immorality from Wilson MacDonald:

He took decent girls whom W. MacD. had introduced to him, and thru his most insinuating graces wrought them to his passion. He lives in a state of sexual excess. He can never write anything great again, I fear. There is no sustained core to his thinking and living. He confessed to W. MacD. that he had been diseased, if indeed he was not so now.

MacDonald circulated his stories so widely that the word got back to Roberts, who reacted in alarm. It was one thing to cultivate the image of an ageless Don Juan, but it was quite another to be pictured as a dissolute old rake. Pierce recorded Roberts' denunciation of MacDonald without comment, but thereafter he appeared to be slightly less censorious.[13]

Pierce and Roberts shared a special interest in the work of Mrs Constance Davies Woodrow, a young British-born poet living in Toronto. In 1926, Pierce chose her small sheaf of poems, *The Captive Gypsy*, to be the fourth volume in the chap-book series, and Roberts wrote an introduction for it. There is no reason to doubt the sincerity of Roberts' graceful compliments to her poetry even though it was his way of meeting his obligations for a brief but tempestuous affair that had just ended between them. The romance appears to have begun during the 1925 Muskoka Assembly and its intensity may be judged from the passionate letters they exchanged while he was on his Maritime tour, although he advised her against confiding in his daughter: 'Yes, Beloved, it is most *wise* not to acknowledge to Edith (bless her) or to *anyone*, that you hear from me, – other than a business note!'[14] The cautionary tone sounds decidedly shamefaced, and the mercurial Constance, whose moods were unpredictable at the best of times, would have been justified in being upset by it. Early in 1926 she visited relatives in England, and by the time she returned the romance had languished.

After Roberts came back from the Maritimes, Dr E.A. Hardy, head of English at Jarvis Collegiate, sent four grade thirteen students to the Ernescliffe to interview him. Roberts was so pleased by one schoolgirl's report of the meeting that he selected her to be his special courier. Throughout the winter months, she collected autographed books from the Ernescliffe and delivered them to Dr Hardy, who sold them to the staff and students. The following year, after the young lady had started training to become a nurse, she began to feel that the distinguished author was 'showing too much interest' in her. Thereafter, she avoided going to his apartment unless she was accompanied by a friend or by her younger sister. His frequent letters, inviting her to visit, would invariably conclude with a courtly flourish: 'I kiss both your hands.' Once she took along a very pretty nurse to whom Roberts was immediately attracted. Soon afterwards, her comely friend confided: 'I've been receiving "kiss both your hands," too.'[15]

In mid-March, after an occasional lecture in Toronto and vicinity, Roberts was off on another tour of the West. Despite Pierce's prediction that he would not be very welcome a second time, he had a heavy schedule – nearly two months of readings that took him to Vancouver and back.

While he was on the road, he found time to complete an essay called 'My Religion' for a series that was running in the *Toronto Star Weekly*. It appeared on the newstands shortly after his return to Toronto, and he was vastly amused to discover that it had been credited to the writer Grace Dean McLeod Rogers, a devout Baptist. Through a blunder in the make-up department, only the last three paragraphs were from the pen of Mrs Rogers. All the rest was by Roberts. 'Imagine the good, Puritan lady's feelings,' he chuckled to Rufus Hathaway, 'when she sees my rather unorthodox screed ascribed to her!'[16]

The first week in July found Roberts back in Muskoka, where he was scheduled to give four lectures at the Summer School of Canadian Literature under the sponsorship of the Muskoka Assembly. The arrangement had been made by Dr Aletta E. Marty, a public school inspector, who happened to be one of Elsie Pomeroy's most cherished friends. The other speakers for the week-long session were Wilson MacDonald and John W. Garvin. The complete series of twelve lectures was offered for five dollars with accommodation at the Epworth Inn ($16-$20 per week for a room; $13 for a tent). The promotional brochure announced that classes would be held out-of-doors in 'The Little Theatre in the Woods' at 11 A.M. and 4 P.M., thus making it possible to take advantage of the boating, tennis courts, and bowling green, and also to enjoy the daily sunset cruise in the early evening.

Among the passengers on board the lake steamer that carried Roberts to the island hotel was Elsie Pomeroy, whose doubts about registering for the summer school had been overcome by her devotion to Dr Marty. Up to that point, she had successfully avoided meeting Roberts, even though she was a member of several societies that were lionizing him in Toronto. She feared that the man might not measure up to the poet as had happened with Wilson MacDonald, whom she had befriended with small donations of money to 'further his art.' Therefore, although she was eager to hear the lectures, she had grave misgivings over the prospect of coming into daily contact with the Canadian poet she idolized above all others.

Somewhat to her dismay, Roberts intercepted her on the deck of the steamer with the unexpected greeting: 'Pardon me, but I can't help wondering if you might be Miss Elsie Pomeroy.' Surprised and flattered, she mumbled an acknowledgment. He continued: 'Your name has come up so often whenever the subject of Canadian literature is mentioned in Toronto that I cannot understand why I have not met you before.' Miss Pomeroy smiled quietly, and Roberts must have been conscious that the warmth of her expressive eyes transfigured a face that was not beautiful in any other respect. By the time the steamer docked at Epworth wharf, they were chatting like lifelong friends. Later, after dinner, she accepted his invitation to go canoeing in the long summer twilight.

Thus began a mutually rewarding friendship that lasted almost until Roberts' death. Finding herself admitted to her hero's select circle of intimates, Elsie Pomeroy soon decided that his stature had not been diminished upon closer examination. For his part, Roberts had rarely found anyone whose knowledge of his work could surpass Miss Pomeroy's reverential familiarity with it. While she felt honoured to be his confidante, Roberts, in turn, was so stimulated by her faith in his art that he turned again to poetry. He told her that the concluding stanza of 'Spring Breaks in Foam' expressed his indebtedness to her:

> And in my heart
>   Spring breaks in glad surprise
> As the long frosts of the long years melt
>   At your dear eyes.

Despite its closeness, their relationship was platonic from beginning to end. She was not the type of woman that Roberts found physically attractive; and, in the beginning at least, she saw him not only as the Father of Canadian Literature but as a father-figure in her life. Wilson MacDonald, who was jealous of her new alliance, tried to spread a rumour that she had spent a night in Roberts' apartment, but no one believed him. When he took the malicious story to Dr Marty, she not only ordered him out of her sight, but threatened him with dire consequences if he ever dared to repeat the scandalous lie to anyone else.[17]

Referring to the Summer School of Canadian Literature in a letter to Lloyd, Roberts reported that his '"conferences" had been a great success,' but he made no mention of his acquaintance with Elsie Pomeroy. However, he noted that Wilson MacDonald was in a 'generous & genial mood,'[18] which may indicate that the involvement with Elsie had not yet reached the point where it could rouse the resentment of his envious fellow poet. Furthermore, just when the friendship had made a promising start, it was interrupted at the end of the week by Roberts' return to Toronto and his subsequent departure for a brief holiday in New Brunswick.

While he was back in his native province, Roberts visited the village of Westcock for the first time in many years. It was a bittersweet experience, for the changes were far greater than those he had lamented in 'Tantramar Revisited.' After more than forty years, his words had taken on a deeper relevance: 'Hands of chance and change have marred, or moulded, or broken, / Busy with spirit or flesh, all I most have adored.' Not only were the old familiar faces missing, but many of his most cherished landmarks had also disappeared. The beloved parsonage had long ago been levelled by fire, and only the well remained to mark the site of the dooryard. The groves of spruce and fir, behind the parsonage, where the crows used to nest, had been felled by the axe; and the wooded hillside of his boyhood was now a grassy clearing. 'Ah, how well I remember,' he had written as he viewed the scene in 1883. Sadly, in 1926, he was mindful of the aspects that no longer existed except in memory.

In August, Roberts went back to the Muskoka Assembly for Canadian Authors' Week, which boasted his old friend Sir Gilbert Parker as one of its special attractions. Lloyd Roberts, who was scheduled for a recital on the thirteenth of the month, was there with his wife and his daughter Patsy. Elsie Pomeroy was also in attendance to applaud her hero when he gave a well-attended reading one afternoon on the huge veranda of the Epworth Inn. His success served to invite comparisons when his son gave a recital the next evening. Lloyd was very anxious to prove himself a worthy writer in the Roberts tradition, but he was well aware that his accomplishments could not match what his father had achieved at the same age. His particular gift for the personal essay had been delightfully demonstrated in *The Book of Roberts* (1923), but that special talent was never enough to remove him from the shadow of his father's reputation.

Returning to Toronto from Muskoka, Roberts moved from his apartment to Suite 25 on the fifth floor of the same building. The new quarters, with their superb view of the city and lake beyond, substituted for a home for the rest of his life. While he was settling in, Elsie Pomeroy, no longer elusive, was frequently in his company. She entertained him in her apartment, which she shared with her brother Howard, also a teacher, and introduced him to her younger sisters, Ada and Dora, who lived elsewhere in the city. Howard and Dora, in particular, had already caught something of Elsie's contagious admiration for Roberts as a writer; and, like her, they soon came to look upon him as a delightful companion and a valued friend. But it was Elsie who remained his most faithful follower; and, as time passed, he came to depend more and more upon her devotion. He later acknowledged his feelings for her in a little jingle from his privately circulated 'Colour Toasts':

144 Sir Charles God Damn

> Here's to the lady who dresses in *black*,
> So demure she is almost secure from attack,
> But there's something about her makes others seem slack;
> So if once you have known her you'll always go back.

With the approach of winter, he set out again for 'my blessed Vancouver,' as he phrased it in a letter to a friend, adding: 'Hope to stay for several months, this time, please the gods!' He had been lured westward by an invitation to deliver several lectures at the University of British Columbia. The summons had been issued in response to considerable agitation, which included an editorial in the Vancouver *Morning Star* requesting the university to ask Roberts to lecture to the students. On 4 December, he reported to Lorne Pierce that the lectures had been 'a huge success,' and that he had been booked for 'many recitals' after the holidays. Shortly afterwards, he took a sixth-floor apartment in the Royal Alexandra on Bute Street, where he remained until he left again for the East at the beginning of March.[19]

Once again he was fêted by the Vancouver Poetry Society as well as by the local branch of the Canadian Authors' Association. Both groups played host to him and Lloyd when the latter visited his father in January and gave several readings. Bliss Carman arrived in the city around the end of February, as did Lorne Pierce. Those three literary men from the East were guests of the Poetry Society at a formal gathering to celebrate the publication of Dr Fewster's first book, *My Garden Dreams*, a collection of nature essays interspersed with poems. Dr Fewster, Annie Charlotte Dalton, and A.M. Stephen posed with the distinguished visitors for a group photograph which shows Roberts looking uncommonly grim. An explanation for his demeanour may be found in the reminiscences of Miss May Judge, a member of the Society, who was present for the occasion:

Also seated in the hall was Charles G.D. Roberts. He looked so utterly depressed and forlorn that I could not help wondering if he had just received some bad news. No one was talking to him, so I ventured the remark that I was surprised not to see him on the platform with his cousin, Bliss Carman. He gazed at me sadly, his pince-nez, with its long, black ribbon attached, giving a finishing touch to his air of gloom. Then, looking first to see if other people might be listening, he said in a low, melancholy whisper, 'I have got toothache.'[20]

It was a malady from which he had been suffering at frequent intervals during the winter.

While he was on a lecture engagement in Victoria during February, Roberts took time out to visit the aging poet Charles Mair, who at eighty-eight was confined to a nursing home in that city. Mair basked in the reputation of being 'our first nature and dramatic poet, the adventurer who blazed the trail,' but in recent months he had been a little disgruntled by all the acclaim that Carman and Roberts had been receiving. He contended that those two Maritimers did not have a monopoly on Canadian poetry. Furthermore, he argued, had Roberts not abandoned poetry long ago in favour of 'imaginary zoology'? Nevertheless, he greeted Roberts in a cordial mood, and appeared flattered that the younger man wanted to dedicate a new book of poems to him. Aware that his death was imminent, he seemed to be waiting 'with zest and anticipation for what he spoke of as the "next and greatest adventure".' Pouring two glasses of whisky, he proposed a farewell toast with a special significance which his visitor fully understood: 'not "good-bye," but "till we meet again"!' When Mair died, five months later, Roberts thought of their parting, and rejoiced that the 'venerable poet' had lived so 'long, and adventurously, and richly.'[21]

Fortunately, Mair had lived to see *The Vagrant of Time*, the new volume of poetry, which was dedicated to him as promised. It came out in April 1927, after Roberts had arrived back in Toronto following a lecture tour from Vancouver across the prairie provinces. The first printing was an attractive deluxe edition of 500 copies, many of which were personally signed by the author. In spite of the book's impressive appearance, however, collectors of Roberts' work must have been disappointed to discover that he had simply reissued the contents of *New Poems* with only fourteen additional selections, including 'The Sweet o' the Year,' which had appeared in his recent chap-book.

The London *Times*, the only major journal outside Canada to review *The Vagrant of Time*, remarked that 'Mr Roberts rhymes pleasantly and experiences life with an agreeable sense of wonder, but he has little specific poetry talent.' This view of Roberts' 'conventional' images and 'discursive' vision was in contrast to *The Times'* enthusiastic commendation of *New Poems* a few years earlier. Canadian critics were generally kinder, but Archibald MacMechan wrote to Pierce: 'I have received Roberts' 'Vagrant,' and I have reviewed it in *The Standard* ... but I am not sure that either you or the poet will be particularly pleased with the result.' He foreshadowed *The Times'* criticism by declaring: 'The intellectual content is *nil*, though the craftsmanship is competent enough.' Although Mac-Mechan was usually a perceptive critic, his displeasure over the predomi-

nant mediocrity of *New Poems* may have blinded him to the special merits
of some of Roberts' more recent work.

MacMechan, who had been the George Munro Professor of English
Language and Literature at Dalhousie University ever since 1889, was
aware that Roberts had competed against him for the position, but had
later withdrawn from the field – for reasons that are no longer clear,
although they may have been well known at the time. It is impossible to say
whether or not the old rivalry made MacMechan any more critical of
Roberts as a writer, but it is no secret that he heartily disapproved of the
man's life-style. Since he deplored Roberts' extramarital affairs, it may not
have been an entirely aesthetic judgment when he complained: 'His
"love" poetry – "makes me sick"...' It was in reference to Roberts that he
stated: 'I wish I didn't know so much about our native geniuses.'[22]

Familiarity does not always breed contempt, however, and the people
who knew Roberts best usually were inclined to take a tolerant view of his
shortcomings. Even Elsie Pomeroy looked upon his amorous escapades as
forgivable human weaknesses in a man whose married life had been
difficult. Some of his detractors called him a sponger, but his close friends
knew how courageously he had tried to cope with his truly straitened
circumstances. Since he had been forced to deal with creditors for most of
his life, he had learned to be ingenious when it came to deferring
settlements. He always had good intentions of paying back everything he
owed, but, as his debts mounted faster than his sales and royalties, it
was usually only the most pressing of the accounts that received his attention.

Lorne Pierce's secretary became very upset when Roberts kept ordering
books on credit from Ryerson Press. Feeling that he had always presumed
too much upon his friendship with her employer, she typed an angry note
which she attached to one request before slapping it down upon Pierce's desk:

I gave the requisition for these copies – six of his own chap-books and 3 of T.G.
Roberts – to Mr Ellins to have sent down to Wholesale. I am not so sure he will
send it down, for he says that Roberts never pays for the books he gets from us. I
see no reason why the books for which he sends should be charged to our
department. That is his idea I suppose in writing to me direct, but I am a turning
worm. It is that sort of thing that keeps our department in financial straits, and in
the last analysis our stipends down. C.G.D. has sacrificed a good many people to
his own selfish ends, I do not propose that he shall make a Roman Holiday of me!

Secretary

ANTI-WORM SOCIETY[23]

One of the friends Roberts 'sponged' upon without reproach for rather extended periods of time was George Frederick Clarke, a dentist in Woodstock, New Brunswick. In June 1927, Dr Clarke arranged a series of recitals for him in the Woodstock area, and uncomplainingly played the customary role as his host. A writer himself, having many poems and several novels for juveniles to his credit, Dr Clarke was a 'brilliant & temperamental' man whose companionship Roberts found extremely congenial. The atmosphere of his social circle was 'cultured & easy, & much less conventional than one is apt to find in Ontario or the West.' In addition, as Roberts happily reported, there was a special advantage in living with a dentist: 'My old toothache is cured, praise the gods, & I'm feeling very fit.'[24]

It was fortunate that Roberts had been restored to his usual health at that time, for he had recently committed himself to a project that required his full strength and concentration. It had begun when the government of New Brunswick approached him to write an ode to commemorate the Diamond Jubilee of Confederation. He was also invited to read the completed work as part of the official celebrations in Fredericton on Dominion Day. At first he had refused the request, partly because he was feeling ill and exhausted, but also, perhaps, because he hesitated to compete with his own long-standing reputation as a writer of patriotic pieces. Times had changed since he had composed the nationalistic lines that had once thrilled Elsie Pomeroy's generation of schoolchildren, and he may well have wondered whether he could speak with the same effect to Canadians of a later and more cynical era.

His reservations about undertaking the project were finally overcome by a lucrative offer from the T. Eaton Company for a new patriotic poem to use as a full-page display in all the newspapers in which they normally advertised. Even with the added stimulus of much-needed cash, he had difficulty getting started, and the deadline was only ten days away when he wrote the first four lines on 20 June, the day he arrived back in Toronto from Woodstock. The poem was completed within a week, more in desperation than in inspiration, as its laboured lines attest. However, although it gets off to a bad start with a sing-song rhythm in the opening stanza, its lines generally have a ponderous dignity that undoubtedly sounded impressive when their author read them to the loyal citizens of Fredericton on the first of July.

CHAPTER ELEVEN

National President, CAA

1927–1929

FROM THE TIME of his return to Canada, Roberts had worked closely with the Canadian Authors' Association. Many of his readings had been given under the auspices of the various branches that had sprung up across the country since the Association's inauguration in 1921. In the summer of 1925 he had appeared at the annual convention, which was held in Winnipeg that year, 'with the shutters of his face all down, but his eye glass ribbon on guard.' His duties at the Muskoka Assembly prevented him from attending the convention in Vancouver the following year, but he accepted an invitation to assume the presidency of the Toronto Branch, whose members were reported to 'keenly appreciate the honour he had bestowed upon them.'[1] At the next convention, held in Ottawa at the end of June 1927, he was elected national president of the Association.

The idea of a Canadian Authors' Association grew out of a chance remark by humorist Stephen Leacock at a private luncheon he had hosted for three literary friends: Pelham Edgar, B.K. Sandwell, and John Murray Gibbon. There should be 'a strong body of authors in Canada,' Leacock declared, which would protect its members against copyright infringements. His guest seized upon the notion with such enthusiasm that plans were made to invite every published Canadian writer to attend an organizational meeting at McGill University on 12 March 1921. Over 100 people turned up in response to the call, and the Canadian Authors' Association was born with Gibbon as the first president and Sandwell as the secretary. Leacock, chief mid-wife at the accouchement, was unable to take an office because he was booked for an extended lecture tour in

Britain. Gibbon, being a publicist for the Canadian Pacific Railway, was a pragmatic choice for leader because he could travel on a free pass to organize branches of the Association across the country.

The foremost aim of the new organization was twofold: 'To act for the mutual benefit and protection of Canadian authors and for the maintenance of high ideals and practice in the literary profession.' The intentions were commendable and their fulfilment highly desirable; and it must be conceded that the Association created a new awareness of Canadian literature by supporting lecture tours, holding Book Weeks, and generally promoting the work of its members. There were even a few modest successes in the ongoing attempts to modify the Canadian government's legislation on copyright. As far as literary standards were concerned, however, the Association seldom lifted its sights above the level of its rank-and-file membership. Dissatisfaction with its dilettantes and poetasters led to an outburst from Earle Birney in 1948: 'The CAA, to my mind, is predominantly a body of aging hacks and reactionaries who maintain a dubious prestige by persuading a number of genuine writers ... to represent them in the public eye.'[2]

Roberts was the fifth president of the Canadian Authors' Association. His predecessors in office, with the exception of Robert J. Stead, were men whose greatest distinction lay in fields other than literature. In fact, he was the most accomplished writer ever to head the organization, up to the present, although, as a poet, Duncan Campbell Scott has stood the test of time at least equally well, and novelist Ralph Connor was more widely popular in his own day. His greatest contribution to the Association was undoubtedly the prestige of his name, although no one could fault him in any way for the manner in which he discharged his duties. The Father of Canadian Literature, as he had so often been called, assumed the paternal role willingly and proudly.

Instead of worrying that the Canadian Authors' Association was attracting too many writers whose talents did not match their aspirations, Roberts took great pride in the 'substantial increase in membership' that occurred during his presidency. He believed, perhaps a little too naïvely, that the best way to insure better writing was to encourage *more* writing. Furthermore, he could not agree with the charge that the Association was guilty of protecting incompetent craftsmen. In his view, every published author was entitled to all the benefits, privileges, and services that the CAA could offer. Nor was he convinced that the founders' lofty ideals were necessarily compromised by the general mediocrity of the membership.

Elsie Pomeroy was among the new CAA members whom Roberts had recruited personally. Because she was the author of numerous articles that had appeared in several educational and religious periodicals, she was already qualified to join the Association, but the thought had always struck her as highly presumptuous. Being too modest at first to bring her published work to the attention of a prominent writer like Roberts, she showed it to him only after he kept reiterating that she should get something into print in order to enjoy the literary contacts that the CAA would provide. Her total output, meagre though it was, took him by surprise. 'You have been holding out on me,' he laughed. 'I command you to apply for membership in the CAA at once!'[3]

A young man name Nat Benson, whom Roberts met in June 1927, at the home of Mrs Constance Woodrow, was a much less diffident CAA recruit than Miss Pomeroy. A graduate student at the University of Toronto, Benson soon turned to teaching to earn his living, but his greatest ambition was to become a celebrated poet. He quickly established himself as Roberts' protégé and marvelled at his 'unparalleled good fortune' in finding so perfect a mentor. Roberts was always generous in his praise of Benson's work, but he also offered sound advice which the impetuous novice frequently failed to follow: 'Work over, – condense, – hold in check your facility & abundance of words, – and again, *condense!*' Privately, Roberts confided to Elsie Pomeroy that young Nat was cursed with a 'fatal facility' which would probably prove to be his undoing. In the course of time, however, Roberts' critical judgment was overruled by his deepening affection for his youthful apprentice. When Benson's poem 'Dollard' (1933) received an unfavourable notice, Roberts consoled him by calling it 'one of the two or three best narrative poems yet written in English-speaking Canada.'

Benson's filial devotion – he called Roberts 'almost a second father' – was useful as well as heartwarming, for it found many practical expressions, including an occasional loan of money to take care of an emergency. It is to Benson's credit that he always felt that he owed a far greater debt than he could ever repay. In one of the many tributes he wrote after Roberts' death, there is a very vivid description of his hero's appearance and personality:

May I try to picture him as I knew him: short, compact, active, tremendously muscular for his slight stature, rugged of feature, with a seemingly 'granite' chin and sturdy pillar of neck, warm-hearted, bright-spirited, debonair, intolerant only of stupidity and wrong thinking. His eyes were strange, almost mysterious, of a remote dark-bluish grey, at times narrowed to slits, at other times wide and aglow with humour. His nature and whole make-up exuded warmth and kindliness.[4]

Roberts began his presidential duties in the fall of 1927 by organizing a New Brunswick branch of the CAA and representing the Association at the American Book Fair in Dayton, Ohio. His travelling was made easier by the complimentary railway passes provided by John Murray Gibbon. In December, while returning to Vancouver for the winter, he visited nearly all of the CAA branches along the way. His ten lectures on Canadian literature, delivered at the University of British Columbia, were not part of his official duties, but they were given welcome support and publicity by the Vancouver branch of the CAA.

Although Roberts professed to be pleased with the reception accorded his lectures at the university, and proudly mailed copies of the outline to his friends in Toronto, Dr G.G. Sedgewick of the English Department was less that enthusiastic about the series. Even before the lectures began, Sedgewick indicated his lack of interest in whatever Roberts might have to say about 'Canadian Literature & Wild Life,' adding: 'The latter topic will neglect many aspects of the subject familiar to Roberts.' Afterwards, according to Lorne Pierce, who got his information second hand, Sedgewick declared that Roberts 'said nothing & said it poorly.' By the second lecture, the students had lost interest, and thereafter the audience consisted mostly of townspeople, but the attendance never exceeded fifty. Roberts intimated to Pierce that he had relied upon the latter's recently published *Outline of Canadian Literature* for his factual material, but Pierce grumbled in his diary that sufficient acknowledgment had not been made during the lectures. In all likelihood, Roberts thought that his random reflections, copiously interspersed with lengthy quotations, was just what his audience wanted to hear. It probably never occurred to him that anyone would expect him to take a critical and analytical approach in order to put the development of Canadian literature into some kind of perspective.[5]

Augmenting his honorarium from the literature course by giving recitals in nearly every educational institution in Vancouver and vicinity from the public schools to the university, Roberts lingered in the city until the second week of April. His sojourn was broken only by a brief visit in February to the League of Western Writers in Seattle, where he represented the CAA and had 'a whale of a time.'[6] His return to the East was marked by more visits to CAA branches and more recitals. He was back in Toronto for less than three weeks before he was off again to Winnipeg to attend a Royal Society meeting at which Bliss Carman received the Lorne Pierce Medal for Literature. During the visit, he and Carman, along with the Reverend C.W. Gordon (Ralph Connor), were tendered a banquet by the Manitoba members of the CAA.

Roberts had two qualities that were a great asset in his work with the branches: his genial nature and his contagious enthusiasm. He could mix easily, and always gave the impression of being sincerely interested in the person to whom he was speaking. Although he was a good listener when the occasion required, he could be quick with a sally or an entertaining anecdote. Wise and witty, he was very persuasive in promoting ideas or causes that were close to his heart. The leg-work of the copyright issue was done by Lawrence J. Burpee, a civil servant in Ottawa, and there were several additional concerns that were handled capably by someone other than the national president, but it was Roberts who worked hardest to keep the CAA active and involved at the branch level.

Roberts' skill as a chairman contributed greatly to the resounding success of the eighth annual convention of the CAA held in Calgary on 4, 5, and 6 July, with a closing banquet in Banff. He was surrounded by loyal cohorts, for a large delegation from Toronto outnumbered any other group except that of the host branch of Calgary. Among his stalwarts were Dr E.A. Hardy, the diligent national secretary, and the ubiquitous John M. Elson, national treasurer. At his side also were three other Toronto members who had become his habitual followers: Constance Davies Woodrow, Elsie Pomeroy, and Nat Benson.

A heavy agenda of business matters and papers related to professional interests was relieved by traditional western hospitality in the form of public and private luncheons, receptions, and other social events. On the first evening, a reception in the ballroom of the Palliser Hotel featured Roberts and Nat Benson in a program of readings from their own poetry. Benson was unknown, except to the Toronto delegation, but Roberts, with characteristic generosity, arranged the joint recital deliberately to bring his protégé to the attention of a wider public. The second afternoon was given over to a drive to the Prince of Wales' ranch for supper, followed by a leisurely return in the long summer twilight. On the fourth day, Saturday, the convention removed to the Banff Springs Hotel for the annual dinner.

En route to Banff, there was a scheduled detour to the Sarcee reserve for the induction of Roberts as an Indian chief. Unfortunately, the early summer rains had made all the roads to the reserve nearly impassable. Some cars became mired to the hubs so that the passengers had to help the drivers rip up fence posts in an effort to extricate the vehicles from the deep mud. Several carloads of frustrated visitors failed to reach their destination, and missed the colourful ceremony on the tree-shaded lawn of the Anglican mission on the reserve where Chief Joe Big Plume presented Roberts with a magnificent war bonnet of eagle feathers and gave him the almost unpronounceable name of Na-Kee-Tlee-Se Ah-Kee-Tcha, meaning 'Chief Great Scribe.'

There were ceremonial Indian dances in which the CAA delegates were too sedate to participate except for Ruth Brotman, a teenager from Montreal, who had been given a scholarship by John Murray Gibbon to write up the convention for the CPR from the viewpoint of youth. Being vivacious and uninhibited, she danced along with the Indians, who bestowed the name 'Princess Laughing Water' upon her. She also caught the attention of Roberts, as she recalled nearly fifty years afterwards:

I met him later at a function in Vancouver after the Convention, and he invited me to lunch. He told me then that he had never had a Jewish sweetheart; and, not liking the trend of the conversation, I told him I had forgotten something and would return shortly, and never did return. But he did call me many times in Montreal, inviting me to various functions, and wrote his letters in *red ink.* I forgave him, as he was probably a lonely old man.[7]

Less forgiving was Kathleen Strange, the petite, attractive wife of a wheat farmer from Fenn, Alberta. Mrs Strange had attended Roberts' recital in Calgary in the spring of 1927 and had written him several effusive letters the following year. 'I warn you, Dr Roberts,' she announced on one occasion, 'if I do come east, I will monopolize as much of your time as you will spare me.' It is uncertain whether such a meeting ever took place, although at another time she wrote that she hoped to be arriving in Toronto after a proposed visit to Montreal

there to meet with your dear self, and interview a hundred and one people I have met so far only by correspondence. Then from Toronto to Calgary. I wish I could arrange to land in Calgary about the same time as you do, as it would save me another trip down and we might perhaps make some part of the journey together. Or would it bother you too much, I wonder? I have so much I want to talk to you about, dear Dr Roberts.[8]

If Roberts read more into those messages than she intended, he was to be disabused at the Calgary convention.

There are several versions of what happened. Thomas H. Raddall, to whom Mrs Strange told the story many years later, embellished the account considerably when he came to record it in his memoirs. According to Raddall, Roberts invited her to his room in the Palliser to look at some photographs of himself taken at the time of his meeting with Isadora Duncan. There was a series showing him in a flimsy pseudo-ancient-Greek tunic, claims Raddall, and then came one, minus tunic, with 'full frontal exposure.' At that moment, Roberts reportedly 'pounced,' only to be rebuffed by a healthy swing from Mrs Strange's 'indignant right arm.' It made an amusing anecdote, and many reviewers of Raddall's book seized upon it without realizing that a professional story-teller had been exaggerating for effect – or expanding upon half-remembered details with his own inventive imagination. Vinia Hoogstraten, Mrs Strange's long-time friend, has set the record straight:

I have heard Kay's version of this story many times. I can recall no mention of photographs. Kay's story featured a telephone. She was tiny and delicately made, and a blow from her right arm wouldn't have much effect, as she realized instantly. The phone was the nearest object to hand and she hit him with it, raising ... a lump on his forehead...

Mrs Hoogstraten, who never met Roberts, added that surely 'a mental image of him in a Grecian toga would have remained with me' if Mrs Strange had ever mentioned it. Also noteworthy is the fact that no photographs of Roberts such as Raddall describes, either in tunic or out of it, have survived among his effects. There is, however, a 1922 snapshot of Lloyd turning away from the camera after skinny-dipping in a wilderness lake. Roberts normally carried that item with him among his family pictures, and it may have shocked Mrs Strange if he ever showed it to her, although the pose is modest enough to appear in a family paper today. Whether or not the truth throws a better light upon Roberts' behaviour, Mrs Strange was outraged, and 'remained less than enthusiastic' about her former idol for the rest of her life.[9]

At the concluding banquet of the 1928 convention, Arthur Stringer, a tall, handsome bon vivant with prematurely white hair, rose on behalf of the delegates to thank the Calgary Local Committee for their outstanding work in arranging for the comfort and entertainment of their guests. 'You opened your hearts to us,' he declared, 'and in your homes we also found your bottles open!' Calgarian Nellie McClung, renowned for her temperance views, interjected good-humouredly: 'Not in my home, Mr Stringer!'

Thus the convention ended on a jovial note which belies the sour view that Frederick Philip Grove reported to his wife when he passed through Calgary in September: 'The town is full of echoes of the CAA convention: Elson lorded it. Roberts was drunk most of the time. Several people called him "a swine".' Ruth Brotman, who took her task as a junior reporter very seriously and kept a sharp eye on Roberts, answered emphatically when Grove's comment was brought to her attention: '*I never saw him drunk.*' As for the 'swine' epithet, we have nothing for it except Grove's word – which, it has been proved, was sometimes an unreliable source for the truth.[10]

With the 1928 convention over, Roberts relaxed in Vancouver, sharing an apartment with his nephew Archie MacDonald for nearly two months before returning to Toronto. However, his term in office still had another year – and one more convention – before he could be free of the duties that took so much of his time and energy. Carman, who was notoriously indolent himself, marvelled at the scope of his cousin's activities on behalf of the CAA: 'He hovers and broods over the whole Dominion.' But having mastered the art of combining business with pleasure, Roberts seemed always to be thoroughly enjoying the responsibilities of his position.

He was still receiving complimentary railway passes, thanks to John Murray Gibbon, and although he had to use them judiciously in travelling to the CAA branches, it was not difficult to combine business with a personal holiday. Near the end of September he went to the Maritimes to accompany Carman on a ten-day visit to the branches there, but the two cousins had such a good time that the trip stretched into a month. Their headquarters was at the Merkel home in Halifax, but their peregrinations took them to the South Shore of Nova Scotia, the Annapolis Valley, and Saint John. Carman outlined their travels in a letter to Mary Perry King, but barely mentioned Roberts because he knew that his benefactress would be jealous of their camaraderie. To Ernest Fewster, however, he wrote: 'We had some fine days together.'[11]

There were joint recitals and individual recitals, and there were extravaganzas of song at the summer home of Robert Norwood in Hubbards, Nova Scotia. It was under the influence of Norwood's merry company of poets, who styled themselves 'The Song Fishermen,' that Andy Merkel came up with the idea of issuing printed 'song sheets' of Maritime verse under the imprint of an imaginary publishing house called the Abernaki Press. After two or three issues lay unsold in the local bookstores, the printing press became a mimeograph machine in Merkel's Canadian Press office, and the distribution was restricted to a select group of friends. About a dozen issues of the sheet appeared at irregular intervals over the next two years. The fifth issue (15 January 1929) contained Roberts' 'Pan and the Rose,' which had been completed the previous August.

Carman was deeply moved by the warmth of the reception given him and Roberts everywhere they went, but he felt particularly welcome in Halifax. 'Heaven is my home doubtless,' he joked to Margaret Lawrence (Mrs B. Greene). 'But Halifax is my haven.' The Nova Scotia branch of the CAA reminded him that they were playing host to the 1929 convention to be held in Halifax in the latter part of June. Roberts, of course, would be there in his role as president, and Carman was urged to attend also. His reply was definite as well as whimsical: 'Just try to keep me away!' But it was a promise he would not be able to fulfil.[12]

The winter of 1928–9 passed pleasantly and uneventfully for Roberts in Toronto. His only absence from the city was a brief trip to address the Montreal branch of the CAA in March. With the approach of spring, he was busy with the final preparations for the forthcoming convention. On the morning of Saturday, 8 June, he decided to take the day off to visit the Toronto Islands – one of his favourite outings. While he was still on the streetcar, on the way to the ferry docks, his eye caught the headline of a newspaper in the hands of a passenger in the seat ahead of him: 'Bliss Carman Falls Dead.'

Carman had been struck down suddenly by a heart seizure while taking his morning shower at his rooming-house in New Canaan. Although he had taken ill in Minneapolis earlier in the year at the beginning of another recital tour, he had recovered quickly and had gone on to complete the itinerary that took him to Vancouver and down into California. He had returned in the spring to Mrs King, whom he hailed as his 'April the immortal, radiant as ever, and all-sufficient,' in apparent good health. Thus the blow of his death came as an unexpected shock to Roberts, who had been counting upon a reunion in Halifax within a few weeks.

Elsie Pomeroy, who saw Roberts the next day after he received the tragic news, never forgot his overwrought state of mind:

I was away out of the city on the Saturday Carman died and so R. was over fairly early Sun. morning. I can never forget the picture as he walked back and forth in my flat, stooped and old-looking, the picture of distress. He told me how he had been down town and so missed Will's telegram, and received the news as he read Wilson MacDonald's interview with a reporter in the *Telegram*, how Carman was visiting *him* and a mutual friend, Roberts, called, etc., etc. 'My anger took the edge off the blow. ... Wilson 'phoned me last night and wanted to come down. ... I told him "No". ... He said the reporter had got what he had said mixed. ... I told him I couldn't see anyone. ... He'll be writing a poem about Carman today. ... You'll see it in the *Globe* in the morning. ... (It was!). ... If only he doesn't go to the funeral. ... I'm afraid to go to the station. ... I'm *childishly* afraid to go. If he is there, I can't tell him to go home ...'

Rufus Hathaway and Lorne Pierce went to the funeral from Toronto, but, to Roberts' great relief, Wilson MacDonald stayed away. There were other worries and annoyances, however. No arrangements had been made to accommodate the contingent of Carman's relatives and friends, which, in addition to the Toronto group, included Will Ganong (his brother-in-law), Mr and Mrs Will Roberts, Frank Edge Kavanagh, and others. Mrs King was too prostrate with grief – or too antagonistic – to look after such details, but, without consulting anyone, she arranged to have Carman's ashes buried in the King plot in New Haven instead of Fredericton. Roberts was outraged by her behaviour and by the spectacle she created at the funeral service. After declaring that she did not wish to be bizarre – 'I am not his widow' – she made her appearance 'in the deepest of crepe, simply swathed in it.'[13]

In exactly two weeks after Carman's funeral, the CAA convention began. Roberts had barely recovered from his ordeal, and Constance Davies Woodrow noted that he looked 'old & worn & broken.' He was without two of his mainstays: Elsie Pomeroy could not attend because the school year was not yet over, and Nat Benson was serving a short stint with the *Free Press* in Winnipeg. Mrs Woodrow, whose devotion had been deflected, was downright malicious in a gossipy account written to Lorne Pierce after the convention. After belittling Roberts' impact upon the proceedings she concluded:

Once I saw a lot of lovely things in Charles. They are still there, but they are over-balanced by evil. But even the latter rouses my pity now, rather than my contempt. I am so secure where he is concerned now, that I can still let him kiss me – on the cheek – or lay my cheek against his in the old way with a difference. It is the little girl side of me that is drawn to him now. The woman is safe for all time – safe in much cleaner hands. I am proof against all his arts, as he learned in Halifax. I see him as he is – a pitifully unhappy & lonely old man, grasping at straws. I owe him much & therefore if I can comfort him a little, I will, but he must be content with that little...

In Mrs Woodrow's view, Roberts had not run a good convention, but, under the circumstances, her remarks must be viewed with considerable scepticism. Roberts himself was extremely well pleased with the outcome. 'Old Man, you *should* have been in Halifax!' he wrote to Nat Benson. 'It was a triumphant success.'[14]

Within a couple of months, Roberts was in the Maritimes again – in Fredericton this time to attend the memorial service for Bliss Carman on 20 August. Carman's ashes were returned to the city of his birth through the efforts of Lorne Pierce, who had enlisted the aid of the Canadian government in persuading Mrs King to release them. A telegram from the prime minister, W.L. Mackenzie King, finally settled the matter, and Mrs King commissioned a mourning outfit from a New York couturier to prepare for her tragic role. She arrived at Christ Church Cathedral, moaning behind her veil, with the ashes in an urn on her lap. A rumour persisted that Carman's ashes had previously been scattered over the Hudson River in accordance with his last wishes, and that the urn that Mrs King carried so possessively contained nothing but coal ashes. Lorne Pierce vehemently denied the story, however, insisting that it was a tasteless joke perpetrated by a waggish civil servant in Fredericton.[15]

Roberts experienced a psychological letdown in the months following Carman's death. His term as president of the CAA was over, and the buoyancy that his duties had given him was gone. Gone also were the free railway passes, which meant that his travelling would be greatly curtailed in the future. For the last two years he had been too busy to do much serious writing, but now that he had the time he seemed to lack the creative energy to begin again. Yet his finances were at such a low ebb that he needed to struggle on with his pen. Finally, to complete his depression, he was nearing his seventieth birthday.

A group of his friends, led by John W. Garvin, proposed to honour his birthday by starting a subscription of money for him, but Roberts would have none of it. He appreciated the concern that was being expressed over his welfare, but he knew that the contributions would simply be charity in disguise. As he pointed out to Garvin, he had not done any writing recently 'to justify my friends in asking the public to take any immediate & special interest in me.' Nor did he like the idea of treating his seventieth birthday as 'a definitive landmark.' Robert Norwood, who undoubtedly understood the bravado behind Roberts' refusal, sent a note to cheer him up:

And so he won't have a seventieth birthday party! Noble Charles, who will not be fooled by the illusion of years. Himself is eternal and he know it; therefore why pose as seventy when he is timeless? O incorruptible and doughty poet!

Roberts, being an old hand at graceful flattery himself, was not one to be deceived by Norwood's playful hyperbole, but the genuine affection that prompted the message must have lifted his spirits, at least temporarily.[16]

CHAPTER TWELVE

Honour
without
Profit

1930–1935

BY 1930, AS THE CANADIAN ECONOMY began
staggering under the impact of a world-wide depression, Roberts found
himself in the direst financial straits he had known since the early days of
his career. Because his meagre royalties were not enough to provide even
the bare necessities of life, he pushed himself doggedly to write magazine
fiction again. To insure an adequate income, he needed to work at the
prolific rate he had maintained during his heyday, but he no longer
possessed the stamina to follow such a rigorous schedule. Furthermore,
the public's reading preferences were changing, and most of the editors
who could afford the top prices were not interested in animal stories any
more, not even when the author was an acknowledged master of the
genre. Roberts' anxiety was further increased when Paul Reynolds, his
New York agent, rejected one of his stories with the implication that the
master might be losing his touch:

I read the cat story as soon as it came and had it read by another person. Our
judgment is against it. Like all your stories, it is well written but, as I remember, the
stories of yours in the past which I sold were about wilder animals and were more
dramatic. They did not only extremely well depict the atmosphere of the
outdoors, but there was an exciting breathless culmination to them, and this, this
story seems to lack. The cat is very vividly described and very naturally described,
but I think the story lacks in suspense and also in drama. Again, I may be wrong
and I hope for your sake I am. I send the story back herewith, but I hate sending
stories back only a little less than I hate offering them when I don't think they will
sell, especially to an old friend like yourself.[1]

It must have restored some of Roberts' self-confidence when that particular story, 'Tabitha Blue, or the Indiscretions of a Persian Cat,' was accepted by *The Windsor Magazine* and appeared in the April issue, 1933.

He was still contributing to the support of his wife and daughter in Ottawa, for May's income from her father's estate was not nearly enough for two women to live on. After Douglas married and moved into an apartment, May stayed on in the nine-room house they had shared, refusing to move to smaller and less expensive quarters. Edith, who had always been indulged and sheltered by the family because of her physical disability, had no skills or training with which she could earn a living. Her father believed (or so he professed) that she possessed a natural poetic gift which she ought to cultivate. When she was nearly fifty, he was still trying to encourage her: 'You are very late *maturing*, but I expect you to *do* things yet!' Unfortunately, she never fulfilled his hopes, either because her talents were too slight, or (as one of her Fenety aunts contended) because she was too indolent.[2] Financially, it made little difference whether or not she did any serious writing, for there was no money in poetry, and she would have remained dependent upon her parents anyway.

Roberts often said: 'Of course I don't *live* with my wife – nobody *could*, God bless her,' but his close friends knew that he was merely trying to sound debonaire. The flippant remark was really a means of diverting attention from his embarrassment over his marital difficulties. He felt that his treatment of May had been unchivalrous, even cowardly, but he simply could not face her again. On one occasion after he had been visiting Lloyd in Ottawa, he rushed from the train to Elsie Pomeroy's apartment in great agitation. Leila had tried to persuade him to see his wife – the poor woman had begged her to do it – but he could not go, even though he felt wretched to refuse. Elsie sympathized with him in his distress, but she 'thought also of the lonely woman in Ottawa' who was still waiting for the reconciliation that would never come.[3]

Despite the long estrangement, Roberts never ceased to worry over May's welfare, and his concern was deepened by a letter from Lloyd on 7 April 1930:

Thanks for the little check. Anything will be acceptable in the state of Mater's finances, but indeed, more is required at an early date. Mater is very poorly, so that I feel sorely depressed every time I see her. She has become thin and haggard during the past year and has to be assisted up steps, into the car, and is forced to forego her walks. Leila or I take every opportunity to give her drives. Douglas and Maud have her at their flat very often. I fear it is her heart...

Lloyd's misgivings about his mother's condition were entirely justified. It soon became necessary to place her in a local nursing home, but the end was not far off. She died on 12 May, and was eulogized in the *Ottawa Citizen* for 'her loyalty to her family and her tranquility of outlook.' Roberts attended the strictly private ceremony conducted by the Christian Science congregation May had joined after her sons had become converts. Although Roberts was no longer a close adherent of the Church of England, he missed the comforting familiarity of the Anglican funeral service. He was not a believer in Christian Science, and its rational principles could not alleviate his grief and self-reproach.[4]

Roberts and his wife had been married for fifty years, but for more than half that time they had lived apart. Had he been free sooner to remarry, he might have been a happier man, but by the time death made the separation final, his one great love had disappeared from his life forever. There had been several other women, charming and sympathetic companions, any one of whom might have made a suitable partner, but they, too, were long since gone. He had cultivated the image of the philanderer so successfully that few people realized the depth of his loneliness. 'For goodness sake don't marry again,' cautioned Major Gordon Casserly from England. 'You are much happier as a bachelor.'[5] It was good advice even though the major was mistaken in his reasoning. Roberts was not especially suited to single blessedness, but, at the moment, he could not support a wife financially, and for him the idea of being dependent upon a spouse's income was unthinkable.

Roberts was attracted to younger women, but he thought it was unseemly for an older man to take a young wife, as his contemporary Ernest Thomson Seton had recently done. Because Grace Gallatin, Seton's first wife, had been unwilling to subordinate her career to that of her husband, they had gradually drifted apart. Roberts learned about their eventual divorce through Will Roberts' wife, Mary, who was one of Grace's closest friends. While Grace was in hospital being treated for arthritis, Mary got wind of Seton's plan to obtain a quick Mexican divorce in order to marry his secretary. Mary marched Grace out of the hospital and rushed her to Mexico, where she obtained the decree a few days before Seton filed his application. That put the stigma of the divorce upon him and gave Grace the upper hand in the financial settlement. Mary chuckled to Roberts over her role in the affair: 'It will amuse me to tell Ernest about it some day.'[6]

Roberts never openly acknowledged that he had a favourite among his three surviving children, but, in many respects, he was closest to Lloyd. They had lived together as adults in New York City for nearly five years, not so much as father and son, but as fellow writers, and Lloyd had been admitted into that Bohemian circle which Roberts remembered with a particular fondness because it had included Carman. The memories they shared of the studios on Ninth Street and Fifth Avenue forged a special bond between them. They had been comrades in those far-off days of struggle and success in a hectic world of which Douglas and Edith had never been a part.

Lloyd always objected to the familiar remark that he was following in his father's footsteps as a writer. It was an unhappy reminder that he was still being recognized, not in his own right, but as the son of Charles G.D. Roberts. The implied comparison was odious: his father had been the leader of a generation of Canadian writers while he, the son, was a mere follower. Adding to his discomfort was the painful realization that his productivity did not begin to match that of his father at the same age. Once when he had the temerity to point out that his sire had slackened off at the age of seventy, Roberts retorted: 'Look, young fellow, when you have sixty books on your shelf written by yourself, you'll have earned the right to get after me.'[7]

Lloyd was thirty by the time his first volume, *England Over Seas*, was published in 1914. After a nine-year interval, those early poems were followed by *The Book of Roberts*, a delightful collection of essays about his remarkable family. In 1927, he published *Along the Ottawa* (poems), and his fourth and final book, *I Sing of Life* (more poems), appeared a decade later. All of them were slim volumes, but they possessed sufficient merit to convince his father that they were worthy of the Roberts literary tradition. It gave the elder Roberts great satisfaction that at least one of his children had become a fellow craftsman, and he was pleased that Lloyd's name seemed always to be linked with his in the minds of the public. Lloyd's feelings were mixed: he was proud of his father's reputation, but he resented the shadow it cast over his own achievements.[8]

The lot of the literary journeyman in Ottawa, which Roberts senior had narrowly missed, fell to Lloyd. After a short period with the *Ottawa Citizen*, he served as an editor of immigrant literature for the civil service from 1913 until 1920, when he resigned to devote his full energy to creative writing. His freelance struggle lasted several years before he gave it up to become a parliamentary correspondent for *The Christian Science Monitor*. In 1939, he accepted an appointment as a liaison and public relations officer with the Royal Canadian Mounted Police. Whereas his father had spent all but ten of his adult years as a full-time writer, Lloyd, during the prime of his life, was nearly always tied to the hack work of journalism and public relations.

Although Lloyd's career was fraught with many frustrations, the circumstances of his domestic and social life filled his father with admiration and envy. He lived outside the city in a long, grey stucco house called 'Low Eaves,' with a frontage on the Ottawa River. During the summer months the family entertained upon the wide veranda which led down to the beach and had a full view of the river and the Quebec shore on the other side. When the weather grew cold, there was always a welcoming blaze in the fieldstone fireplace of the long combined living-room and dining-room. A constant flow of visitors to Low Eaves bore testimony to the wide circle of literary, artistic, and political friends that Lloyd and Leila had built up over the years. It was the kind of company that Roberts had yearned to preside over in his own home, but with which May would never have felt at ease.

Leila Roberts was a kind-hearted woman who not only shared her husband's interests but ran his household smoothly and efficiently. In fact, her friends often wondered how she managed so successfully on Lloyd's small salary. She had endeared herself to her father-in-law by arranging his first Canadian tour, although he did not altogether appreciate her good intentions in attempting to manage his budget. Roberts was as surprised as anyone when Lloyd fell in love with a young nurse and arrived in Toronto with her in the spring of 1943. One of the most painful tasks of his life was a subsequent trip to Ottawa on Lloyd's behalf to plead with Leila to agree to a divorce. Elsie Pomeroy was furious that anyone of Lloyd's age (he was in his fifty-ninth year) would impose such a strain upon an old man like his father. Roberts defended his son with a gentle but firm reproach: 'Hush, my dear, you have no idea what Lloyd has been through.' Elsie, fuming silently, was mindful of the old adage that blood is thicker than water.

Aside from the period that Douglas Roberts spent in France, his relationship with his father is only sparsely documented. Nor is there much known about the man himself except that he fitted unobtrusively into the Department of National Revenue, and did not make much of an effort to emulate the achievements of either his father or his brother. His apprenticeship in writing at Pontlevoy had borne little results, but the fluency he had gained in the French language during that time was undoubtedly an asset to him in his civil service post. He was reputedly devoted to his wife, Maud, whom he married in 1925, and when her eyesight began failing because of the cataracts – an operation was contrary to her Christian Science convictions – she became increasingly dependent upon him. Remaining childless, they lived quietly in a rented city flat which Roberts found considerably less attractive than the rustic charm of Low Eaves. It was always Lloyd's house, never Douglas' flat, that served as the gathering place for family celebrations.

Of his three children, Edith was by far the most critical of Roberts. As a young girl in Fredericton she had been infected with her mother's bitterness over his desertion of his family, and her disapproving attitude persisted into adulthood. In later years, she became extremely conscious of his importance as a public figure and did not hesitate to warn him if she felt that he might do anything to jeopardize his image. After her mother's death, she wanted to live with him, partly to cut down expenses, but also to keep a watchful eye upon him. Roberts would have none of it, however, and threatened to cut off her monthly allowance of twenty dollars – which he increased whenever he could manage it – if she said anything more about it. Elsie Pomeroy thought that he needed his daughter to help take care of him, but, after having Edith as her guest for a couple of weeks, she changed her mind and concluded that it would only end with the father waiting upon the daughter.[9]

Edith remained in Ottawa, sharing rooms with a friend and keeping in touch with her father by means of weekly letters in which she was often more charming that she was in person. Not enough of her correspondence has survived to judge it, but Roberts was so pleased with some of her letters that he showed them to Elsie Pomeroy, who agreed that they were 'very clever & original.' On one occasion, she regaled him with an account of a talk she had given at the reading club she had joined. 'Delighted to hear of your success at the reading club with your paper on one C.G.D.R.!' he replied. 'I trust you gave the old vagabond beans.'[10]

When the ship that brought Roberts back to America docked in New York harbour in 1925, the first familiar faces he saw were those of his brother Will and sister-in-law Mary. Unfortunately, there could be only a hurried reunion in a taxi-cab before he caught the train to arrive in Toronto in time for his first recital. However, in the years that followed, he paid frequent visits to his brother's home where he enjoyed the congenial company of old acquaintances and met many new and interesting people. The cordiality of his relationship with Will (variously called Bill or Billy) and Mary may be deduced from the letters that passed between them. 'I have no words to tell you, Dear, how much I enjoyed my visit and your lovely hospitality,' Roberts wrote to Mary after one lengthy stay. 'It was even more enjoyable than ever before.'

In the same letter, replying to a bemused query from Mary, he declared:

Honestly, Dear, I am utterly at a loss to explain 'those shoes.' *No* girl friend of mine left her shoes behind her! The only feminine callers I had were known, – & *their calls were known* to you & Billy. And I can't imagine them taking off their shoes & going home in their 'sock feet.' Those shoes I am not connected with in any way, – & if I were, I should have no hesitation at all in confessing it! But alas, no!

But he did admit to running out of money in New York. 'I hope you cashed that cheque of mine in good time to meet Bill's needs!' he wrote from Toronto. 'I had it well provided for here.' He was anxious that Mary should not consider him a drain like his brother Theodore. 'Thede is a tough proposition, all right,' he conceded. 'I suppose as long as Billy will meet the drafts, he will be drawn upon.'[11]

His relationship with his youngest brother was always a trifle uneasy. 'They got into quite vehement conversations at times,' Thede's daughter, Dorothy, recalled. 'My brother Goodridge sometimes thought Uncle Charles held the floor too much, but I had no such feeling.' The two men were so unalike in temperament that it is not surprising that their attitudes frequently differed and their opinions often clashed. Charles was more optimistic, inclined to take a positive view of everything, while Thede (like his mother) was more cynical and difficult to please. Both men had lived on the brink of poverty most of their lives, despite the prodigious output from their pens. However, whereas Thede felt that he had been underrated by his contemporaries, Charles had the satisfaction of being more widely acclaimed – even though the honour was lacking in substantial profit. Because he understood the reasons for the bitterness, Charles was able to 'view the jealousy of his brother Theodore philosophically.' Outsiders, on the other hand, were often surprised – even shocked – by the vehemence of Thede's verbal attacks. 'I recall only too well,' wrote Wilfrid Eggleston of his first meeting with Theodore Roberts in 1931, 'that he deflated the popular image of his famous older brother in a diatribe which lasted several minutes.'[12]

Meanwhile, the maligned brother was doing his utmost to boost the career of Theodore Goodridge Roberts. Shortly after his own chap-book had initiated the new series by Ryerson Press, he urged Lorne Pierce to publish one by Thede. '*Very* great stuff, to my mind,' he said in recommending the latter's poems. 'And never yet in book form!' When Pierce expressed some interest in the proposal, Roberts was quick to reply:

So glad you like my brother Theodore's poems. I think that in authentic *essentially poetic* quality, he ranks with our best. It is the fact that he has not yet published in book form that has so long delayed his due recognition. But the *best* American magazines have long accepted him, – & American anthologies. I am writing him to send you more stuff. A Chap Book of his verse would be one of the choicest of the series.

That bit of lobbying led to the publication in 1926 of *The Lost Shipmate* by Theodore Goodridge Roberts, the seventh volume of Ryerson Poetry Chap-Books.

Roberts sent out many letters on his youngest brother's behalf. In the latter part of 1931, when Thede was contemplating a recital tour, Roberts wrote to several friends in Toronto, including William Grant at Upper Canada College, asking if they could give his brother 'a little show.' W.A. Deacon came to his aid with a column in the *Mail and Empire*, announcing the expected arrival of Theodore Goodrich [sic] Roberts in the city. Roberts appreciated the gesture, although he felt that the heading, 'Another Roberts Coming,' was 'not exactly a happy way of putting it.' Two years later, after a skilful campaign of letters, Roberts succeeded in gaining Thede's election to the Royal Society of Canada.[13]

When Thede moved to Toronto in 1934, he took a house that was only a few minutes walk from his brother's apartment. During the next four years, while Thede and his family remained in the city, the two men were often in each other's company. Charles was happy to have his brother nearby. Despite Thede's unpredictable moods, he was generally a stimulating companion whose 'humour was a warming attribute, although it could cut deeply on occasion.' As much as they differed in personality, they had many qualities in common. Their nephew, Goodridge MacDonald once said of his Uncle Theodore: 'Chivalry, love of the old traditions, were as inherent in his nature, as his love of the outdoors.' The same phrases could have been used to describe his Uncle Charles.[14]

Once, while Thede was living in Toronto, Will and Mary came from New York on a fortnight's visit to the two brothers. Since neither Charles nor Thede had enough room to accommodate their guests easily, Elsie

Pomeroy generously relinquished her apartment to the visitors and went to stay with her brother and his wife in North Toronto. For that final reunion of the surviving children of Canon Roberts, it was fitting that many of their days together were spent canoeing and picnicking among the Toronto Islands in a manner reminiscent of the family camping expeditions on the Saint John River.

Even after Roberts reached the age of seventy, he was in remarkable physical shape and still justified Sir Gilbert Parker's remark: 'You are the youngest and sturdiest man for your years that I have ever known.'[15] However, his anxiety over finances and family problems kept him under an emotional strain that was taking its toll of his nerves. Being faced with abject poverty was bad enough in itself. On top of that, while he was recovering from the blow of Carman's sudden death, he was enervated by the nagging remorse that followed the death of his wife. He was in no condition, mentally, for the unveiling of the Carman memorial which he attended in Fredericton on 18 October 1930. Two weeks later, to the day, he was seriously incapacitated by an attack of hypertension. Robert Norwood, who happened to visit Toronto while that illness was at its height, took his old professor back to New York for a prolonged rest. Roberts' recuperation was almost complete by the time he returned home, although there were several minor relapses later on.

Robert Norwood, the one-time student who had been privileged to use Roberts' study at Kingscroft, had been keeping a solicitous watch for several years over the welfare of his former mentor. He had come a long way since his impoverished student days when he had been 'unable to dress properly for the social functions at Windsor.' As the rector of St Bartholomew's Episcopal Church in New York City since 1925, he presided over one of the largest Protestant parishes in the western hemisphere. He had gained such a reputation as an orator that he 'preached almost invariably to a full church of more than 2,000 persons,' and was in great demand as a special speaker at various public functions. But, as Roberts said of him, 'the power of the preacher came from the spirit of the poet,' and poetry was 'his most serious concern, his ever-present enthusiasm and enduring aspiration.'[16] That side of his personality, as well as his unfailing generosity, greatly endeared him to Roberts.

In August 1931, Roberts spent the last of what had been a series of annual visits to Norwood's summer home in Hubbards. Wilfrid Eggleston, a young journalist who was touring the Maritimes with his wife and two other couples (one of which happened to be Lloyd and Leila Roberts), had a memorable glimpse of the 'bonhomie and youthful hilarity' of Roberts and Norwood during their final holiday together by the sea. Many years later, he recalled the impression that Roberts made upon him:

Charles G.D. was a revelation, especially in his own Maritime setting. Witnessing as we did, his sheer physical enjoyment of life, more like that of a lad of eighteen than a veteran of 71, the way the 'Dean of Canadian Letters' joined in all the fun, it defied probability to recall that Archibald Lampman, a Victorian, who had died thirty years earlier, had been first inspired to write poetry by reading *Orion and Other Poems*, written by this lean and athletic swimmer who was still the life of the party at every evening campfire! It was impossible to believe that as long ago as 1885 this lively spirit was editing a Toronto magazine for Goldwin Smith, or in 1895 was 'retiring' from college teaching to write for future generations of schoolboys like myself those inimitable animal stories I had first met in *Kindred of the Wild*. I am sure I gained a new conception of the potential of life in reflecting on some of these unlikely by unquestionable facts.[17]

With the same high spirits that had been so evident to Eggleston, Roberts met Lloyd in North Bay, Ontario, on 30 September 1931, for a month of adventure. As a special correspondent for *The Christian Science Monitor*, Lloyd was being sent to make a report upon the recent completion of the Hudson Bay Railway to Churchill, Manitoba, and the concurrent construction of the town. Father and son crisscrossed Manitoba, travelling northwestward on the Canadian National Railway from Winnipeg to The Pas before proceeding northeastward to Churchill via the weekly 'Muskeg Special.' They spent several days in the 'ocean port of the north,' ever mindful that they were witnesses to the opening of a new frontier.

Another anticipated highlight of the trip was to be a meeting with Grey Owl, the supposed half-breed who had recently been publishing articles on wild life in *Forest and Stream* and *Country Life*. Through chance circumstances, before he ever met Grey Owl, Lloyd had seen the contract that the former's English publishers were offering for his forthcoming book, *The Men of the Last Frontier*. Horrified to discover that the manuscript was to be bought outright without the payment of royalties, Lloyd took the law into his own hands and cabled a rejection which he signed with Grey Owl's name. This was followed by an explanatory letter to Grey Owl, who was so grateful for Lloyd's intervention and advice that he invited him to visit his camp near Cabano on the Quebec-New Brunswick border.

After their first meeting, Lloyd kept in touch with Grey Owl and was partly instrumental in obtaining a salaried position for him as a naturalist in Riding Mountain National Park in Manitoba. Shortly before Lloyd and his father began their westward trek, however, Grey Owl had arranged a transfer to Prince Albert National Park in Saskatchewan. It was in Prince Albert that the Roberts men were hoping to meet him, but he had returned to his former quarters by the time they arrived. Retracing their steps back to Manitoba, they set off to find their quarry, deep in the woods of the huge Riding Mountain Park. The final miles of the journey had to be covered on horseback over rough and difficult trails.

Grey Owl was a striking-looking man in his early forties, tall and lean, with a handsome face in spite of his rather hawk-like features. His pose as a half-breed was so convincing, in manner as well as appearance, that neither Roberts nor Lloyd ever doubted his story that he was the son of an Irish father and an Apache mother. They were as stunned as anyone to learn after his death, seven years later, that he was really an Englishman who had probably never even seen an Indian before he arrived in Canada at the age of seventeen.

As an amateur naturalist, Roberts was fascinated by Grey Owl's impressive knowledge of the woods and wild life. He quickly made friends with Jelly Roll, Grey Owl's pet beaver, who had gained fame by starring in a remarkable film, *The Beaver People*, made by the Parks Department. Unfortunately, as Roberts could see for himself, the park site assigned to Grey Owl was not suitable for Jelly Roll, her mate Rawhide, and their four beaver kittens. The lake beside the lodge was so shallow that it had shrunk to a level of slimy stagnation during the summer drought. Grey Owl's concern for the beaver had prompted his upcoming transfer to Saskatchewan, although his pretty Iroquois companion, Anahareo, was saddened at the thought of leaving the cosy lodge, which she described as 'a castle' compared to the tents and shacks to which they had been accustomed. To Roberts, however, it was 'very rough and ready accommodation' which took him back to the cherished camping jaunts of his youth.[18]

It was the end of October when Roberts returned to Toronto to settle down for the winter. By that time, he was flat broke even though he had been free-loading upon Norwood's hospitality in the Maritimes and upon Lloyd's expense account during the trip to the West. The following summer, when Norwood again issued his customary invitation, Roberts was still too strapped financially to afford the train fare. Being too proud to admit the real reason for not going, he pretended to be swamped with engagements and assignments. In late September 1932, he received the shocking news that Norwood had died suddenly of a cerebral hemorrhage.

The autumn of 1931 had seen the first appearance in print of his lengthy free verse narrative, 'The Iceberg.' The poem had been produced after a long period of gestation. The introduction

> I was spawned from the glacier
> A thousand miles due north
> Beyond Cape Chidley

had been written as early as January 1929. Two years passed – with his intervening breakdown – before he added any further lines; but, on a wall map above his desk, he often traced the route the iceberg would follow. At the beginning of February 1931, when he began regaining his health, he finished the first two stanzas of the poem, but at first he doubted whether he would ever find the energy to complete it. As the work progressed, however, he felt rejuvenated by the stimulus of composition, and he grew steadily stronger. He persisted so tirelessly that by the middle of March he was able to announce to Rufus Hathaway: 'I have just written a poem of 260 lines.'

He was pleased with his accomplishment for two reasons: first, because he had proved that he was still capable of the physical and mental labour of creation; and, second, because (as he wrote to Lloyd) he thought it was the best thing he had done since *Ave*. 'I'm so glad you like my "Iceberg",' he told Lorne Pierce. 'I do feel that the old quality is in it.' He agreed to read the poem at the closing banquet of the Canadian Author's Association, which held its annual convention in Toronto during the latter part of June. 'It is an effective poem to read, so I have no fear of its reception,' he wrote to the Association's secretary. Sir Robert Falconer, president of the University of Toronto (and a fellow Maritimer) paid him the honour of introducing the poem in the inaugural issue of the university *Quarterly* (October 1931). It was not the policy of the new periodical to publish fiction or poetry – 'a rule,' declared Sir Robert, 'which it is our pleasure to ignore in the case of *The Iceberg*.'[19]

It is obvious to anyone familiar with Roberts' work that the iceberg narrative follows one of the patterns that he had developed in his animal stories: the chronicle of events in the lifespan of a typical individual of a species. Indeed, this autobiography of an iceberg is almost an animal story in free verse. As Roberts portrays it, the iceberg is hardly a lifeless object, especially since it is the narrator and uses the pronoun 'I' throughout. In this respect the poem differs from his stories, for none of his animal characters speak. The supposedly inanimate iceberg, on the other hand, not only tells its life story, but does so after it has melted 'in the all-solvent sea' – speaking from the dead, as it were, and displays withal an amazing knowledge of geography, biology, and navigation. The resulting poem could have been absurd, but we are willing to suspend disbelief because the action rings true and the detail is convincing.

Ever since Roberts' trouble with his nerves, his friends in Toronto had been deeply concerned about his welfare. They knew that his chief worries were caused by his desperate financial circumstances. Elsie Pomeroy and Nat Benson belonged to a small but close circle of admirers from whom he could not hide the nature of his personal problems. In their individual ways, they did all they could to help him. There was another group, people such as Lorne Pierce, W.A. (Bill) Deacon, and Pelham Edgar, who were intimate enough to be well aware of his difficulties. This second company of friends were mostly men of considerable influence, and they decided that something significant had to be done to ease the burdens of the acknowledged 'Dean of Canadian Literature.'

As early as 26 January 1931, Lorne Pierce appealed on Roberts' behalf to the prime minister, R.B. Bennett, for 'a small honorarium, say $100 a month,' from the Canadian government. He stated the case eloquently:

It is tragic that such a man, three score and ten, the founder of the Canadian School of writers, Dean of his craft, should come to want. Outrun in the economic struggle, he is also bewildered by the new cries, and, at his age, unable as he is unwilling to write that sort of pablum which the public desires. It is useless, I suppose, to charge such men with being poor managers and bad accountants. Bankers, even Editors, might find themselves criticized for being no poets at all!

Bennett, a former Maritimer, was personally acquainted with Roberts and admired his literary work, but he did not approve in principle of handouts from the public treasury. He gave Pierce the noncommittal answer that he 'was looking into the whole question.'[20]

Meanwhile, Pelham Edgar, of the English Department at Victoria College was spearheading a movement to establish a Canadian Writers' Fund of which Roberts was to be the first beneficiary. The latter was hopeful of the results, although (as is apparent from a letter to Lloyd, written 29 March 1931) he could not shake the uncomfortable feeling that he would be accepting charity:

Yes, these committees of the 'Fund' are getting to work from ocean to ocean, and I imagine something fairly substantial will come of it, in course of time. Of course, what I would like best would be a senatorship, if only that were possible; because that would be a real 'job,' where I could do *real service* & *give full value* for money received. Better value, I believe, than most senators can give! But I think that is too much to hope. The men in power are apt to think of me as a 'mere' poet, not knowing that I am a very practical economist & publicist.

If long experience in juggling credit is enough to make a man a 'practical economist,' then Roberts was indeed qualified.

Under Edgar's direction, the Canadian Writers' Foundation Fund held a promotion rally at Toronto's Convocation Hall in October 1931. Sir Robert Falconer presided over the meeting, which was addressed by several distinguished guests, including Prime Minister Bennett. Typical of the sentiments expressed were the remarks of Dr H.J. Cody (soon to be president of the University of Toronto) who said: 'It is a well founded hope that in the future those men of letters who are not men of money will no longer be haunted to death.' In spite of the Foundation's good intentions, however, the spectre of poverty did not immediately disappear for Roberts. The federal government arranged for him to receive $2,500 annually, but bureaucratic red tape delayed the first payment for another three years.

Although the money was intended for Roberts, his name was discreetly not mentioned when the amount was finally passed by the Supplementary Estimates. That led to the first cheque being made out to the Canadian Authors' Association and sent to Winnipeg, addressed to Charles W. Gordon (Ralph Connor), the president, who had no idea what it was for. It was then passed on from one person to another in a comedy of errors while Roberts tried desperately to track it down. 'My tongue is hanging out!!' he wrote to Howard Angus Kennedy, secretary of the CAA. The cheque was two months in the mails before it reached the rightful recipient. Roberts' letter of appreciation to Bennett was dated 6 November 1934:

I have no words to express my gratitude to you for this pension which you have arranged for me through Professor Edgar, – with Mr King's hearty endorsement, as Professor Edgar doubtless informed you at the time. It has lifted a crushing blow from my old shoulders, and given me new life.[21]

To Pelham Edgar, Roberts declared on one occasion: 'I can't begin to thank you for all you have done for me!' Even while he thanked Bennett most profusely for the pension, he knew that it would never have materialized without Edgar's determined efforts. But aside from his indebtedness to his younger friend (born 1871), he liked and admired him as a person. They enjoyed each other's company because they shared many of the same interests (in wine and women as well as song), although, of the two men, Edgar appeared outwardly to be far more reserved and austere in temperament. A casual acquaintance once referred to Professor Edgar as 'a great teacher and fosterer of talent disguised under a rather pompous manner,' but Roberts saw him in a different light. 'He plays a good game of golf – and poker –' he wrote to a friend in the West, 'and is one of the boys.' Two of the 'boys' with whom he was frequently found were E.J. Pratt, the fun-loving Newfoundland poet, and Hugh Eayrs, the nimblewitted head of Macmillan of Canada. Roberts rarely made a fourth when they played golf, although he sometimes joined them in the clubhouse, but when it came to poker he was always one of the first persons at the table.[22]

Roberts' pension did not begin in time to cover his expenses when he accompanied a group from the Canadian Authors' Association on a 'literary tour' of Britain in the summer of 1933. At first the trip had seemed an impossible dream, even at the modest cost of $310, which covered all the travelling expenses, accommodations, and meals. He was flattered when H.A. Kennedy, the tour organizer pointed out that his presence would add distinction to the party, but he could not be tempted because his finances were 'completely on the rocks.' Then, to his great surprise, he received word from Kennedy that someone, who wished to remain anonymous, had paid his fare for him. He immediately wrote a joyful letter of acceptance, expressing his gratitude to Kennedy '& the generous unknown one, & the Gods who look after poets.' He confided to Edith: 'I expect the sea-voyage will do me a lot of good – but *between ourselves* it is a bit humiliating not being able to pay my own way.'[23]

The tour had been given much advance publicity, and arrangements had been made for many official receptions and many opportunities to meet some of Britain's best-known writers. More than fifty people were in the group that left on board the *Empress of Britain* on 1 July; but, of that number, only the names of Charles G.D. Roberts and 'Ralph Connor' (the newly-elected CAA national president) were likely to be recognized outside Canada. Over half the delegation came from Ontario, but no one overseas had ever heard of such local scribblers as Dr E.A. Hardy, Mrs M.M. Howard, Marial Jenkins, and Elsie Pomeroy.

Landing at Southampton on 7 July, the Canadian pilgrims took two days visiting the literary and historic shrines en route to London. Hardy's widow gave a reception in their honour, and they were met by the mayors of Salisbury and Winchester. For six days in London and vicinity they visited all the important sites, had tea with Lady Pentland (daughter of former Governor-General Lord Aberdeen), lunched at Claridge's with the Royal Society of Literature, and had a guided tour of Number 10 Downing Street conducted by Prime Minister Ramsay Macdonald himself. During the following week, they had a triumphal progress from Stratford-on-Avon to the Lake District to Edinburgh and the Trossachs. With the exception of Roberts, who returned to London, the travelling authors, sated and happy, sailed for home from Greenock on 22 July.

Of all the writers the Canadians met, only George Bernard Shaw was not bound by the conventional restraints of good manners. He told the visitors quite frankly: 'Of course no one believes there is a Canadian literature!' The scene was the Forum Club dinner and reception at the Victorian mansion which housed the club's headquarters in London. About 100 British literary celebrities attended the function, and there was a rumour that Shaw might appear later. Around 10:45, after the inevitable speeches had ended and the meeting was breaking up, an excited whisper sent the company scrambling back to their seats: 'Shaw has come!'

Having just arrived from a dinner party, the controversial gentleman entered the room smiling, although Helen Creighton of Halifax swore that she heard him mutter: 'Disgraceful hour to be going anywhere.' He was ushered to the platform where he pirouetted playfully for his audience. 'Ladies and gentlemen, you have all come to see me this evening,' he began in his habitually strident voice. 'Well, here I am; take a good look.' There was a mischievous twinkle in his eye, and his face 'was a marvel of continuous changes' as he set out to be deliberately provocative.

'I do not see any difference between Canadians and Americans!' was his opening salvo. He probably spoke for the majority of Britishers, if the truth be told, but he outraged the nationalistic feelings of the Canadian Authors' Association, who protested against his remarks in a loud chorus. 'I know nothing about Canada,' he confessed, 'never having been there,' but the Canadians in the audience did not find that admission very flattering. It was even worse when he told them that, in particular, he knew nothing about Canadian literature. Moreover, he declared bluntly, nobody in England ever bothered to read a Canadian book. He spoke in hyperbole, but his point was more accurate than his audience was ready to acknowledge. With all the red carpet treatment they had received, the visiting authors had been deluded into thinking that their hosts really took them as seriously as they took themselves.

When Shaw sat down, the Forum Club's chairwoman looked from Ralph Connor to Charles G.D. Roberts for a rebuttal, but they both declined. H.A. Kennedy stepped into the breach, saying that the busy schedule had left him with no brains, 'And I am sure that Mr Shaw will agree with me that I have no brains left when I say that I enjoyed his speech.' Kennedy was roundly applauded for giving the *enfant terrible* his come-uppance. The whole episode lasted less than fifteen minutes, but the impact was destined to reverberate long after the other events were forgotten. It would scarcely be an exaggeration to say that the tour is still remembered solely as the occasion for Shaw's remarks.[24]

Elsie Pomeroy omitted any mention of Shaw when she wrote a detailed account of Roberts' participation in the tour. The contention that Canadian writers were ignored in Britain was not in accordance with her conviction that her hero was internationally famous. After all, even though the sales had been negligible, there had been British editions of five of his volumes of poetry. And his animal stories had found a dedicated (if limited) following among the British public. In fact, he had taken advantage of the tour to arrange in person with J.M. Dent & Sons, London, for the publication of his latest collection, *Eyes of the Wilderness*. He had also negotiated with Dent to draw upon his last three prose volumes (including *Eyes of the Wilderness*) for a selection that would appear three years later as *Further Animal Stories* in the King's Treasury series.

Roberts remained in London for six weeks, living in the same rented flat at 10 Buckingham Street that he had occupied briefly during the war. Combining business with pleasure, he divided his time among his publishers, his literary agents (Hughes Massie & Co.), and his former cronies whom he had not seen for more than eight years. A few familiar faces were missing – Sir Gilbert Parker, for example, had died the previous September – but the old friends who were left welcomed him warmly. He was childishly pleased and flattered to be remembered by the boathouse attendants at Richmond, who had not forgotten his preference for a Fredericton Chestnut canoe. 'Dear old unchanging England!' he commented in a letter to Elsie Pomeroy. Yet, before he left for home on 15 September, he wrote to H.A. Kennedy that as much as he loved England, it was 'good to be getting back to Canada.' On the homeward voyage, he was fortified against the Atlantic winds by a gift of long underwear that Elsie Pomeroy had foreseen he would need in the autumn.[25]

Eyes of the Wilderness was already off the press by the time Roberts arrived home at the beginning of October. It appeared simultaneously in Britain, the United States, and Canada, and received brief but favourable notices from several important British and American critics, although *The Times* (London) got his middle initials wrong. In Canada, it was widely reviewed – in many instances by Roberts' personal friends, who praised it in very flattering terms. Nat Benson, whose effusions in *Saturday Night* must have been downright embarrassing, undertook to redress the recent Shavian insult by declaring that Roberts was a good example of a septuagenarian whose faculties 'unlike Mr Bernard Shaw's have not been affected by the senescence of the seventies.'

W.A. Deacon, whose mother had read Roberts' animal stories to him on Sunday afternoons when he was a child, admitted quite frankly that he was unable to be objective:

Meanwhile quite a bit has gone on as a result of those first years of foxes and wolves and other kindred of the wild. I had met, also for the first time, the still rarer animal known as the Canadian author. Soon, at the appropriate age, I was to lose myself in Roberts the poet, and through him to be led to Lampman, Scott and Carman. An interest in native literature was to develop, which eventually led to this chair and this typewriter. Roberts has become not only a personal friend, but that courageous pioneer who showed the way to an independent national literature. I feel towards him a personal allegiance which precludes sour remarks.

Roberts was touched by 'the warm personal note' of Deacon's introductory paragraphs, and hailed the comments that followed 'as a model of what a review ought to be, – comprehensive, illuminating, & exquisitely understanding.'

Two notable detractors were the critics for the Winnipeg *Free Press* and *The Canadian Forum*. Roberts was especially irritated by the tone of the former's review. When Gerald Wade sent him a clipping of the notice, he replied rather coldly: 'It is hardly pleasant to say that I "like to think of" myself "first and foremost as a poet" or to say that I "claim" to be "the modern reviver" of this kind of story.' H.K. Gordon, in *The Canadian Forum*, conceded that the stories were 'competent' and would probably attract a new set of readers. 'But those who knew the old Roberts,' he advised, 'had better leave them alone.' He was saying that the old magic was gone, but Roberts had the satisfaction of knowing that Mr Gordon had been contradicted by a declaration in *The New York Times*: 'The hand of Charles G.D. Roberts, the veteran Canadian naturalist and writer on life in the wilds, has not lost its cunning.'[26]

Late in 1934, all of Roberts' new poetry of the last seven years was issued by Ryerson Press as *The Iceberg and Other Poems*. Around the same time, Ryerson also brought out *The Leather Bottle*, the selected poems of Theodore Goodridge Roberts. The two books were not in competition on the market, however, since *The Iceberg and Other Poems* was printed in a special deluxe edition of which only 100 copies were on sale to the general public. Because of its limited availability, *The Iceberg* was not reviewed on the book page of most daily and weekly newspapers. Its most important notice was written by Pelham Edgar for *Saturday Night*. Calling the title poem 'an event in our literary history,' Edgar also commended Roberts' lyrics for combining 'the freshness of youth with the tender reflectiveness of age that remembers past delights.' And everywhere throughout the book he found 'the precision and control of the classically trained mind and the sure touch of the accomplished artist.' Roberts was deeply appreciative of the review, for he knew that Edgar had too much critical integrity to be unduly influenced by friendship. 'It warmed the cockles of my heart,' Roberts told him. 'It is so strong & generous & inclusive, & says *just* what I would want you to say – and feel!'[27]

The Iceberg and Other Poems was not the only book that Roberts saw through the press in 1934. As general editor of the *Canadian Who Was Who*, a project of the Trans-Canada Press, he was responsible for Volume I, which appeared in September. He had not returned willingly to the drudgery and meagre remuneration of an editorial job, but he was desperately in need of more cash than he could earn from his sales and royalties. He still gave an occasional recital or lecture; but, since he had already spoken – sometimes more than once – in most of the easily accessible centres, he could not count upon regular engagements without embarking upon a tour. In spite of the remarkable stamina he possessed for a man of his age, he did not want to face the rigours of another series of one-night stands. He was ready to settle for the hack work of editing, as long as it kept him in Toronto.

Early in February 1933, a form letter bearing Roberts' signature had been sent by Trans-Canada Press to various persons whose names had 'been suggested to the Editors' as 'desirable' contributors to a proposed encyclopedia of Canadian biography. Most of the recipients were personal acquaintances of Roberts, including college professors and other non-professional writers, whose literary competence he felt he could trust. Only people who had died in the twentieth century were to be the subjects of the first volume.[28]

All of the preliminary work in the preparation of the biographical dictionary was done by Arthur Tunnell, the managing editor of Trans-Canada Press. It was Tunnell who contacted relatives and / or intimates of the subjects, and put together as much biographical and bibliographical material as possible for the convenience of the contributors. Since the latter were being paid only two dollars per sketch, they could hardly be expected to do all of the necessary research as well as the writing. In spite of the inadequate remuneration, most of the people who were invited to contribute agreed to do so quite willingly. Some of them – such as Elsie Pomeroy, who wrote four of the pieces – seemed to feel that the honour of being associated with the volume was enough payment in itself.

It was Roberts who made all the important decisions about the contents of the dictionary. He selected the contributor-writers, approved all of the manuscripts, and made all the final revisions. It was he, also, who badgered, cajoled, and flattered all of the temperamental and delinquent contributors. The work was exhausting; and, just as the manuscripts were coming in, Tunnell contracted scarlet fever and was off work for a month. Roberts' friends feared that he was working too hard, and he admitted to Pelham Edgar: 'I have been slogging *past* the limit of my strength.' On 23 June 1934, he wrote wearily to Lorne Pierce: 'At last, at last, I have finished this first vol of *Who Was Who*, & I'm just about all in.' Even before Volume I was off the press, however, work had begun on its sequel.[29]

Assisting with the second volume was Joan Montgomery, Roberts' latest protégé, for whom he had tried in vain to secure a position at Ryerson Press. On 28 April 1934, he had written to Lorne Pierce:

Will you, at your earliest convenience, grant an interview to a *very* well-equipped and intellectual girl, – & extremely charming girl, – who is most anxious to form a connection with a publishing house with a view to working her way up in it. (She does not write herself!) She, Miss Montgomery, is a graduate of the University of Toronto (B.A. 32), in English, Italian, Spanish, History & Economics, and has since passed the Librarians' course. She is a specialist in Spanish, having taken two years of it in Chicago & then five years of it here under Buchanan. She is a friend & protégé of mine & I have a very high opinion of her abilities. If you could find a place for her *to begin* on the Ryerson Press, I would trust her to make her way.

It was not the first time that Pierce had been approached to assist one of Roberts' female acquaintances – including several aspiring writers looking for a publisher – and, as always, he gave the request his serious consideration. He congratulated Roberts for having 'the art of finding beauty and brains in one body,' and promised to do his 'level best' for Miss

Montgomery. Unfortunately, there were no openings in the company just then. In the end, Roberts used his influence at Trans-Canada Press to give her a research assignment which held no prospects for advancement, but would have an unforeseen impact upon the course of her life.[30]

Roberts and Joan Montgomery had first met at a tea party given by the latter's college chum, Muriel Miller, whose M.A. thesis on Bliss Carman had been written in consultation with Roberts. At that time Joan had completed her library science course, and was living in Toronto with her recently widowed mother while she searched in vain for a job that suited her qualifications. Although born in Scotland, she had spent her early childhood in India where her father, the son of a British army officer and a high-caste Indian lady, served in the British Engineering Department. By the time Joan was in high school, Mr Montgomery's work had taken him to Chicago. After beginning at the University of Chicago, she transferred to the University of Toronto because her parents preferred to have her educated in the British tradition.

Joan was a slender girl with a Mona Lisa face that may have been inherited from her Indian grandmother. Aside from her distinctive appearance, Roberts was attracted by her winning manner and the intellectual quality of her mind. She had been devoted to her scholarly, cultured father; and when Roberts came into her life, so soon after the bereavement, she appears to have transferred much of her father-worship to him. Working together as closely as they did on the biographical dictionary, they developed a partner-like relationship that came to have special significance for both of them. With their growing dependence upon each other, and the deepening of their mutual affection, the difference in their ages grew less and less important.

It was while Roberts was helping Joan Montgomery out of her financial difficulties that his own circumstances were at their 'very worst.' He was 'living largely on porridge,' he confessed to Nat Benson, '& borrowing a dollar or two on all sides.' Meanwhile, the prime minister, who had revived the practice of conferring titles, abolished in 1919, was debating whether a title, rather than a pension, might be a more appropriate award for Roberts. Pelham Edgar told Bennett bluntly that the need for cash was far greater than the need for honours. However, after the pension was granted, rumours persisted that a knighthood might also be bestowed upon the veteran writer. The official word came to Roberts from Bennett on 18 May 1935: 'it will give me very great pleasure if you would permit me to recommend to the King that you receive the honour of Knighthood.'[31]

The public announcement of the honour was made on 3 June, and Roberts was overwhelmed by the 'general favour' with which it was immediately greeted. 'All this acclaim makes me feel rather humble,' he replied to one of the many congratulatory letters. 'I know I am no better poet than Duncan Campbell Scott, – nor as good a one as Carman, – but I tell myself that no one of my colleagues has written so with the definite purpose of developing a national consciousness in Canada.' Although Pelham Edgar had been right in saying that Roberts needed money more than he needed a title, the knighthood had a value that could not be measured. In a grateful letter to Bennett, he expressed its importance to him: 'It puts the crown on my life's work.'[32]

The pension had lifted the burden of debt and worry under which Roberts had been staggering, but he still had difficulty in making ends meet. He could not even afford to attend the Investiture of the King's Honours which Lord Bessborough held at Government House on 6 September, but he was sent his Letters Patent of Knighthood in the mail the following day. Three weeks later, he received a reminder from the Governor-General's secretary that he had not remitted the necessary payment of £30 for the aforesaid Letters Patent. He was highly embarrassed that his friends had to come to his aid to pay the debt and clear the blot from his escutcheon. Obviously, he was not a prophet without honour in his own country, but – had he been addicted to puns – he might have reflected that he had honour without much profit.

CHAPTER THIRTEEN

The Final Years

1936–1943

CHARLES G.D. ROBERTS had been a personage in Canadian literary and social circles ever since his return from England in 1925. If the magic of his name had worn off somewhat through familiarity during the ensuing decade, the added fillip of a title gave it new lustre. When the honour was conferred upon him, there was no way of knowing that his knighthood would be among the last to be created in Canada. A few weeks after the investiture, Bennett's Conservatives suffered a crushing defeat at the polls; and the Liberal government under Mackenzie King, responding to a heightened spirit of nationalism, renewed the ban on English titles for Canadian citizens. However, although there was a growing tendency to reject any lingering vestiges of colonialism, many Canadians were still impressed by titles. As time took its toll upon the remaining recipients, the honour took on an added distinction because of its increasing rarity. 'Sir Charles' had an air that lent prestige to any group with which Roberts was associated.

No Canadian literary gathering of any pretensions was complete unless Roberts attended. He was, for example, a natural choice to officiate at the opening of the first Book Fair, which was held in Toronto by the Association of Canadian Bookmen in 1936. The Canadian Authors' Association was proud to bear his name as honorary president on its masthead, and organizers of the annual CAA conventions always arranged the programs to accommodate any contributions he might be prevailed upon to make. It was left to him as to what form his participation would take; but, if nothing else, he could usually be counted upon to read several of his most recent poems. The Toronto branch of the CAA organized a huge party for him on the occasion of his eightieth birthday. There was standing room only at the celebration, but, as Dorothy C. Herriman reported reverentially in *The Canadian Author and Bookman*, it was not necessary 'to turn a single worshipper from the presence.'[1] Around the same time, the Canadian Literature Club instituted a 'Roberts' Night,' which was held annually to mark his birthday until many years after his death.

While Madge Macbeth of Ottawa was national president of the CAA, from 1939 to 1942, Roberts got caught in the cross-fire of a savage feud between the Ottawa and Toronto branches. There was an element in each group that was jealous of the control that the other had over the membership, and the bitterness of the animosity threatened to wreck the Association. Roberts had first met Mrs Macbeth at Low Eaves, where she was often a guest. She had a vibrant personality which he found attractive. When the battle lines were drawn between the branches, however, he came to regard her as his enemy, along with Eric Gaskell, a member of her executive. He came close to being a casualty of the fighting, as he explained to Lorne Pierce after the 1941 convention in Vancouver and Victoria:

Madge & Eric had been getting things all cut & dried, & carrying on some very 'slick' intrigue, so that the original nominating committee, picked by her, ousted me from the Hon. Presidency! Topped over from my pedestal!! And then a lot more 'politics'! But this particular item was changed, *and how*, when it came to the general meeting, – which was pretty tumultuous! I was put back, – & after refusing, I had to accept. Murray Gibbon led the attack to have me reinstated, & there was some pretty violent language used. A.M. Stephen told the Committee it was the most disgraceful case of barefaced 'engineering' he had ever seen.[2]

During the following winter, Roberts swung into action by recruiting a group of 'responsible men' in the membership to defeat 'the Gaskell faction,' as he called it. He was in a mood to agree with Murray Gibbon, who bluntly declared: 'to hell with women presidents.' He objected strongly to the supposed Macbeth / Gaskell conspiracy to fix the next election of officers in order to 'put in my very dear little friend K. Strange as *President*, who, with all her charm, is not the stuff for President, at least not yet!' After further intrigue on both sides, much of it petty and unworthy of the participants, the national presidency finally went to

Watson Kirkconnell, a professor at McMaster University, who modestly described himself as a 'tame dray horse who would not run away with the milk-wagon.' Under Kirkconnell's competent leadership, most of the explosive issues were diplomatically defused, and Roberts retained his position and influence in the Association.[3]

Never one to stand unduly on ceremony, Roberts was noted, nevertheless, for his unfailing ability to meet any situation with the dignity required. He was conscious of his position as the unofficial dean of Canadian Literature and managed to act the part without pomposity. If he felt he was being given less than his due, however, he was likely to counter with a gentle but firm rebuke. When Charles Clay, national secretary of the CAA, used an injudicious phrase in asking Roberts for some autobiographical material to use in a reference work being prepared by the Wartime Information Board, the 'dean' of Canadian literature was mildly indignant. 'You say it has been suggested that my name "should be included",' he replied. 'Would it not be rather singular if my name were *not* included?'

In fairness, it must be stressed that sharp remarks were not characteristic of Roberts. 'If Charles was one thing, he was gracious,' his daughter-in-law Judy Roberts has said of him. 'He was probably the most gracious man I ever met.' His courtly manner, so befitting a knight, came as naturally as breathing, but he was also noted for his impish sense of humour – which, among his cronies, sometimes took a ribald turn. 'You are "a verray parfit gentil knight",' his friend E.K. Broadus had said in congratulating him upon his title, 'but if you think that a royal tag can dispel the picture of your blessed self, clad in scandalous purple pyjamas, reciting the unprinted and unprintable scurrilities of Bliss Carman, you have another think coming.'

Both Carman and Roberts had written verse for 'private circulation only.' Some of Roberts' pieces, such as his 'Colour Toasts,' were innocuous enough that he often recited them for the amusement of a mixed company. There were others, such as this revision of an old army song, that he reserved for 'the boys':

> There was a young lady of Kew
> Who said to the Curate, 'You'll do!
>   But I must say the Vicar
>   Is quicker and slicker
> And longer and thicker than you.'[4]

Unlike Lorne Pierce, who was always offended by Roberts' off-colour verse, E.K. Broadus took a tolerant view of the ribaldry: it was further proof that there was nothing stuffy about the new knight.

There was a group of young intellectuals, however, who had long regarded Roberts as the symbol of stuffiness. The year of his return to Canada had seen the appearance of *The McGill Fortnightly Review*, a student-run journal of literature, the arts, and campus affairs, edited chiefly by two graduate students, A.J.M. Smith and Frank R. Scott. Those aspiring young poets and the small but brilliant coterie they soon attracted (young men such as Leon Edel, A.M. Klein, and Leo Kennedy) did not share the general veneration of the 'dean' of Canadian literature. For the next two years in the *Review*, and afterwards in the short-lived *Canadian Mercury*, they campaigned against the kind of poetic tradition for which they held Roberts' generation responsible – the Maple Leaf brand of Victorianism that had dominated Canadian literature much too long.

As most of this Montreal group later admitted, they knew next to nothing about the so-called Confederation poets at the time (although Smith expressed an admiration for Duncan Campbell Scott's work as early as 1928). Their main acquaintance with Canadian poetry, apart from contemporary periodicals, seems to have been some bad anthologies, particularly John W. Garvin's *Canadian Poets* (1916; revised 1926). Smith confessed in 1963 that once he became an anthologist himself he 'found that Lampman, Roberts, and Carman had written some very fine poetry.' But in the 1920s and 1930s, those radical young intellectuals thought of Roberts, who had written most of his poetry before they were born, as nothing more than a literary dinosaur. Patricia Morley has written of their reaction:

One look at a contemporary photograph of Charles G.D. Roberts, then in his mid-sixties, goes far to explain their opposition to the poetic ideals he embodied. Picture a dark, three-piece suit, a monocle complete with black ribbon, a haughty expression, and an establishment air. Any young intellectual would hate his guts on sight.

Of course, the camera cannot always be trusted. No one who knew Roberts ever described him as being 'haughty.' In repose, his face was sometimes misleadingly severe, especially in his photographs, and his expression might have been mistaken for arrogance by anyone already disposed against him.

The Montreal group vehemently rejected conventional poetic diction and romanticism, and strongly advocated imagism and free verse. 'Canadian themes are improved by modern treatment,' A.J.M. Smith declared in *The Canadian Forum*, a journal which from the late 1920s became a vehicle for launching attacks against the Maple Leaf school of poetry. The models for Canadian modernism were to be found in the United States and Britain, where the imagist movement spearheaded by Ezra Pound had prepared the way for the poetry of T.S. Eliot and the later Yeats. Not only the Montreal group but a scattering of poets, writing independently of each other in various parts of Canada, were profoundly influenced by the new techniques from abroad. Unfortunately, the literary establishment which ran the CAA, with Roberts as the honorary president, was generally antagonistic to change.

Roberts himself was not particularly hostile to the new experiments in poetry. He was, in fact, far more tolerant of the Canadian modernists than they were of him. His essay 'A Note on Modernism' (1931) stressed that reaction to long-established forms is both inevitable and desirable. Five years later, when he wrote the 'Prefatory Note' to his *Selected Poems*, he was still of the same mind:

It seems to me it is all a matter of the succeeding cycles of reaction. Reaction is life. The more healthy and vigorous the reaction, the more inevitably does it froth up into excess. The excess dies away of its own violence. But the freshness of thought or of technique that supplied the urge to the reaction remains and is clarified, ultimately to be worked into the tissue of permanent art.[5]

The foregoing statements represent his public pronouncements. In his private correspondence he wrote more frankly about his mixed feelings:

March 11th, 1937 (to Harrison Smith Morris): Tell me, how do you feel about these extreme modernists in Verse? How do you like Spender? Auden? And can you always understand T.S. Eliot? Or put up with Ezra Pound?

October 18, 1938 (to John Huston Finley): ... I love T.S. Eliot's 'Ash Wednesday,' even though I cannot profess to understand it. It has the compelling power of *incantation*.

December 14, 1938 (to Lorne Pierce): T.S. Eliot, a great poet who achieved *notoriety* with his 'Wastelands' [sic], really handled the modernists, as such, in his wonderful poem 'The Hollow Men,' which has everything that a great poem ought to have. And his 'Ash Wednesday,' though wilfully obscure in spots, has a most thrilling power of incantation. Spender & Day Lewis have, to my mind, the stuff in them, and will do fine things when they realize that propaganda is not poetry.

March 24, 1940 (to Walter McRaye): I know Ezra Pound personally, – & I thoroughly dislike him as a man, & still more thoroughly as a poet. ... Nowadays people are always looking for something violently new in verse, & indeed in all art, & when they get it, how they like to pretend they like it!
Have you seen photos of Epstein's new Masterpiece – 'Adam'? To me it seems like the abortion of a sick hippopotamus who had been raped by a gorilla. (Gorillas please pardon!)

February 1, 1941 (to Ralph Gustafson): My criticism [of your poetry], if any, would be that occasionally in your aim to be swift and concise (stripped for the race!) you permit yourself the modernistic sin of obscurity. *My* passion is for *lucidity* – when possible. Yet sometimes I am impassioned by such a wonderful poem as Eliot's 'The Hollow Men,' – which is an incantation.[6]

Dorothy Livesay was another home-grown poet who had been influenced by contemporary movements outside Canada. Unlike the Montreal group, however, she had not repudiated Roberts, and in an 'Open Letter' (*Canadian Bookman*, April 1939) she praised him for having kept abreast of the times. 'Who amongst us,' she asked, 'could have written your last poem: "Peace with Dishonour"?' Her letter was a plea for Roberts to exercise his influence in order that Canadian poetry might be required to measure up to world standards. In her view, the existing poetry groups were nothing more than 'mutual admiration societies,' and the Canadian critics were merely 'tripping bridegrooms.' She felt that a special strategy was needed to improve the performance of the country's poets:

We need a group of people whose first concern is poetry itself, not poets. Who would be content to study poetry as it is being sung all over the world, and who would not insist that their own efforts be regarded. From such a group could come critics, Canadian critics, who would have the necessary background and culture to be objective when they turned to the writing of their own people.

Before the Livesay letter appeared in print, it fell into the hands of Lorne Pierce, whose Ryerson Press published the *Canadian Bookman*. Pierce showed it at once to Roberts for his opinion. 'The gist of it is good,' was Roberts' reaction, 'but the scolding tone of it does not seem to me quite worthy of Dorothy Livesay.' He felt that her argument was damaged by intemperance: 'It makes an urgent plea for competent criticism, but the demand is hardly couched in terms of competent criticism!' Neverthe-less, he urged Pierce to allow the letter to be printed. The gesture was typical of his magnanimity towards the younger pack of poets whether or not they were snipping at his heels.[7]

The Selected Poems of Sir Charles G.D. Roberts (prepared by the poet himself) was published in 1936 by Ryerson Press. Its contents were chosen from his nine books of verse from *Orion and Other Poems* (1880) to *The Iceberg and Other Poems* (1934). The latter volume, because its only previous appearance had been in a limited deluxe edition, was reprinted in its entirety. In his 'Prefatory Note' Roberts contended that the whole range of his work would indicate that he had 'always been alive to the moment, keenly aware of the contemporary currents of thought, action and emotion.' Change was not necessarily growth, he admitted, but he felt that such 'divergence' should 'be taken into account in any serious evaluation ... which the critics may find it worth while to make.'[8] Some critics have complained, however, that since he grouped the poems together, either according to their form or their subject-matter, it is almost impossible to trace the development of his work.

Many of Roberts' friends, men such as W.A. Deacon, H.A. Kennedy, and G.H. Clarke, acknowledged *Selected Poems* with glowing reviews that paid warm personal tributes to the poet. In contrast, Burns Martin in the *Dalhousie Review* wrote only a brief notice of the book, concluding: 'It is almost too late to say anything new about Sir Charles' poetry, and too early to assign him his permanent place in our literature.' E.K. Brown, in the *University of Toronto Quarterly*, was equally laconic and noncommittal. His entire review in the yearly 'Letters in Canada' issue consisted of three sentences:

Sir Charles Roberts in his *Selected Poems* reprints the entire contents of *The Iceberg and Other Poems*, along with a generous selection from eight earlier volumes all of which are out of print. The claim made in the prefatory note that the poems illustrate a great variety of tendencies and techniques, and show the author's responsiveness to successive waves of thought and attitude, is a sound one. The collection contains no new material.

Subsequently, when some of Roberts' admirers protested that the *Quarterly* had not given the poet his due, Brown replied rather lamely that any justification for such a claim 'lies in the fear that I had lest his great age, the strong loyalties he evoked, and the immense influence he had come to wield should prejudice the reception throughout the country of some kinds of poetry that he did not fully appreciate.'[9]

Selected Poems came off the press late in the year, in time for the Christmas trade, but the sales were disappointing. On 17 February 1937, he received the following statement from Ryerson Press:

> *Selected Poems* – regular edition – $2.00
>> Printed 950 (450 sheets)
>> Sales 131 (@ 20%)
>> Reviews 30
>> Author 6
>> On hand 333 (bound)
>> On hand 450 (sheets)
>> Royalty total: $26.20
> *Selected Poems* – *de luxe* edition – $2.50
>> Printed 50
>> Sold 26 (@ 20%)
>> Royalty total: $13.00

The fact that he always earned more money from his prose was underscored by the success of *Further Animal Stories* (1936), seven selections which J.M. Dent had reprinted from *Wisdom of the Wilderness*, *They that Walk in the Wild*, and *Eyes of the Wilderness*. The advance royalty alone on the little volume was £50.[10]

Within three years' time, Roberts was horrified to discover that Ryerson Press was remaindering both *Selected Poems* and *The Iceberg and Other Poems*. The move was a violation of his contract, which specified that the author should be given first chance to purchase any 'remainders.' In a fiery letter to the general manager of the company, he wrote:

Permit me to interpolate, at this point, that in all these years no one of my other publishers – Macmillans, Ward Lock & Co., Methuens, J.M. Dent & Sons – has ever subjected me to having one of my books 'remaindered off,' even when its sales had temporarily dropped to one or two copies a year. It remained for a Canadian company to do this!

He was further aggrieved that he had been deceived over the disposal of *The Iceberg and Other Poems*. Although 500 copies had been printed, there was a declaration right in the book itself that only 100 copies were for sale. 'It was definitely stated to me,' he fumed, 'though not in writing, that the rest of the copies, except for the author's copies and the review copies, were for use by the firm as gift copies solely and would not be put on sale.' He raised such a storm that he was guaranteed 'full retail royalties' on all the copies remaindered of both titles.[11]

Over the years, Roberts had many complaints against Ryerson Press, such as their lack of push in handling book promotions and the unbusinesslike practices of the accounting department. Yet he had many reasons to be grateful to them. The editor-in-chief, Lorne Pierce, was more generous towards Roberts, perhaps, than he was to any of his other writers. For example, Pierce collected four poems that Roberts had written in 1937 and had 165 copies privately printed and copyrighted by Ryerson Press in little booklets to be sent as Christmas gifts to Roberts' friends and his own. Called *Twilight over Shaugamauk and Other Poems*, the collection contained (in addition to the title sonnet) 'Those Perish, These Endure,' 'As Down the Woodland Ways,' and 'Two Rivers.'

At one time, Pierce toyed with the idea of writing Roberts' biography, but he was already committed to so many literary projects, including a biography of William Kirby, that he hesitated to undertake something new. Pierce appears to have been Roberts' personal choice for biographer, but when it became apparent that the work would be delayed indefinitely, the biographee turned to A.M. Pound, who had been indicating for a long time that he was eager to take on the task. Pound's premature death in 1932, before he had begun the actual writing, left only one aspirant for the role of biographer: Roberts' son Lloyd. The thought of the indiscretions that Lloyd might find irresistible filled Roberts with alarm.

Once when someone commented to Lloyd Roberts that he was following in his father's footsteps, he replied: 'No, my father's footsteps are very large and of a peculiar shape; I have to mark out a path for myself.' The remark pleased the elder Roberts, but he knew very well that Lloyd's filial feelings were ambivalent. Although he regarded his father as a hero whose footsteps were difficult for lesser men like himself to follow, he had been known to imply that his father's feet were made of clay.

In *The Book of Roberts*, written from the viewpoint of childhood, Lloyd had pictured his father as the complete hero: 'We were sure that he possessed no frailties; he never lost his temper, or grumped, or nagged, or talked loud, or swore, or did any of the things that lesser mortals did.' Roberts liked that portrait of himself, but he expressed his displeasure over the candid description of George E. Fenety (C.G.D.R.'s father-in-law), who was called a '"self-made man" who, now that he was made, could not altogether get rid of self.' He told Lloyd that should a new edition be brought out, the comments on Fenety should be revised 'thoroughly into key with the rest of the book.' If there were any family skeletons, they were to remain in the closet.

The Book of Roberts was never reissued, but Lloyd wrote a sequel, called 'Dark Houses,' and this time it was his father who received the 'warts-and-all' treatment. Roberts was so alarmed that he threatened to cut Lloyd off forever if he allowed it to be published. Lloyd agreed that his father might show it to Elsie Pomeroy for an outside opinion. Her reaction was outrage. In a letter to Lorne Pierce she declared: 'I have refused to allow R. to bring Lloyd to my flat since I read a few chapters.'

To appease his father, Lloyd gave fictitious names to all the people in the book and disguised it as a novel. The last of many drafts bore a new title: 'Hell and High Heaven' – obviously influenced by Gwethalyn Graham's enormously successful *Earth and High Heaven*. Even in its final version, however, the disguise is transparent. All the significant events in the lives of the Roberts family are covered right up to the time of Lloyd's first marriage and the birth of his daughter. Lloyd, who is renamed David North, is the central figure of the story. When his father, Stephen, goes to New York to earn his living by his pen, the family are left to fend for themselves with insufficient financial aid from the struggling author. Stephen's wife is full of self-pity over her 'desertion.' She feels neglected and humiliated and worries about what her relatives and neighbours are thinking and saying. Her bitterness clouds the whole household and Stephen's infrequent visits are far from harmonious. The incidents are all lifted from life, and the reader cannot help feeling that Lloyd has given a very faithful account of the upheavals and resentments in the Roberts household.

For someone who truly admired, respected, and indeed loved his father, Lloyd exhibited a curious perversity by persisting in his revelations. Perhaps his compulsion to tell the story was a way of exorcising the resentments he still harboured. As a child it must have seemed to him that his mother was right, that his father had deserted the family. In later years, he and his father often debated the point. Roberts would maintain that under the circumstances he had had no alternative. 'Yes, I know,' Lloyd would agree, 'but ...'[12]

Sometime during the 1930s, when Roberts was fretting that Lloyd might someday attempt an unauthorized biography, Elsie Pomeroy showed him a sketch she had based upon some incidents he had told her about his childhood. That led to the idea of a biography, written by Elsie, but with himself not only supplying most of the information but also exercising strict editorial control over the whole writing process. In that way he could make sure that the record would be 'set straight' as he saw it – or as he wanted the world to see it – and he would, perhaps, forestall any plans that Lloyd might have.

Lorne Pierce expressed great interest in the undertaking, practically assuring Elsie Pomeroy that Ryerson Press would publish her book. Earlier, Pierce had been on the point of publishing 'Dark Houses,' but he had given it up in deference to Roberts' strong objections. After Lloyd failed repeatedly to place the manuscript elsewhere, Pierce asked for a copy of the final version, which he deposited in the Lorne Pierce Collection at Queen's University. One cannot help wondering about the motivation behind his action. Did he think that he might reconsider the publication of the work someday? Did he feel it should be accessible to future researchers? Obviously, he did not want the material to be lost.

Lloyd made it clear that he was not pleased with his father's choice of biographer. 'It was jealousy, pure and simple,' Elsie Pomeroy always maintained. 'Lloyd wanted to write the biography himself, but his father didn't trust him.' Perhaps she was not being entirely fair to Lloyd. Maybe he had honest reservations about her suitability for the task. As she herself confessed, she was 'always given to "hero-worship",' and she was too much in awe of Roberts ever to challenge his judgments or to oppose his wishes. 'It is *his* biography,' she told Lorne Pierce when the latter questioned certain items that Roberts wanted included, 'and I feel that I must let them stand.' She was, in fact, dedicated to the task of preserving the image by which Roberts wanted to be remembered. Once when Lloyd implied that too much was being left unsaid, his father retorted: 'Remember, Lloyd, if anyone attacks me after I am gone, Elsie will keep the wires burning in my defence!'[13]

Just as Elsie was drafting the framework of the biography, in close co-operation with the subject himself, the work was interrupted by an unexpected opportunity for Roberts to travel to Trinidad. His companionable cousin, Major Lionel Hannington, after returning to America from London, had settled in Port-of-Spain, where he became editor of the *Trinidad Guardian*. Early in 1936, Hannington sent Roberts a cordial invitation to pay him an extended visit, and offered to arrange a recital to help pay the expenses of the trip. Accordingly, Roberts left for the Caribbean in March and did not return to Toronto until early May. While he was away, his letters to his friends were rapturous about 'lovely, tropic Trinidad ... where I am lecturing a *little* & loafing & enjoying myself a lot.'[14]

In the biography that she was soon to write, Elsie Pomeroy devoted several pages to the Trinidad interlude, indicating how refreshing a respite it was from Roberts' ordinary routine. However, she made no mention whatever of his next lengthy holiday, which took him to a residential suburb of Chicago for about six weeks in the spring of 1938. Oak Park, famous as the birthplace of Hemingway and the home of Frank Lloyd Wright, was significant to Roberts as the girlhood home of Joan Montgomery. The latter fact was not one that he was likely to discuss with Elsie Pomeroy, from whom he concealed as much as possible about his relationship with his assistant at Trans-Canada Press. Nor was he likely to have divulged that Joan was also in Oak Park during part of the time that he was staying there.

Following his return from Oak Park, Roberts and Elsie resumed their work in earnest during the latter's summer holiday from school. To freshen his memory and to give her a better understanding of his background, it was decided that she should accompany him to New Brunswick for a fortnight in August. They arrived in Sackville together, but, although her detailed account of the visits to Westcock and vicinity took up several pages of the biography, she omitted any reference to her own presence there. Nor did Roberts mention her in the letter that he wrote to Joan Montgomery:

I have been on the go ever since my arrival, but just in a leisurely, irresponsible way, being driven all over the countryside & seeing places which I had never seen since I was 13 or 14 years old. It is very wonderful & re-invigorating to me; & the weather is bright and freshly warm – & it is my native salt air! I am feeling 'made over.' The only fly in my ointment is that my Beloved One is not with me, but is steaming in the heat of Toronto.

When he went on to Halifax, Elsie proceeded to Fredericton, where he had prepared the way for her by writing several letters of introduction. To Dr C.C. Jones, president of the University of New Brunswick, he announced: 'She is doing my *authorized* biography! Any facilities which you can give her will be deeply appreciated by myself as well as by her.'[15]

The summer and autumn of 1939 were extremely busy periods for Roberts. Leaving for the Maritimes with Elsie at the end of June to attend the CAA convention in Halifax, he spent a hectic fortnight in Nova Scotia before returning to Toronto. After crossing by ferry from Saint John to Digby, they took the train to Halifax. Another passenger, noticing the fuss that the crew were making over Roberts, came forward and introduced himself. He was Angus L. Macdonald, premier of the province. Thus the tone was set for the three-day convention that followed, for it soon became apparent that the most popular delegate with the press and the general public was Sir Charles G.D. Roberts.

On the opening day of the convention, Roberts regaled his fellow delegates with reminiscences which kept them 'in a continual ripple of amusement and applause.' Some of his more important statements were made the next day, however, when he conducted the Poetry Group discussions (and firmly curbed several poets who were bent upon giving a recital from their own works). He defended contemporary trends in Europe and America by observing that 'much of the published work of the so-called "modernistic" poets is really poetry.' Moreover, in the light of the world political situation, he felt, 'that there was some justification for the pronounced note of futility in present-day verse.' Therefore, although his private utterances confirm E.K. Brown's assertion that Roberts did not 'fully appreciate' some of the recent poetry, it is on record that he used his influence to give the 'modernists' a fair hearing from the CAA.[16]

The day after the convention ended, a group of delegates, including Roberts and Elsie Pomeroy, took an excursion to the 'Land of Evangeline.' Their visits to Windsor, Grand Pré, and Wolfville were conducted in the spirit of a literary pilgrimage, and Elsie was thrilled to see the landmarks associated with Roberts and Carman in the far-off days about which she had been writing. Following their return to Halifax, Roberts was whisked off as a week-end guest on a railway party to Sydney and Louisburg. He had wanted to see Louisburg since his early days as a writer when he had contemplated using it as the setting for a piece of historical fiction. The time had long since passed for that type of project; nevertheless, the visit was a dream come true.

He was back in Toronto for only a month before returning to Halifax as an honoured guest at the sesquicentennial celebrations of King's College. His affection for King's had deepened in retrospect, and he apparently forgot many of the frustrations he had felt while he was there. He had spent most of his tenure, from 1885 to 1895, trying to get away to something more stimulating; but, looking back at the past from the perspective of 1939, he saw the Windsor years in a different light:

Those ten years were assuredly among the richest and most formative of any similar period of my whole career. They gave me of my best work, both in prose and verse, and supplied me with memories and inspiration which through all my later years have never faded out or failed to move me. True, a great sorrow came upon us during that period, in the sudden death of my beloved younger brother, Goodridge, then a student at the College. But in the main my days were very happy and very productively filled. I was happy in the friendship of my colleagues on the staff and in the sympathetic understanding and comradeship of the student body, – for I was always a *student's* professor, belonging to their organizations and taking always a prominent part in them – usually, I think, as president.[17]

As it turned out, his adventures were not yet ended for the summer. 'I went to Chester, N.S.,' he explained in a letter to Lorne Pierce, 'met there an old friend of the New York days, now a very rich retired Philadelphia banker, who insisted on taking me back to New York with him & then on a wonderful luxury trip to the West Indies & Venezuela.' Before they departed on *The Rotterdam* of the Holland-American line, however, World War II had begun and many passengers had cancelled their reservations; but, for Roberts, the knowledge that the ship might be dodging submarines only added zest to the voyage. His generous friend, who made all of that possible, remains unnamed in the correspondence to Pierce and others. Nor does Elsie Pomeroy reveal the man's identity in Roberts' biography even though she felt obliged to include the names of nearly all the other people to whom her subject had ever been indebted. Upon returning to New York, Roberts spent a few days with Will and Mary and visited briefly with some friends in Washington before arriving back in Toronto on 4 October, commenting with satisfaction: 'I've had a fine time this summer.'[18] With the coming of winter, he settled down to a regular schedule for collaborating on the biography.

On 3 June 1940, Roberts wrote to Pierce: 'Elsie and I have the Biography about finished at last; and will be sending it to you in a few days, D.V. I've worked, and she has worked tremendously hard over it. ... It is almost a sort of *camouflaged autobiography*.' In due time the manuscript came back from Pierce with what Roberts acknowledged as being 'painstaking, thorough, and invaluable suggestions and criticisms.' On 27 February 1941, Roberts reported on the progress of the revisions: 'We are working hard and successfully on it three nights a week; and she's at it alone the rest of the time!'

Unfortunately, Pierce was not satisfied with the final results of their efforts. First of all, the manuscript was still too long; second, it seemed to lack distinction and he felt that Roberts was entitled to something better. On 24 August 1942, he wrote an evasive letter to Elsie Pomeroy advising her that that he feared the publication would have to be postponed. In great dismay, Roberts wrote back at once: 'I have put five years of very hard work on this biography ... and ... it is of vital interest to me that it is published during my lifetime. ... I cannot accept your decision to postpone the publication of the book indefinitely.'

After what he considered further evasions by Pierce, Roberts dispatched more letters and made several angry telephone calls. Eventually, Pierce was badgered into an agreement that he would 'give it a final sandpapering for the printers and put it into their hands as soon as possible.' Roberts was irritated by the 'sandpapering' idea, complaining that Pierce had 'harped upon this continually.' Although he declared that he would not allow any more of it, a further 10,000 words were deleted, and Pierce informed Elsie on 1 April 1943 that the book was being sent to press.

It was ready for distribution on 12 June, and Elsie sent Pierce an ecstatic acknowledgment of her author's copy. 'Your letter reads like a lyric,' he wrote in reply. 'I am thrilled that you are so happy over this child of yours.' In guarded praise, he added: 'It is a useful book and will be referred to a good many times in the future.'[19]

Pierce was right. The book is useful, and subsequent students of Roberts' life and work have been greatly indebted to it. Even though the significant facts are often buried among the trivia, there is a wealth of valuable information that would now be lost if Elsie Pomeroy had not recorded it first-hand. Of course, her literary insight was often blinded by her hero-worship, but there have been many literary critics since her time to correct, sometimes too rigorously, her lack of objectivity. She was, as *The Times Literary Supplement* said of her, 'an appreciator, not a critic, of her subject whether as a writer or man.' One of the best appraisals of the book was written by Pelham Edgar:

It would be possible to cavil at its lack of critical discrimination, its failure to relate Roberts in any large way with the movements of his time, its episodic fullness and its dearth of general conclusions. Yet these negative features in the book do not seem greatly to matter. A living and lovable figure emerges from her pages, and we attune ourselves readily to the full confidence of the author's assumptions and to her unquestioning belief in the high importance of her theme.

In a private conversation with Roberts, however, Edgar was overheard posing this question to his friend: 'The truth, but not the whole truth?' When Roberts did not dispute the observation, Edgar suggested gently, 'It lacks salt, perhaps.'[20]

It is possible that something of Roberts' private feelings may be deduced from a favour he asked of Elsie Pomeroy before the book went to press. He had looked so serious and anxious as he led up to the question that she braced herself for something very difficult, but all he wanted was to have her name appear as 'E.M. Pomeroy' on the cover of the forthcoming publication. It would be more dignified, he suggested, and she quickly agreed to the change, which, in her opinion, signified an eccentricity of taste, nothing more. However, his request may have reflected a secret uneasiness over the public's possible reaction to the adulation of a middle-aged spinster – especially one whose name might suggest the insipidity of the 'Elsie Dinsmore' series.

While there is no other evidence that Roberts was ever embarrassed by Elsie's devotion, he was well aware of the ridicule that some of his family, particularly Lloyd and Thede, were heaping upon his biographer. One of Lloyd's more temperate comments, made five years after his father's death, appears in a letter to Wilfrid Eggleston: 'Pomeroy wrote a guide-book and gazetteer of Charles, leaving Charles completely out of the picture.' Thede never acknowledged the complimentary copy that Elsie sent him, but word got back to her that he was 'damning both book and Sir Charles.' In view of those attitudes, it must have given Roberts some satisfaction to enumerate the favourable reviews for the benefit of his daughter Edith. He listed notices from several of the leading Canadian papers, but omitted to mention that the reviewers were his personal friends. 'They all recognize what a brilliant piece of work Elsie has achieved,' he assured Edith. 'It puts her at once "right on the map" as a consummate biographer.'[21]

While the biography had been in progress, the threat and actual outbreak of World War II had given Roberts the stimulation to write topical and patriotic verse again. Curiously enough, World War I, in which he had served, had inspired only three of his poems; but between 1938 and 1942 he wrote ten poems on the theme of war. Perhaps his frustration at being barred at last from active service found an outlet in verse. Writing to Lorne Pierce on 19 October 1939, he declared:

How it galls me to feel I'm out of it this time. Perjury would not help me out now, alas! But what would I not give to get up to our 'Front' again & reel exultantly to the cracking of the big guns. That always thrilled me. But when the machine guns got chattering, my tail went between my legs – & I lit a cigarette if possible, & looked as if I was not scared stiff.

Early in 1937 he had written 'Those Perish, These Endure,' a comment upon the Spanish Civil War. In it he regarded war philosophically: the horrors would pass, the routine of the seasons and normal living would endure. His 'Peace with Dishonour,' written in September 1938 after the Munich crisis, expressed the same view of the crimes of war, but the concluding stanza is a bitter denunciation that shows how deeply he was affected by the 'dishonour':

> But oh, for faith betrayed cringes my soul.
> For long dishonour, brief cowed peace.
> For Freedom stripped and cast to the loud pack.
> The stain endures. For this cringes my soul.

He confided to Lorne Pierce: 'That bit "Peace with Dishonour" was forced from me suddenly by strong emotion.' He was similarly affected during the anxious period of 1940 when Britain was experiencing her 'darkest hour' as her allies fell one by one. Every month or so he produced a new poem. In February 1940 when Watson Kirkconnell contacted him about signing a protest against the neutrals, he replied:

Yes, indeed, I will eagerly sign your Protest, – & would that I could sign it with ten million bombs and bayonets. I enclose a bit of verse – still in the rough, – which I have just written, & which feebly expresses my sentiments.

The poem in question, 'In Time of Earth's Misuse,' was featured in the 15 March issue of *Maclean's*. In calling Lorne Pierce's attention to it, he described it as 'a fierce *anti-neutral* blast! Not poetry perhaps, but "polemics".' His next poem, 'Too Long We Wait' (later retitled 'Forget Not Thou'), he classified as 'another such' polemic. June and July saw the completion of 'To France' (retitled 'Canada to France') and 'Not Here Comes Spring' (retitled 'The Ravaged Lands'). 'I have several more "on the stocks," of similar timelessness,' he wrote to Pelham Edgar on 1 August. 'They are so different from my peace-time stuff that I can't tell whether they are good or not. At least they are darn well *felt*.'[22]

When he completed 'The Empire Speaks of Britain' (retitled 'Canada Speaks of Britain') on 19 August 1940 he submitted it to *Maclean's*, where it was prominently displayed in a subsequent issue. Its appearance was greeted with '*extravagant* praise' from Pelham Edgar, E.J. Pratt, George M. Wrong, and B.K. Sandwell. In fact, Sandwell asserted that 'it ought to be most widely distributed as a significant war document.' Ryerson Press took up the idea and the result was a fifteen-page booklet called *Canada Speaks of Britain* (1941) which contained all of his war poems since World War I plus three recent miscellaneous poems. It sold at the modest price of sixty cents, with the author's royalties and the publishers profits being assigned to the War Services Council for the purchase of books for the armed forces of Canada. Roberts' opinion of the title poem is expressed in a letter to Ralph Gustafson regarding the latter's impending *Penguin Anthology of Canadian Poetry*: 'I have done a sonnet called "Canada Speaks of Britain" which is undoubtedly one of the best things I have ever written and I should consider it the most essential thing for the anthology.' Gustafson obligingly included the sonnet in the first edition of his anthology (1942), but when he revised the collection fifteen years later he eliminated several of his earlier choices from Roberts' work, including 'Canada Speaks of Britain,' although he increased Roberts' total representation from five poems to eight.[23]

'Canada Speaks of Britain' was followed by 'Epitaph for a Young Airman' (completed 18 October 1940) and then there was over a year's silence until the early months of 1942 when he completed 'A Song for Victory Delayed,' of which he wrote to Pelham Edgar on 21 March:

Here's a bit of timely verse which I have just been delivered of. What do you think of it? Perhaps not poetry exactly, but possibly it has a punch to it.

Monday night was a *great* night. It did me a world of good – sort of rearranged my molecules, so that I feel like writing verse again after a long preoccupation with prose & editing.

However, he wrote only one more poem. It was entitled 'Resurgant' ('I think it one of my best,' he told Lorne Pierce), and it was completed just in time to be included in *Flying Colours*, his anthology of war poems in English which Ryerson Press published in 1942.[24]

Having passed the age of eighty, Roberts was visibly slowing down. At the beginning of 1940, unlike the previous year when he had boasted of dancing the night away on New Year's Eve, he was almost too ill to participate in the eightieth birthday celebrations planned for him. As soon as the festivities were over, he underwent a series of tests at Toronto General Hospital. The results showed that he was in good physical condition for his age. 'So it was proved to be just my trouble of long years ago,' he reported to Lorne Pierce, ' – nervous indigestion.'[25] The doctor treated him for 'heart burn,' as Roberts called it; in reality, he was suffering from mild angina.

Roberts was often heard to say that moderation was his guiding principle in maintaining his general well-being. 'I think *a little* of whatever you like,' he advised, 'is the secret of keeping your interest, & yourself, alive and keen.' The only excesses to which he admitted were drinking (water!) and cigarette smoking (without inhaling!). This cautious formula for controlling his various appetites undoubtedly contributed to his overall good health, which in turn influenced his mental state. He had no safeguards against worry or loneliness or any other vexations, but his bodily fitness helped him shake the maladies of the mind more easily. His outlook was almost always cheerful, since nothing could quell his optimistic spirit for any length of time. Perhaps he did not exactly believe that 'God's in his heaven / All's right with the world,' but he did have a comforting faith in 'a power outside and above ourselves that one might call God.'[26]

Roberts loved to travel, but when his wanderlust was hampered by his age and lack of money, he found pleasure in the familiar scenes close to home. In Toronto, 'the place he liked best was Centre Island,' a fifteen-minute ferry ride across the harbour. During the summer, whenever he was in the city, he visited the Island several times a week. 'If he were worried,' Elsie Pomeroy recalled, 'the Island was his comforting haven.' Elsie often accompanied him on those expeditions, and it was their custom to go canoeing among the lagoons and have their lunch in some secluded nook among the reeds. After returning the canoe to the boathouse, they would pause on the bridge leading to the docks, 'drinking in the beauty,' as Roberts called it, 'first from one side and then from the other.'[27]

He was too poor to take advantage of many of the attractions that Toronto had to offer. 'I never go to the theatre,' he lamented, 'because I have to have the best seats in order to see, & I can't afford them.' But a widow named Gertrude Baker invited him to 'some big thing once in a while,' Joan sometimes asked him to a performance at Hart House, and Elsie occasionally took him to the Royal Alexandra Theatre. 'They buy the tickets & I do the *escorting*!!' he explained. He was especially pleased to attend a performance of Mazo de la Roche's *Whiteoaks* with Elsie. He had taken a special interest in Miss de la Roche's work ever since she had won the *Atlantic Monthly*'s literary prize of $10,000, and he had presided over the banquet that the CAA held in her honour shortly thereafter. He enjoyed the production of the play and raved that 'Ethel Barrymore was splendid' in the role of Grandmother Whiteoak. Miss de la Roche had a different reaction: 'Never for a moment did Miss Barrymore make me believe in her.'[28]

The announcement of Mazo de la Roche's enviable prize for *Jalna* in 1927 had sparked a request from the CAA that the Canadian government establish an award 'for the most notable work published each year by a resident Canadian.' Although the CAA continued to press, nothing came of their efforts for nearly ten years until a new Governor-General, Lord Tweedsmuir, gave vice-regal consent to a system of annual awards to begin with the 1936 publications in fiction, poetry, and general literature. For several years Roberts was one of the judges for Canadian poetry written in English. In the first year there was no poetry winner in English, but Roberts' cherished friend, Annie Charlotte Dalton, received a special Tweedsmuir Award for *The Neighing North*, published five years earlier. E.J. Pratt was the winner in 1937 for *The Fable of the Goats*, although Roberts maintained that Lloyd Roberts' *I Sing of Life* was 'decidedly one of the three or four most important books of poetry of the year.' Of the 1938 award, Roberts wrote to Pelham Edgar, a fellow judge:

I have examined all these eight volumes of verse submitted for the Governor General's Medal. As I judge them, Kenneth Leslie's *By Stubborn Stars* is easily preeminent. This is *big* stuff – fresh, individual, full of a sinewy strength. It has passion & tenderness, & a music essentially its own. And its craftsmanship is sure.

Edgar agreed with that evaluation – which indicates the qualities that he and Roberts both admired most in poetry – and the award went to Leslie, one of the congenial spirits of the disbanded 'Song Fishermen.'[29]

For some reason, Roberts' *Selected Poems* was not considered eligible for the Governor-General's Award in 1936, possibly because he had already agreed to be a judge. His *Canada Speaks of Britain* booklet was passed over in 1941 for Anne Marriott's eight-page chapbook, *Calling Adventurers!* As if to make up for his failure to capture the new literary award, other honours continued to come his way without being sought. At the spring convocation of Mount Allison University in 1942, for example, he was granted the degree of Doctor of Laws. His visit to Sackville for the presentation was charged with emotion, for he was conscious of the possibility that he might be seeing his beloved Tantramar country for the last time.

There had been many reminders within recent years that his connections with the past were rapidly disappearing. A letter dated 4 October 1941, from his sister-in-law in Connecticut, Mary Fanton Roberts, had brought ominous tidings:

We do long to hear from you, especially as Bill is quite ill, rather serious heart trouble. He is not allowed to work or drive, and is fearfully depressed. If you can spare us a few weeks, do come. I should so like you to see our home. It is really lovely, and Bill has done such fine things with it – too much work I fear. We could make you quite comfortable – with a room and bath of your own.[30]

Unfortunately, Roberts was unable to get away before it was too late. Just six weeks after Mary's letter had arrived, William Roberts suffered a fatal heart attack while out upon his customary evening stroll. Roberts grieved, not only for a beloved brother, but for the breaking of another link with the old days.

Despite his nostalgia for the times beyond recall, Roberts probably lived less in the past than most other people of his age. He still believed firmly in the philosophy he had expressed long ago that 'whatever be gained, yet the reach of the morrow is more.'[31] He always had many projects planned for the future: there were new poems and stories 'on the stocks'; there were special articles to write (among the pieces he completed was an essay on New Brunswick for a souvenir book commemorating the royal tour of 1939); and he still dreamed of completing 'Overlords of Earth,' his partially finished sequel to *In the Morning of Time*. As soon as Volume II of *The Canadian Who Was Who* came off the presses in 1938, he was busily at work on Volume III, although it was unfinished at the time of his death and never was completed. Among the public engagements for which he had to prepare was a nation-wide reading over the CBC network on 10 January 1939, to mark his seventy-ninth birthday. Regrettably, since the CBC did not see fit to record the broadcast on a phono-disc, as could have been done, the sound of the poet's voice was not preserved for posterity.

His last public performance was given on the evening of 22 February 1943, under the sponsorship of the Toronto branch of the CAA, to raise money for the Aid to Russia Fund. Reading in the large auditorium of the Toronto Conservatory of Music, Roberts never appeared in better form as his voice, strong and resonant, carried throughout the hall. He showed no signs of tiring, not even after finishing all 264 lines of 'The Iceberg.' He read poem after poem but still the audience lingered for more until he finally closed his book. 'No,' he said firmly, 'you have had enough. I know when to stop.'[32]

CHAPTER FOURTEEN

The Final Months

1943

THE LAST SIX MONTHS of Roberts' life, following the appearance of his biography, were a mixture of happiness and stress. After his anxiety about Pierce's hesitation over publishing the book, he was greatly relieved to see it actually in print with nothing revealed therein that did not meet with his approval. There was very little that he needed to hide, but his Victorian sensibilities recoiled at the public exposure of linen whose freshness was even slightly open to question. Elsie Pomeroy was fully in sympathy with his feelings, and it never occurred to her that, in the long run, the full story of his struggles, failures, and triumphs might do him greater justice than an obviously laundered account that allowed too much latitude for rumour and conjecture. His satisfaction with Elsie's bland story of his life was soon marred by complications that arose out the book's existence. The time came, also, when Elsie almost wished that it had never been written.

At first, she was enveloped in the euphoria of authorship. With Roberts by her side, she was the centre of attention at a series of receptions and publisher's promotions. She autographed copies of her book by the dozen and accepted numerous invitations to speak in public about the experience of writing an authorized biography. In her classroom at King Edward Public School she had become a celebrity overnight. And at the CAA convention in Toronto in September she was overwhelmed by congratulatory greetings. Over the years, CAA delegates had grown accustomed to her discreet presence in the background whenever Roberts was on hand, but at last she was sharing the limelight with him. Their names were forever coupled in the public mind, and many of their acquaintances (unaware of his enchantment with Joan Montgomery) thought it was inevitable that Elsie would soon become Lady Roberts. There are even some indications that Elsie may have thought so herself.

Roberts had been captivated by Joan Montgomery almost from the first moment he saw her. After persuading Tunnell to hire her on a trial basis, he was delighted to find that she soon justified his faith in her capabilities. The work on the biographical dictionary was to her liking; and she became an able researcher, interviewing surviving relatives and friends, writing and rewriting sketches, editing, proofreading, and generally making herself useful.[1] Not only was she indispensable at the office, but Roberts was finding her companionship increasingly important to his private life. The age difference proved to be a bonus instead of a handicap to their relationship: he was refreshed and stimulated by her youth and active mind; she was enriched and instructed by his years and experience.

By 1937, they had become utterly devoted to each other. 'My love is yours while life shall last,' he declared in a letter from Ottawa where he was spending Christmas with his family. That seems to have been the occasion when he announced his May-December romance to his children. In a second letter, written two days later, he assured Joan that Lloyd and Leila wanted her to visit Low Eaves, and that Edith was looking forward to seeing her. 'And I know,' he added 'the others will love you when they meet you.'[2] The tone was a trifle anxious, as if he might still be worried about his family's reaction to his choice of a woman who was young enough to be his granddaughter. Age did not matter to either him or Joan personally, but they knew that society in general disapproved of an alliance between an old man and a young woman. It was important to Roberts that his children should disregard public opinion and welcome Joan into the family circle.

Instinct told him that Elsie Pomeroy would consider his involvement with Joan to be a shameful liaison. Therefore, he kept it from her, but some time in 1940 she heard a rumour that Roberts and Joan were planning to be married. Although she insisted that she did not believe it, even for a moment, she confronted him with the gossip the next time she saw him. He repudiated it emphatically. 'Nothing is more undignified than for a man in his 80's to marry a young girl,' he told her. 'If I ever do that be assured that I am approaching senility.'[3]

Around the time that the final revisions to Elsie's manuscript were under way, Joan moved into an apartment in the Ernescliffe buildings where Roberts lived. Because the complex was on a corner lot, her address was 477 Sherbourne Street while his was 197 Wellesley Street. About three times a week he would spend the evening working with Elsie and then go home to Joan. For the most part his social contacts were divided into two groups: one consisted mainly of people in the literary societies to which he and Elsie both belonged; the other was the circle in which he moved with Joan. Only a few intimates who overlapped with both groups were fully aware of the double life he was leading. Elsie, who had been reassured by his denial of intended marriage, had absolutely no idea of the extent to which his life was committed to Joan.

Roberts felt deeply indebted to Elsie for her work on the biography. She had always listened to his advice and had tried hard to tailor the book to suit his wishes. It had been a labour of love for her – the culmination of her unceasing devotion for seventeen years. Therefore, his feelings must have been full of self-reproach over his deception. He could see that because she had played Boswell for so long to his Johnson she was convinced that she was his closest confidante. Consequently, it was becoming easier for her to imagine that she was the most important person in his life. To make it still harder for him, he was probably aware that some of their mutual friends expected that his gratitude would lead to yet a closer bond between them, possibly even marriage. It is also quite possible that he was indebted to her financially.

His emotions were thrown into further turmoil by Lloyd, who had left Leila and moved to Toronto just a few weeks before the biography appeared. Since Joan Montgomery was already almost a wife to Roberts, Lloyd felt strongly (or so he claimed) that it would be unfair to her for them to continue as they were. He urged his father to marry her, but Roberts was daunted by the likelihood that they would become the butt of public ridicule and coarse jokes. The pain that the marriage would cause Elsie Pomeroy was also uppermost in his mind. It seemed to Lloyd that the latter objection was the only one with which they needed to be concerned. He insisted that the best way was to tell Elsie at once, but it was as difficult for Roberts to do it as it had been for him to tell May the truth about their separation. He could not bear the thought of hurting Elsie, nor did he want to forfeit the comforting warmth of her friendship.

Lloyd was a trial to his father in another respect as well. Nearing sixty, he had literally run away from home and his old responsibilities to begin his life over again. With less than $400 to his name, and a companion with whom he was deeply in love, he dreamed that freedom from the hack work of journalism and publicity would give him at long last the chance to fulfil those early prophecies of literary fame. His father could sympathize with those aspirations, and he was delighted with Judy, Lloyd's young love, but he worried whether his son could succeed in the boarding-house business which he had bought on Jarvis Street by borrowing heavily 'on nerve and faith, at 6%.' Nevertheless, Roberts was happy to have Lloyd 'living only a couple of blocks' away and to be able to see him 'almost every day.' Judy and Joan, who were close in age, became good friends, and the foursome 'had some marvellous times together.'[4]

Roberts still tried to find time for his customary outings with Elsie: visits to the Riverdale Zoo and trips to the Island. One mild Saturday early in September they met for the noon ferry to the Island, and as they approached the boathouse he asked, 'Do you think it's mild enough?' She knew that he meant mild enough for her to paddle, since he would not allow her to use the oars if there were any breeze. She persuaded him that it was safe, and they glided away to eat their lunch on the banks of the lagoon as they had done so many times in the past. As they returned the canoe, he said: 'Now I can face the winter much better; I knew I could never paddle again so I didn't tell you how much I've been longing to lunch once more among the reeds.' As they walked slowly across the park to the wharf, he spoke again: 'When I can't come with you to the Island, I won't be here much longer.'

It had long been his custom to go to the Island with Elsie to pay a special farewell visit for the year, usually on Thanksgiving Day. In the beginning they marked the occasion by having dinner downtown afterwards, but in later years they usually went back to her apartment. Early on Thanksgiving morning in 1943, he telephoned to say that he would call at her apartment after lunch. Her suspicions were aroused since he normally would have said: 'I'll meet you for the twelve o'clock boat.' When he arrived, around one o'clock, his first words were: 'I'm too sick to go to the Island. I'm much too sick.' His angina had been keeping him awake, but in his favourite chair in her apartment he fell asleep.[5]

Elsie always blamed Lloyd for the decline in Roberts' health during the summer of 1943. She told Lorne Pierce in the autumn:

He *is* slipping. Those attacks, *mild* angina the doctor calls them and some are not so mild, are more frequent than ever. Up to the time he went to Ottawa in July to ask Leila to divorce the 59 year-old son ... he would say 'I haven't had a pellet for four days or five,' etc. Sometimes it would be a week. This fall he has been taking several attacks a day, has been *eating* the pellets [nitroglycerin].

Judy Roberts, on the other hand, has wondered about the connection between her father-in-law's attacks and his worry over Elsie:

Charles was upset. He knew that he had treated her shabbily, and his behaviour did not match the image he wanted to have of himself. It was after this that he began to have the angina pains. Until then, he had not had any pains. I do not say that his distress over Elsie caused them; probably he was ripe for them anyway. It *may* have precipitated them, or their occurrence at this time may simply have been a coincidence.[6]

In the early autumn when Nat Benson, who had been editing *The Canadian Poetry Magazine*, left Toronto to live in New York, Roberts agreed to take over the editorial duties. 'This will force me to concentrate,' he remarked grimly to Elsie when he told her about the appointment. He also insisted that she accept the position of associate editor, which would keep them working together as they had done on the biography. On the evening of 25 October, they spent over an hour in her apartment getting the next issue ready. He seemed troubled, as if he wanted to tell her something, but all he could say was 'I want you to promise that no matter what happens you will always let me come here.' Elsie replied lightly, trying to jolly him out of his serious mood: 'Well, now, you'll have to be careful not to get thrown into the Don Jail or you won't be able to come here.' To her astonishment and consternation, he broke down and wept, but not a further word was spoken.

The next day, when Elsie arrived back at her apartment late in the afternoon, she found a letter from Roberts tucked under her door, announcing that his marriage to Joan Montgomery would take place on the evening of 28 October. With a trembling hand he had written:

It is my dearest wish – & it would give Joan great pleasure, too – that you, as my biographer & closest friend, should attend. ... Your presence would be a declaration & an explanation to your family & to our mutual friends.

At first Elsie reacted more in horror than in anger. Then, in a rage over her betrayal, she telephoned to refuse the invitation and announce that she would have nothing more to do with him. Until then, she had feared that he would have a coronary thrombosis, but for the next two days she prayed 'but without faith ... that the thrombosis would take him off before the ceremony.'[7]

At the time of her wedding, Joan Montgomery had given up her job at Trans-Canada Press and was working as a radio operator at Dominion Skyways, Malton, a commercial organization for training men in the RCAF. For the brief ceremony in Holy Trinity Church, she wore her duty uniform of navy blue with tie and stewardess-type hat. In addition to Lloyd and Judy, only her mother and two friends were present to see her become Lady Roberts. Afterwards, Lloyd held a reception for the newlyweds and released the news to the press. The next day the story appeared in the daily papers, along with pictures of Roberts and Joan holding two of Lloyd's house pets, Solomon, the cat, and Chang, the dog. Just as Roberts had feared, the public's attention focused upon the difference between his age and that of his bride, the reaction ranging from scorn to amusement. Lorne Pierce's tacit disapproval is evident in this one-line entry in his diary: 'Roberts was married last evening – he 83, the bride 33.'[8]

Elsie, in a somewhat calmer mood, defended Roberts to his daughter: 'I hope you and Douglas will not be too hard on him. Many old people would do equally silly things if they had no protecting influence, and remember your poor old father had no one but his jealous and partially crazed son.' She had softened enough towards Roberts to say: 'I still believe the man is exactly as I have pictured him in the book and his work will live long after this is remembered even as a distressing incident.' While she was feeling conciliatory, she telephoned him without having decided beforehand what she was going to say. Unexpectedly, Joan answered, saying, 'Lady Roberts speaking.' All at once, Elsie's anger flared again in full fury. 'Go to hell!' she shouted, and slammed down the receiver.

Elsie still accepted speaking engagements to promote her book, but her admission to Lorne Pierce that 'It's really no joke to speak now' was undoubtedly a huge understatement. She steadfastly refused all invitations to gatherings at which Roberts and Joan were likely to be present. One of their hostesses told her that Roberts had asked plaintively: 'Has Elsie forgiven me yet?' After the president of the Arts Club telephoned to invite her to a reception for Sir Charles and Lady Roberts, Elsie reported the conversation to Lorne Pierce:

ELSIE
Thank you very much, but unfortunately I could not under any circumstances meet that woman.
MRS SMYTHE
I fear you misunderstand her.
ELSIE
Not at all. Through her a distinguished name is now only a lewd jest on the street.
MRS SMYTHE
I can't understand you. I never heard anyone speak like that.

ELSIE

If you really mean what you say, my dear lady, you must be dumb. Everyone knows that this is the ignominious ending to a great career.

MRS SMYTHE

Well, anyway, she's his choice.

ELSIE

A very old and very sick man makes no choice.

MRS SMYTHE

Well, anyway, I am sure she will be a help to him.

ELSIE

She! A help! After dragging his name through the mud! Really, as much as I admired Sir Charles I could never let anyone see me speaking to such a person. Good-bye!9

Elsie's outrage, for all its sincerity, was grossly unfair. Roberts' young wife did not deserve the vilification that was being heaped upon her. Far from being a selfish opportunist, she was deeply concerned about the welfare of the man upon whom she had lavished her loving care for upwards of a decade. She was terribly hurt by the cruel remarks of all the people who misunderstood her motives.

Elsie's greatest wrath was directed against Lloyd, who, in her view, was the chief villain in the whole affair. For the rest of her life, she remained convinced that he had engineered the marriage just to spite her for writing the biography. Her letter to Harold Child, one of Roberts' friends in England, contains a typical tirade:

He (the son) begged Lorne Pierce, the Editor of the Ryerson Press, not to take my book. ... Then to be revenged upon me for the Biography, and to get his father away from me completely, he planned the marriage with one of those persons whom Sir Charles had tried to help. The father was most unhappy. His mind could still function, but he was not strong enough to stand against the son.10

She believed so strongly in the revenge theory that for a long time she actually regretted having written the biography. In the end, however, she decided that no matter what the consequences had been, it was still more important (as she phrased it) 'to have the record set straight.' What she really meant (for she knew how selective she had been with the facts) was that she had successfully thwarted Lloyd's plans to present his version of his father's career. No publisher would be interested in another biography of Roberts during Lloyd's lifetime.

The end was nearer for Roberts than anyone realized. Less than three weeks after his marriage, he was admitted to Toronto's Wellesley Hospital. Twelve days later, on 26 November, he died. At Lloyd's request, Lorne Pierce took charge of the funeral, quietly enlisting Elsie Pomeroy, who gave him 'great help with the arrangements.' The biggest problem lay in trying to cut down on expenses. Roberts' assets at the time of his death consisted of a $500 bond, a 1931 Buick which he had bought for $400 as a wedding gift, and $600 in the bank. Pierce had no choice but to order a cheap casket and dispense with limousines.

At the largely attended funeral in St Stephen's Anglican Church, Toronto, representatives came from all walks of life to pay tribute to the man whom W.A. Deacon called the symbol of Canadian literature ('In spite of everything,' Lorne Pierce conceded in his diary, 'a glorious symbol'). Elsie Pomeroy was there in sorrowful reconciliation ('She has been very bitter about the O.M.'s wedding,' Pierce commented, '& her friends hope she says nothing more'). She and Pierce had selected several of Roberts' poems on immortality to be read by St Stephen's rector, Canon J.E. Ward, including the closing stanza of 'The Vagrant of Time':

> In sleep too deep for dreams I'll lie, –
> Till One shall knock and bid me rise
> To quest new ventures, fare new roads,
> Essay new suns and vaster skies.

'In the hushed solemnity of the crowded church,' Elsie wrote afterwards, those poems 'became his requiem,' but Pierce felt that Canon Ward had spoiled the effect by reading them 'poorly.'[11]

The following spring, Joan Montgomery, Lady Roberts, took Roberts' ashes to Fredericton to be interred in Forest Hill Cemetery, overlooking his 'Dear and great River,'[12] the Saint John. While that last service was being performed for him by the woman he had called 'My dearest and loveliest,' his 'biographer and closest friend' sat writing an elegy in the room where they had worked so many hours together:

> There will be no visits to the Island this summer,
> No leisurely walk from the wharf to the boat-house,
> No loving study of each plant that grows in all the many
> flower-beds,
> No long rest on the bridge, drinking in the beauty first from
> one side and then the other.

There will be no paddling on the lagoon this summer,
No running the canoe among the rushes, there to lunch
While listening to the song of the red-shouldered blackbirds,
No visit to the little backwater with its cool dark shade.

There will be no such visits any more.
The lilac trees will bloom and the red hawthorns;
The plants he loved will blossom as before.
But there will be no visits – any more – any more![13]

This sentimental poem was not Elsie Pomeroy's only memorial to Roberts. Using her royalties from the sale of the biography, plus a considerable sum from her savings, she paid for the impressive monument that stands at the head of his grave.

Epilogue

ROBERTS' EARLY ACCLAIM may have been too easily won, too undiscriminating, and too excessive, but by the mid-twentieth century he was well on the way to becoming one of the most underrated writers that Canada has produced. The Canadian modernists who began emerging in the 1930s had focused upon Roberts in their repudiation of the so-called Confederation poets. After all, he was still living, still practising his art in a manner they rejected, and still able to exert considerable influence upon the course of Canadian literature. His high profile, which had always eclipsed that of Duncan Campbell Scott, his fellow survivor from the past, caused the Canadian disciples of Pound and Eliot to denounce him as Charles *God Damn* Roberts. In response, Pelham Edgar wrote in 1943, just a few weeks before Roberts' death: 'Our younger poets of today may not recognize their debt ... but in the long perspective of history the pervasive quality of Roberts' influence will be recognized in its true importance.'[1] Edgar's long-range view became increasingly difficult to share, however, as an even greater antipathy developed towards Roberts in the succeeding decades.

The publication of Irving Layton's *A Red Carpet for the Sun* in 1959, and the fact that it won the Establishment's biggest literary prize, the Governor-General's Award, marks the extreme shift away from the supposedly fustian trappings of the late Victorian tradition in Canadian poetry. The age of redblooded frankness had begun, and to the hasty eye the verse of Roberts and his generation seemed pallid to the point of irrelevancy. As for his once popular animal stories, not only were they considered to be old-fashioned, but they were relegated to 'the uncomfortable limbo between deliberate fable and true understanding of animal psychology.'² No wonder that on the centenary of Roberts' birth, the year after Layton's *Red Carpet* appeared, there was no official or public recognition of any kind to honour the 'Father of Canadian Literature.' The anniversary went completely unnoticed except for a booklet called *Tributes through the Years* which Elsie Pomeroy published privately at her own expense.

More recently, however, there have been indications that the tide of critical opinion is again on the turn. Through the efforts of scholars such as Joseph Gold and W.J. Keith, the animal story has become more widely regarded as a respectable art form and Roberts' work in that genre is being taken seriously once more. The beginning of the 1980s, 100 years after the publication of *Orion*, was marked by a reappraisal of Roberts' poetry. New works or works-in-progress by critics such as Fred Cogswell and Terry Whalen have refuted or modified much of the adverse criticism of the past. A Roberts symposium held at Mount Allison University in 1982 and another at the University of Ottawa in 1983 produced papers that show a renewed appreciation of Roberts' importance as a writer. Further evidence of that attitude may be found in the publication of Roberts' *Complete Poems* (Wolfville, NS: Wombat Press 1985) and in the task of collecting his letters – a project initiated by Desmond Pacey but completed by Laurel Boone.

It is unlikely that the final verdict is in yet upon Roberts the man or Roberts the writer. 'Life and literature are far more strange and puzzling than most of us can imagine,' Louis Dudek has reminded all biographers and critics. 'We should not try to simplify them too much, or to pass quick judgment.' At the moment, the consensus seems to be that he possessed a blithe if restless spirit, that he wielded a wide influence as a diligent craftsman and as a generous critic, and that he was Canada's first important man of letters in the post-Confederation period. He is credited with a hundred or so poems that are 'accomplished and satisfying,' and at least a comparable number of animal stories that are classified as being 'unequalled in their genre.' His total achievements, according to current assessments, would appear therefore to be considerable.³

Notes

ABBREVIATIONS

CLP   Carman Correspondence, Lorne Pierce Collection, Queen's University
      Archives
FUT   Thomas Fisher Library, University of Toronto
LP   Lorne Pierce Collection, Queen's University Archives
LPD   Lorne Pierce Diaries, Queen's University Archives
PAC   Public Archives of Canada
QU   Queen's University Archives
SJC   St John's College Library, Winnipeg
TPL   Toronto Public Library
UBC   Library, University of British Columbia
UNB   University of New Brunswick Archives
VUT   Victoria College Library, University of Toronto

CHAPTER ONE: CHILD OF THE TANTRAMAR

1 *Standard Dictionary of Canadian Biography*, Vol. 1 (Toronto: Trans-Canada
   Press 1934) 440
2 Roberts, *The Heart that Knows* (Boston: Page 1906) 72, 128; Lloyd Roberts,
   Book of Roberts (Toronto: Ryerson 1923) 71
3 Pauline Johnson, *Massey's Magazine* (Jan. 1896) 15; *Standard Dictionary of
   Canadian Biography*, Vol. 1, 440
4 Roberts, *Kindred of the Wild* (Boston: Page 1902) 39, 40, 41
5 *The Heart that Knows* 21; Roberts, *The Watchers of the Trails* (Boston: Page

1904) viii; *Kindred of the Wild* 205; Roberts, *Eyes of the Wilderness* (London: Dent 1933) 4

6 *Kindred of the Wild* 40; Roberts, *Orion* (Philadelphia: Lippincott 1880) 3; Elsie Pomeroy, *Dream World of Sir Charles G.D. Roberts* (privately printed 1959) 10

7 *The Heart that Knows* 75

8 *Book of Roberts* 77, 81

9 *Kindred of the Wild* 41; Parker to Roberts, 22 May 1928, J.C. Adams

10 *The Heart that Knows* 209

11 *Book of Roberts* 77

CHAPTER TWO: APPROACHING MANHOOD

1 Lloyd Roberts, *Book of Roberts* (Toronto: Ryerson 1923) 65

2 Bliss Carman in *Sir George Parkin* by John Willison (London: Macmillan 1929) 35, 36

3 Roberts, *Dalhousie Review* (Jan. 1930), 413

4 Desmond Pacey, *Essays in Canadian Criticism, 1938–1968* (Toronto: Ryerson 1969) 182; *Sir George Parkin* 36

5 *Essays in Canadian Criticism* 186

6 Roberts, typescript, UNB

7 *Standard Dictionary of Canadian Biography*, Vol. II 429–30; I.L. Hill, *Fredericton* (Fredericton: York-Sunbury Historical Society n.d.) 220

8 Carman to Pierce, 7 Oct. 1925, LP

9 *Book of Roberts* 117, 122, 121

10 Pomeroy to Pierce, 15 Mar. 1936, LP

11 Roberts, New Brunswick, *Picturesque Canada*, ed. G.M. Grant (Toronto: Belden 1882) 785

12 T.G. Marquis, *Canadian Magazine* (Sept. 1893) 572

13 Quoted from *The Independent* in *Life and Times of the Right Honourable Sir John A. Macdonald* by J.E. Collins (Toronto: Rose 1883) 465; *The Gazette*, 9 Oct. 1880; Archibald Lampman, *Lyrics of Earth* (Toronto: Musson 1925) 8–9

14 Information supplied by Julia Roberts; Pomeroy to Pierce, 15 Mar. 1936, LP

CHAPTER THREE: CHOOSING CAREERS

1 Roberts to Pierce, typescript of interview, 3 June 1927, LP

2 Roberts to Carman, 12 Dec. 1882, CLP

3 Information supplied by Elsie Pomeroy

4 Roberts to Carman, 12 Dec. 1882, CLP; Roberts to Lampman, 28 Sept. 1882 (copy), Hammond Papers, TPL
5 Roberts to Carman, 10 Mar. 1883, CLP
6 J.E. Collins, *Life and Times of the Right Honourable Sir John A. Macdonald* (Toronto: Rose 1883) 465, 479–80
7 *Rouge et Noir* (Feb. 1883) 13
8 Roberts, *Selected Poetry and Critical Prose*, ed. W.J. Keith (Toronto: University of Toronto Press 1974) 243–59
9 Roberts to Carman, 10 Mar. 1883, CLP; Elizabeth Wallace, *Goldwin Smith* (Toronto: University of Toronto Press 1957) 90
10 *New Brunswick Reporter and Fredericton Advertiser* (18, 21 Apr. 1883)
11 Smith to A.D. White, 8 Oct. 1883, Smith Papers, TPL; Roberts to Carman, 8 Dec. 1883, CLP
12 Roberts to Carman, 28 Feb. 1884, CLP
13 *Ibid.*, 11 Jan. 1884, CLP
14 Roberts, *In Divers Tones* (Boston: Lothrop 1886) 130; Roberts to Carman, 25 Oct., 28 Nov. 1884, CLP
15 Roberts to Carman, 25 Oct., 28 Nov. 1884, CLP
16 *Selected Poetry and Critical Prose* 268
17 Roberts to Carman, 22 Mar. 1886, CLP
18 *Saint John Telegraph-Journal* (24 Oct. 1925); Pomeroy, *Sir Charles G.D. Roberts* (Toronto: Ryerson 1943) 65

CHAPTER FOUR: THE KINGSCROFT YEARS

1 Lloyd Roberts, 'Hell and High Heaven' 1, unpublished ms, LP
2 Roberts to Carman, 31 Jan. 1892, CLP
3 *Ibid.*, 11 May, 17 Aug. 1890, 17 Mar. 1891, CLP
4 *Ibid.*, 6 Feb. 1895, CLP
5 Information supplied by Elsie Pomeroy, who obtained it from Roberts
6 Roberts, *Barbara Ladd* (Boston: Page 1902) 45–6; autographed copy in my possession
7 Roberts to Carman, 17 Aug. 1890, 20 July, 28 Dec. 1891, 31 Jan., 19 Mar., 19 Apr. 1892, CLP
8 Elsie Pomeroy to Lorne Pierce, 15 Mar. 1936, LP
9 Roberts to Carman, 31 Dec. 1892, 19 Dec. 1891, CLP
10 Annie Prat to Carman, 10 Jan. 1892, CLP
11 Lloyd Roberts, *Book of Roberts* (Toronto: Ryerson 1923) 55 and 'Hell and High Heaven' 8; Maude Clarke to Pierce, 27 Apr. 1928, LP
12 Pomeroy to Pierce, 15 Mar. 1936, LP; Roberts to Carman, 6 Apr., 26 Sept. 1892, 25 Aug. 1895, CLP

13 *Book of Roberts* 36
14 Roberts to Carman, 30 Aug. 1891, CLP; *Book of Roberts* 37
15 *Dalhousie Review* (Apr. 1930) 8
16 *Ibid.* 9; Roberts to Carman, 26 Sept. 1892, CLP
17 Roberts to Carman, 17 Mar., Mrs C.E. Hovey to Carman, 14 July 1893, CLP
18 Helen Lynn, ed., *An Annotated Edition of the Correspondence between Archibald Lampman and Edward William Thomson, 1890–8* (Ottawa: Tecumseh 1980) 78
19 Mrs Hovey to Carman, 14 July, 5 Sept. 1893, CLP
20 Pomeroy to Pierce, 15 Mar. 1936, LP
21 Roberts to Carman, 17 Aug. 1890, 27 Feb. 1892, CLP
22 Information supplied by Elsie Pomeroy, who obtained it from Roberts
23 Prat to Pierce, (?) Apr. 1928 and Clarke to Pierce, 28 Apr. 1928, LP
24 *Book of Roberts* 24, 20–1; 'Hell and High Heaven' 4
25 Roberts to Carman, 19 May 1890, 6 Apr. 1892, CLP
26 'Hell and High Heaven' 8 (in this work Goodridge's nickname of 'Gool' is disguised as 'Deedy'); Jean Hunter Bliss to Carman, 9 Feb. 1892, CLP
27 Roberts to Carman, 14 Feb. 1890, CLP; Clarke to Pierce, 27 Apr. 1928, CLP
28 Roberts to Carman, 20 Nov., 31 Dec. 1892, CLP
29 *Ibid.*, 6 May 1894, CLP
30 *Selected Poetry and Critical Prose*, ed. W.J. Keith (Toronto: University of Toronto Press 1974) 270
31 Roberts to Carman, 17 Aug. 1890, 17 Mar. 1891, CLP
32 *Ibid.*, 10 Mar. 1883
33 Pacey, *Creative Writing in Canada* (Toronto: Ryerson 1952) 38; Lighthall, introduction, *Songs of the Great Dominion* (London: Walter Scott 1889) xxiv
34 E.M. Pomeroy, *Charles G.D. Roberts* (Toronto: Ryerson 1943) 69
35 Roberts, *History of Canada* (Toronto: Macmillan 1915) 446
36 Macdonald's last address to the people of Canada, reprinted in *Memoirs of the Right Honourable Sir John A. Macdonald*, by Joseph Pope (Ottawa: Durie 1894) 334; Roberts to Carman, 17 Mar. 1891, CLP
37 Roberts to Carman, 19 May, 31 Jan., 19 Mar., 1 Aug. 1892, CLP
38 Roberts to Denison, 7 May 1888, Denison Papers, PAC; Roberts to Mair, 4 Jan. 1889, Mair Papers, QU; Roberts to Carman, 5 May 1881, 19 Dec. 1891, CLP
39 Roberts to Carman, (?) Apr. 1895, CLP
40 Roberts to Parkin, 6 June 1895, Sir George Parkin Papers, PAC
41 Roberts to Carman, 25 Aug. 1895, CLP; Roberts, *History of Canada* v; Pacey, *Essays in Canadian Criticism, 1938–1968* (Toronto: Ryerson 1969) 189

42 Frye, 'Haunted by Lack of Ghosts,' *The Canadian Imagination*, ed. David Staines (Cambridge, MA: Harvard University Press 1977) 33
43 Pacey, *Ten Canadian Poets* (Toronto: Ryerson 1955) 49
44 Lighthall, *Songs* xxiv

CHAPTER FIVE: THE TURNING POINT

1 Roberts to Carman, 10 Jan. 1895, CLP
2 Roberts to Parkin, 6 June 1895, Parkin Papers, PAC
3 Roberts' stock remark about poetry and prose, often quoted; Roberts to Parkin, 6 June 1895, Parkin Papers, PAC
4 Roberts to Carman, 25 Aug. 1895, CLP
5 *The Dial* (1 June 1896); *The Globe* (17 Oct. 1896); *The Academy* (13 June 1896)
6 *The Nation* (18 Mar. 1897); *The Critic* (14 Aug. 1897); *The Chap-Book* (15 Apr. 1897)
7 *New Brunswick Reporter and Fredericton Advertiser* (31 Mar. 1897); *New York Times* (6 Mar. 1897); *The Critic* (10 Apr. 1897); *The Bookman* (Apr. 1897); *The Nation* (15 Apr. 1897); *The Chap-Book* (1 Apr. 1897); *The Academy* (5 Nov. 1898); *The Athenaeum* (18 Dec. 1897)
8 Roberts, 'The Vagrant of Time'
9 E.M. Pomeroy, *Sir Charles G.D. Roberts* (Toronto: Ryerson 1943) 3
10 Lloyd Roberts, 'Hell and High Heaven' 73, unpublished ms, LP
11 *Ibid.*
12 'Hell and High Heaven' 8; Jean Bliss to Carman, 11 Oct. 1892, CLP

CHAPTER SIX: ASSAILING MANHATTAN

1 Quoted in *The Illustrated American* (15 May 1897)
2 Eve LeGallienne, *With a Quite Heart* (New York: Viking 1953) 282
3 Richard LeGallienne, *The Romantic '90s* (New York: Doubleday, Page 1925) 271
4 Lloyd Roberts, 'Hell and High Heaven' 79, unpublished ms, LP
5 *Reporter and Fredericton Advertiser* (20 Oct. 1897); information supplied by Elsie Pomeroy
6 'Hell and High Heaven' 79, 81
7 *New Brunswick Reporter and Fredericton Advertiser* (25 Mar. 1896); A.B. deMille, *The Canadian Magazine* (Sept. 1900) 429
8 *Reporter and Fredericton Advertiser* (19 Jan. 1898)
9 *Ibid.*

10 Pomeroy to Pierce, 15 Mar. 1936, LP
11 Pomeroy to Pierce, 15 Mar. 1936, LP; Roberts to Pierce, typescript of interview, 3 June 1927, LP
12 'Hell and High Heaven' 185; Pomeroy to Pierce, 15 Mar. 1936, LP
13 Theodore Roberts, *The Independent* (21 July 1898)
14 'Hell and High Heaven' 104, 107
15 Lloyd Roberts, *Winnipeg Free Press* (31 Jan. 1948)
16 E.T. Seton, *Lives of the Hunted* (Toronto: Morang 1901) 10; *Evening Telegram* (27 Feb. 1903)
17 *The Canadian Author* (Sept. 1936) 11
18 Roberts, *The Bookman* (Dec. 1913) 147
19 E.M. Pomeroy, *Sir Charles G.D. Roberts* (Toronto: Ryerson 1943) 182
20 LPD, 4 June 1927
21 Hamlin Garland, *Roadside Meetings* (New York: Macmillan 1930) 408

CHAPTER SEVEN: THE UPSWING

1 Roberts to Parkin, 29, 13 Apr. 1899, Parkin Papers, PAC
2 Roberts to Carman, 13 Aug. 1899, CLP
3 LPD, 4 June 1927
4 Roberts to Carman, 13 Aug. 1899, CLP; E.M. Pomeroy, *Sir Charles G.D. Roberts* (Toronto: Ryerson 1943) 160
5 Roberts to May Roberts, 19 July 1899, UNB
6 Roberts to Carman, 13 Aug. 1899, CLP
7 *Reporter and Fredericton Advertiser* (12 July 1899); Roberts to Carman, 13 Aug. 1899, CLP
8 *Reporter and Fredericton Advertiser* (20 Dec., 25 Oct. 1899)
9 Henry James, *Washington Square* (New York: New American Library 1961, originally published 1881) 16
10 *New York Daily Tribune* (28 July, 14 Apr. 1900); *The Nation* (23 Aug. 1900); *The Globe* (2 Feb. 1901); *Times Literary Supplement* (12 Dec. 1903); *The Athenaeum* (16 Feb. 1901)
11 *Sir Charles G.D. Roberts* 173
12 *Evening Telegram* (27 Feb. 1903)
13 *Evening Telegram* and *Toronto Daily Star* (27 Feb. 1903)
14 *The Nation* (11 Dec. 1902)
15 *The Nation* (3 July 1902); *The Globe* (14 June 1902); *The Athenaeum* (10 Oct. 1903); *Evening Telegram* (27 Feb. 1903)
16 John Burroughs, *Atlantic Monthly* (Mar. 1903) 298–9
17 Roberts, *The Watchers of the Trails* (London: Nelson 1904) viii–ix

18 Roberts, *Dalhousie Review* (Jan. 1935) 421–2
19 Information supplied by Julia Roberts
20 Lloyd Roberts, 'Hell and High Heaven' 135, 176, 75, 177, unpublished ms, LP
21 'Hell and High Heaven' 148; Pomeroy to Pierce, 15 Mar. 1936, LP
22 'Hell and High Heaven' 148, LP
23 Jean Bliss to Carman, 19 Sept. 1914, CLP; 'Hell and High Heaven' 148; Wilfrid Eggleston, *Literary Friends* (Ottawa: Borealis 1980) 69
24 'Hell and High Heaven' 199, 184
25 Lloyd Roberts, *Book of Roberts* (Toronto: Ryerson 1923) 41–2; *The Athenaeum* (4 Mar. 1905)
26 Roberts to Parkin, 29 Apr. 1899, Parkin Papers, PAC
27 Elsie Pomeroy, *The Novels of Sir Charles G.D. Roberts* (privately printed 1950) 5
28 *New York Times* (25 June 1904, 10 Apr. 1909); *The Athenaeum* (5 Dec. 1905)
29 Lloyd Roberts, *Winnipeg Free Press* (27 Mar. 1948)
30 *Saint John Daily Sun* (12 Oct. 1905); *Sir Charles G.D. Roberts* 210
31 Roberts, *Dalhousie Review* (Jan. 1935) 442
32 E.B. Clark, *Everybody's Magazine* (June 1907) 770
33 W.J. Keith, *Charles G.D. Roberts* (Toronto: Copp Clark 1969) 93
34 Stedman to Roberts, 15 May 1907, UNB
35 Clark, *Everybody's Magazine* 773
36 *Daily Telegraph* (10 Aug. 1907)

CHAPTER EIGHT: EUROPEAN INTERLUDE

1 Lloyd Roberts, 'Reminiscences of Days Spent at Pont Levoy,' typescript based upon the recollections of Douglas Roberts, LP
2 Roberts, *A Balkan Prince* (London: Everett 1913) 63, 38, 97
3 'Reminiscences of Days Spent at Pont Levoy'
4 *The Bookman* (Aug. 1909)
5 Roberts to Mr Alexander, undated, PAC
6 'Reminiscences of Days Spent at Pont Levoy'
7 Jean Bliss to Carman, 4 May 1909, CLP
8 Information supplied by Elsie Pomeroy; Carman to J.C. Young, 20 Oct. 1910, Harvard University
9 E.M. Pomeroy, *Sir Charles G.D. Roberts* (Toronto: Ryerson 1943) 230
10 Elsie Pomeroy, *Atlantic Advocate* (Mar. 1962) 57

CHAPTER NINE: MOTHER ENGLAND

1 Gilbert Frankau in *Lauds and Loves* by Henry Simpson (London: Such 1930) 9
2 *The Bookman* (June 1913) 140
3 Roberts to Lloyd Roberts, 16 Feb. 1914, UNB; John Garvin, *Canadian Poets* (Toronto: McClelland, Goodchild & Stewart 1916) 430
4 Jean Bliss to Carman, 22 Feb. 1915, CLP
5 Roberts to Parkin, 5 Nov. 1914, Parkin Papers, PAC
6 Roberts to the War Secretary, 5 Nov. 1914, Parkin Papers, PAC
7 Dorothy Roberts Leisner to the author, 23, 4 Mar. 1980
8 Roberts to Pierce, 19 Oct. 1939, LP
9 Lord Beaverbrook in *Canada in Flanders*, Vol. III by Roberts (London: Hodder & Stoughton 1918) v, xi
10 *Times Literary Supplement* (5 June 1919) 314; *New York Times*, Section III (26 Mar. 1922) 19; *The Spectator* (10 Nov. 1923) 705; Roberts to R.S. Kennedy, 26 Jan. 1937, UNB
11 *New York Times*, Section III (22 June 1924) 12
12 Roberts, 'The Vagrant of Time'; *Ottawa Journal* (28 Feb. 1923)
13 LPD, 8 Sept. 1925

CHAPTER TEN: THE HOMECOMING

1 E.M. Pomeroy, *Sir Charles G.D. Roberts* (Toronto: Ryerson 1943) 273
2 E.M. Pomeroy, *Canadian Author and Bookman* (June 1944) 5; information supplied by Elsie Pomeroy
3 A.A.E. Smythe, *Canadian Bookman* (Feb. 1925) 25; *The Globe* (6 Feb. 1925)
4 Patricia Roberts Henderson to the author, 21 Nov. 1977; Roberts to Lloyd Roberts, 14 Feb. 1925, UNB; Roberts to Katherine Hale, 24 Feb. 1925, Hale-Garvin Papers, QU
5 LPD, 14 June 1928
6 Mair to Lighthall, 22 May 1925, Mair Papers, QU; *Saturday Night* (28 Mar. 1925) 9; McBeth to Mair, 22 May 1925, Mair Papers, QU; Earle Birney, *Spreading Time* (Montreal: Véhicule 1980) 20
7 Constance Davies, *Canadian Bookman* (Aug. 1925) 130
8 R.H. Hathaway, *New Outlook* (30 Dec. 1925) 30; Constance Davies, *Canadian Bookman* (Aug. 1925) 130
9 *Halifax Herald* (7 Oct. 1925)
10 Norwood to Roberts, 21 Sept. 1925, UNB
11 Dorothy Roberts Leisner to the author, 27 Nov. 1977

12 Roberts to Lorne Pierce, 10 Dec. 1925, 6 Apr. 1926, LP
13 LPD, 19 Sept., 20 Aug., 30 Dec. 1925
14 Roberts to Constance Davies Woodrow, 3 Nov. 1925, Woodrow Papers, Kings College, Halifax
15 Interview with Dorothy McKee Miner, 12 Jan. 1978
16 LPD, 20 Mar. 1926; Roberts to Hathaway, 29 May 1926, LP
17 Information supplied by Elsie Pomeroy
18 Roberts to Lloyd Roberts, 18 July 1926, UNB
19 Roberts to R.L. Reid, 11 Nov. 1926, UBC; Roberts to Pierce, 4 Dec. 1926, LP
20 *Vancouver Poetry Society, 1914–1946: A Book of Days* (Toronto: Ryerson 1946) 29
21 *Canadian Poets*, ed. John W. Garvin (Toronto: McClelland & Stewart 1926); Mair to Lighthall, 22 May 1925, Mair Papers, QU; Roberts, *Authors Bulletin* (Dec. 1928) 8
22 *The Times Literary Supplement* (20 June 1927) 459; MacMechan to Pierce, 28 May 1927, LP
23 Note attached by Blanche Hume to a letter to her from Roberts, 21 Dec. 1926, LP
24 Roberts to an unidentified correspondent, 16 May 1927, PAC

CHAPTER ELEVEN: NATIONAL PRESIDENT, CAA

1 *Authors Bulletin* (Aug. 1925, Nov. 1926) 12, 22
2 Lyn Harrington, *Syllables of Recorded Time* (Toronto: Simon & Pierre 1981) 19; Earle Birney, *Spreading Time* (Montreal: Véhicule 1980) 127
3 *Authors Bulletin* (Dec. 1928) 8; information supplied by Elsie Pomeroy
4 Benson to Roberts, 6 Dec. 1939, UNB; Roberts to Benson, 27, 18 July 1929, Emma Benson; information supplied by Elsie Pomeroy; N.A. Benson in *Leading Canadian Poets*, ed. Percival (Toronto: Ryerson 1948) 191–2
5 *Spreading Time*, 21; LPD, 14 June 1928
6 Roberts to H. Gerald Wade, 9 Mar. 1928, Wade Papers, SJC
7 Brotman to author, 30 Nov. 1977
8 Strange to Roberts, 22 May, 31 July 1927, UNB
9 Thomas H. Raddall, *In My Time* (McClelland & Stewart 1976) 252; Hoogstraten to the author, 13 Apr. 1978
10 Information supplied by Elsie Pomeroy; *Letters of Frederick Philip Grove*, ed. Pacey (Toronto: University of Toronto Press 1976) 150; Brotman to the author, 30 Nov. 1977
11 Carman to Fewster, 21 Nov. 1928, CLP

12 Carman to Lawrence, 10 Nov. 1928, Lawrence Papers, University of Western Ontario; *Authors Bulletin* (Dec. 1929)
13 Carman to Fewster, 27 May 1929, LP; Pomeroy to Pierce, 15 Mar. 1936, LP; Mrs William Whitman to Mrs Margaret West, UNB
14 Woodrow to Pierce, 30 July 1929, LP; Roberts to Benson, 27 July 1929, Emma Benson
15 Information supplied by Elsie Pomeroy
16 Roberts to Garvin, 2 Dec. 1929, Hale-Garvin Papers, QU; Elsie Pomeroy, *Sir Charles G.D. Roberts* (Toronto: Ryerson 1943) 308

CHAPTER TWELVE: HONOUR WITHOUT PROFIT

 1 Reynolds to Roberts, 9 Apr. 1932, UNB
 2 Roberts to Edith Roberts, 26 June, UNB; information supplied by Elsie Pomeroy
 3 Interview with Dorothy McKee Miner, 12 Jan. 1978; Pomeroy to Pierce, 13 Mar. 1936, LP
 4 Lloyd Roberts to Roberts, 7 Apr. 1930; UNB; *Ottawa Citizen* (12 May 1930)
 5 Casserly to Roberts, 13 Aug. 1930, UNB
 6 Mary Fanton Roberts to Roberts, undated, UNB
 7 Wilfrid Eggleston, *Literary Friends* (Ottawa: Borealis 1980) 35
 8 Interview with Julia Roberts, 21 Jan. 1978
 9 Information supplied by Elsie Pomeroy; interview with Julia Roberts, 21 Jan. 1987; Lloyd Roberts, 'Hell and High Heaven' 177, unpublished MS, LP
10 Roberts to Edith Roberts, 24 May 1933, 31 Oct. 1930, UNB
11 Roberts to Mary Roberts, 2 July 1931, Mary Fanton Roberts Papers, Yale University
12 Dorothy Roberts Leisner to the author, 27 Nov. 1977; Pomeroy to Harold Child, 18 Dec. 1944, Susan Rice; *Literary Friends* 35
13 Roberts to Pierce, 2 Nov., 10 Dec. 1925, LP; Roberts to Grant, 18 Nov. 1931, W.L. Grant Papers, PAC; Roberts to Deacon, 19 Dec. 1931, Deacon Papers, FUT
14 Goodridge MacDonald, *Canadian Author and Bookman* (Spring 1953) 12
15 Parker to Roberts, 22 May 1928, J.C. Adams
16 *Standard Dictionary of Canadian Biography*, Vol. II (Toronto: Trans-Canada Press 1938) 325; *New York Times*, 30 Sept. 1932; Roberts in *Issa* by Robert Norwood (New York: Scribner's 1931) ix
17 *Literary Friends* 35, 42–3
18 Anahareo (Gertrude Moltke), *Devil in Buckskins* (Toronto: New Press 1972)

145; I remember seeing this letter from Roberts in the correspondence that Miss Pomeroy later destroyed

19 Roberts to Hathaway, 15 Mar. 1931, UNB; Roberts to Lloyd Roberts, 29 Mar. 1931, UNB; Roberts to Pierce, 1 May 1931, LP; Roberts to H.A. Kennedy, 29 May 1931, UNB; Editorial, *University of Toronto Quarterly* (Oct. 1931)

20 Pierce to Bennett, 26 Jan. 1931 (copy), LP; Bennett to Pierce, 10 Feb. 1931, LP

21 Roberts to Lloyd Roberts, 29 Mar. 1931, UNB; E.M. Pomeroy, *Sir Charles G.D. Roberts* (Toronto: Ryerson 1943) 312; Roberts to Kennedy, 6 Oct. 1934, Kennedy Papers, PAC; Roberts to Bennett, 6 Nov. 1934, UNB

22 Roberts to Edgar, 10 Nov. 1935, Edgar Papers, VUT; J.M. Gray, *Fun Tomorrow* (Toronto: Macmillan 1978) 164; Roberts to H. Gerald Wade, 15 July 1931, Wade Papers, SJC

23 Roberts to Kennedy, 26 Mar. 1933, UNB; Roberts to Edith Roberts, 24 May 1933, UNB

24 W.D. Lighthall, *Canadian Author and Bookman* (Spring 1977) 4; Lyn Harrington, *Syllables of Recorded Time* (Toronto: Simon & Pierre 1981) 153

25 The author gleaned information from correspondence that Miss Pomeroy later destroyed; Roberts to Kennedy, 4 Sept. 1933, Kennedy Papers, PAC

26 *Saturday Night*, Autumn Literary Supplement (14 Oct. 1933) 10; *Mail and Empire* (30 Sept. 1933); Roberts to Deacon, 10 Oct. 1933, Deacon Papers, FUT; Roberts to Wade, 23 Oct. 1933, Wade Papers, SJC; *The Canadian Forum* (Dec. 1933) 116; *New York Times*, 22 Oct. 1933

27 *Saturday Night* (19 Jan. 1935) 8; Roberts to Edgar, 27 Jan. 1935, Edgar Papers, VUT

28 The form letter from Roberts may be found in many repositories, including LP

29 Roberts to Edgar, 23 June 1934, Edgar Papers, VUT; Roberts to Pierce, 23 June 1934, LP

30 Roberts to Pierce, 28 Apr. 1934, LP; Pierce to Roberts, 6 Mar. 1934, UNB

31 Roberts to Benson, 20 Feb. 1934, Emma Benson; Bennett to Roberts, 18 May 1935, UNB

32 Roberts to J. Clarence Webster, 13 July 1935, New Brunswick Museum, Saint John; Roberts to Bennett, 30 June 1935, UNB

CHAPTER THIRTEEN: THE FINAL YEARS

1 Dorothy Herriman, *Canadian Author and Bookman* (Jan. 1940) 50

2 Roberts to Pierce, 4 Sept. 1941, LP
3 Roberts to A.M. Stephen, 26 Mar. 1942, Stephen Papers, UBC; Watson Kirkonnell, *A Slice of Canada* (Toronto: University of Toronto Press 1967) 294
4 Roberts to Clay, 7 July 1943, Clay Papers, PAC; interview with Julia Roberts, 21 Jan. 1978; Broadus to Roberts, undated, UNB; Roberts Papers, QU
5 A.J.M. Smith, *The McGill News* (Autumn 1963) 16; Patricia Morley, *Canadian Poetry* (Fall / Winter 1982) 67; A.J.M. Smith, *The Canadian Forum* (Apr. 1928) 600; Roberts, *Selected Poems* (Toronto: Ryerson 1936) viii
6 Roberts to Morris and Finley, American Academy of Arts and Letters, New York; Roberts to Pierce, LP Roberts to McRaye, McRaye Papers, McMaster University; Roberts to Gustafson, Gustafson Papers, University of Saskatchewan
7 Dorothy Livesay, *Canadian Bookman* (Apr. 1939) 5; Roberts to Pierce, 12 Feb. 1939, LP
8 *Selected Poems* vii–viii
9 *Dalhousie Review* (Vol. XVII) 115; *University of Toronto Quarterly* (Apr. 1937) 343; *Letters in Canada* (1943) 314
10 UNB
11 Roberts to the Rev. C.H. Dickinson, 18 Feb. 1940, LP; Roberts to Pierce, 9 Mar. 1940, LP
12 E.M. Pomeroy, *Sir Charles G.D. Roberts* (Toronto: Ryerson 1943) 289; Lloyd Roberts, *Book of Roberts* (Toronto: Ryerson 1923) 22, 121; Roberts to Edith Roberts, 12 Dec. 1934, UNB; Pomeroy to Pierce, 15 Mar. 1936, LP; interview with Julia Roberts, 1 Apr. 1978
13 Information supplied by Elsie Pomeroy; E.M. Pomeroy, *Canadian Author and Bookman* (June 1944) 6; Pomeroy to Pierce, 1 Nov. 1943, LP
14 Roberts to Mary Josephine Allison, 30 Mar. 1936, F.G. Allison
15 Roberts to Montgomery, 13 Aug. 1938, UNB; Roberts to Jones, 28 July 1938, UNB
16 Roberts to Montgomery, 3 July 1939, UNB; *Canadian Author and Bookman* (Oct. 1939) 20
17 Roberts to the editor of the King's College Record, 17 Apr. 1939, University of King's College, Halifax
18 Roberts to Pierce, 19 Oct. 1939, LP; Roberts to H. Gerald Wade, 17 Nov. 1939, Wade Papers, SJC
19 Roberts to Pierce, 3 June 1940, 20, 27 Feb. 1941, 28 Aug. 1942, LP; memo from Frank Flemington to Roberts, LP; memo from Flemington to Pierce, LP; Pierce to Pomeroy (copy), 3 May 1943, LP
20 *Times Literary Supplement* (21 Aug. 1943) 404; Pelham Edgar, *Across My*

Path (Toronto: Ryerson 1952) 99; Wilfrid Eggleston, *Winnipeg Free Press* (10 Jan. 1948)

21 Wilfrid Eggleston, *Literary Friends* (Ottawa: Borealis 1980) 69; Pomeroy to Pierce, 1 Nov. 1943, LP; Roberts to Edith Roberts, 29 June 1943, UNB

22 Roberts to Pierce, 19 Oct. 1939, 14 Dec. 1938, 9 Mar., 3 June 1940, LP; Roberts to Kirkconnell, 12 Feb. 1940, Kirkconnell Papers, Acadia University; Roberts to Edgar, 1 Aug. 1940, Edgar Papers, VUT

23 Roberts to Pierce, 1 Oct. 1940, LP; Roberts to Gustafson, 14 Jan. 1941, Gustafson Papers, University of Saskatchewan

24 Roberts to Edgar, 21 Mar. 1942, Edgar Papers, VUT; Roberts to Pierce, 8 June 1942, LP

25 Roberts to Pierce, 13 Feb. 1940, LP

26 Roberts to J. Clarence Webster, 2 Feb. 1937, N.B., Museum, Saint John; *Literary Friends* 49

27 Pomeroy, *Canadian Author and Bookman* (Winter 1961) 8

28 Roberts to Edith Roberts, 26 Mar. 1938, UNB; de la Roche, *Ringing the Changes* (Toronto: Macmillan 1957) 272

29 Roberts to R.S. Kennedy, 2 June 1938, UNB; Roberts to Edgar, 23 Feb. 1939, Edgar Papers, VUT

30 Mary Roberts to Roberts, 8 Oct. 1941, UNB

31 Roberts, 'On the Road'

32 E.M. Pomeroy, *Canadian Author and Bookman* (June 1944) 5

CHAPTER FOURTEEN: THE FINAL MONTHS

1 Lady Roberts to the author, 9 Feb. 1978

2 Roberts to Montgomery, 24, 26 Dec. 1937, UNB

3 Pomeroy to Pierce, 1 Nov. 1943, LP

4 Wilfrid Eggleston, *Literary Friends* (Ottawa: Borealis 1980) 49; Roberts to Edith Roberts, 29 June 1943, UNB; interview with Julia Roberts, 21 Jan. 1978

5 Elsie Pomeroy, *Canadian Author and Bookman* (Winter 1961) 8

6 Pomeroy to Pierce, 1 Nov. 1943, LP; interview with Julia Roberts, 1 Apr. 1978

7 Information supplied by Elsie Pomeroy; Roberts to Pomeroy, 26 Oct. 1943 (copy made from the letter shown to the author by Pomeroy); Pomeroy to Pierce, 1 Nov. 1943, LP

8 LPD, 29 Oct. 1943

9 Pomeroy to Pierce, 1 Nov. 1943, LP (Pomeroy quotes from her letter to Edith); information supplied by Elsie Pomeroy

10 Pomeroy to Child, 14 Dec. 1944, Susan Rice
11 LPD, 8 Dec. 1943; E.M. Pomeroy, *Canadian Author and Bookman* (June 1944) 5
12 Roberts, 'Two Rivers'
13 Elsie Pomeroy, *Canadian Poetry Magazine* (Sept. 1944)

EPILOGUE

1 Pelham Edgar, *University of Toronto Quarterly* (Oct. 1943) 117
2 Roy Daniells in *Literary History of Canada*, Vol. I, ed. Klinck (Toronto: University of Toronto Press 1973, 2nd ed.) 418
3 Louis Dudek, review of *The Roots of Treason* (*Globe and Mail*, 28 Jan. 1984); W.J. Keith in *Selected Poetry and Critical Prose* by Roberts (Toronto: University of Toronto Press 1974) xiv; Fred Cogswell in *Canadian Writers and Their Works, Poetry Series*, Vol. II, ed. Lecker, David, Quigley (Downsview, Ont.: ECW Press 1983) 197

Index

PICTURE CREDITS

QUEEN'S UNIVERSITY ARCHIVES: Roberts ca. 1925 (frontispiece); Rev. George Goodridge Roberts and Emma Bliss Roberts ca. 1870; King's College football team ca. 1891; May Roberts ca. 1893; Roberts at 'Kingscroft' 1893; Roberts on the Nictau and in New York 1905; Lloyd Roberts as 'wood god' and Roberts at Brighton 1922; with Charles Mair in Victoria 1927; 'Great Scribe Chief' Calgary 1928; with Duncan Campbell Scott at Lampman memorial 1930; unveiling Carman memorial 1930; with Lorne Pierce ca. 1940; with Pratt, Edgar, and Benson ca. 1940; at work ca. 1940

METROPOLITAN TORONTO LIBRARY (MANUSCRIPT COLLECTION): watercolour sketch of Westcock Parsonage

PUBLIC ARCHIVES OF CANADA: Roberts and May Fenety 1880; Roberts during First World War; with Lloyd at 'Low Eaves' 1925

PROVINCIAL ARCHIVES OF NEW BRUNSWICK: Roberts family camping 1891

UNIVERSITY OF NEW BRUNSWICK ARCHIVES: Roberts and Edith canoeing 1921

DR M.L. STOCK: with Wilson MacDonald and Bliss Carman in Muskoka 1925; with Dr Aletta Marty and Elsie Pomeroy in Muskoka 1926

DOROTHY McKEE MINER: Roberts at 'The Ernescliffe' 1926; at Hubbards Cove, Nova Scotia, 1930

MURIEL MILLER: Joan Montgomery 1932

ELSIE POMEROY: Roberts on the *Empress of Britain* 1933; Centre Island, summer 1940; with Elsie Pomeroy, Centre Island, 1943

TORONTO CITY HALL ARCHIVES, *Globe and Mail* COLLECTION: Roberts' eightieth birthday with Elsie Pomeroy and Nathaniel Benson, 63278; Roberts and Joan Montgomery 1943, 87707